CW01647482

Refreshing Reiki

Usui First Degree: 'the light within'

Marion Eaton

Usui Reiki Master 1997

Karuna® Reiki Master 1998

Published by Touchworks Ltd.
a company registered in England, no. 03668464.
Registered Office: 7 Wellington Square,
Hastings, East Sussex TN34 1PD.

Also by M L Eaton

Mysterious Marsh series
#1When the Clocks Stopped
#2 When the Tide Turned
#3 When the Earth Cracked

Faraway Lands series
#1 The Elephants' Child
#2 The Lion Mountains
#3 The Snaking River

Short Read
Norfolk Twilight

Meditation
Spinning into Form book/CDs and MP3s

all books available in print from Amazon
and as an ebook from digital stores at www.books2read.com
A catalogue record for this title is available from the British Library
Marion's websites: www.marioneaton.co.uk and www.marioneaton.com

靈氣

For

my dear, warm-hearted, 'belle soeur'
Janet Chapman

LIGHT

'Light gives of itself freely, filling all available space.
It does not seek anything in return; it asks not
whether you are friend or foe.
It gives of itself and is not thereby diminished.'

Michael Strassfeld

Contents

FOREWORD

I FELL IN LOVE with Reiki more than twenty years ago.

Just remembering this, I feel a smile spreading through the whole of my being.

I am sitting in the summer sunshine on the deck that overlooks my wonderful wild garden, where, now, in July, the reds and oranges of day-lilies and montbretia vie with the mauve of rosebay willow herb, the pink stars of rambling roses, the purplish blue of wild geraniums and a magnificent clematis the colour of an evening sky. The perfume of honeysuckle and roses is heavy in the late afternoon air. A light breeze ruffles the leaves of the rowan tree. The complaints of squabbling jackdaws interrupt the contented buzzing of bees. A child laughs in the garden next door.

As the smile reaches my lips, I can think of no other love in my life that compares with my love for Reiki. I am privileged to have known many loves and to have been loved much in return, but Reiki is more than any tense of the verb 'to love' … it is Love itself….

I believe that Reiki is simply love, an energy from the Divine — whatever you perceive that to be — that moves within us all and informs the whole of life itself.

Reiki is energy. It can be perceived but it cannot be seen. It can be felt, but it cannot be touched. It can be heard, but its sound is that of the universe and cannot be recreated. Some few individuals are aware of its perfume, but are unable to describe it. Others see it as light, but the colours are so intense and vibrant that comparison is almost impossible.

Reiki is wisdom.

Reiki is that undefinable life force — known variously as prana in India, qi in China, ki in Japan, vital force or orgone in Europe — that gives us aliveness.

All I say in this little volume is my own opinion, my own personal understanding of the nature and uses of Reiki, all of which I have learned by allowing it to flow through me. For the past twenty years and more, it has been part of my own energy field, informing and educating me, healing and comforting me, but most of all, teaching me about the nature of compassion and unconditional love.

I am not perfect, by any means. I am human, having chosen to incarnate on earth at this time in a human body with a human mind and human emotions and the spirituality that is vouchsafed to us all. I have foibles and weaknesses. I judge, and I make mistakes. I know that I have accepted others' opinions as truth. But I have learned to see that this is all part of the richness of life, and that nothing is stuck, nothing is permanent. When I catch myself thinking, doing or saying something that I dislike — that *something* might be my opinion, it might be my judgement, or it might be some form of conditioning that I have believed to be the truth — I remind myself that I have the power to change it.

I honour myself by accepting that I am not perfect. Nor would I wish to be… for where is the excitement, the richness, the lesson in that? But I can do my best to see where I can also honour myself by adapting and changing. I believe that in doing so, I demonstrate to others that they, too, can adapt and change as they need.

Marion Eaton
Whisperwood,
Westfield, England
Summer 2017

INTRODUCTION

SEVERAL OF my Reiki Master students have asked me to help them as they begin to teach Reiki. I have told them, as I am saying now, that I no longer give the same class that I gave when I started to teach Reiki — over 20 years ago now.

Not only have I changed and developed in my Reiki practice, but the energy of Reiki itself has changed as it has become more widely known, used and accepted. Similarly, those who decide to learn this wonderful energy healing modality are different from those whom I taught way back then.

Change is a natural organic process. Whether we like it or not, we all alter. If we embrace change, everything in our lives will run more easily. And so will our thoughts and emotions.

In the second decade of the twenty-first century, people accept the whole concept of energy more easily, they appreciate that we have a bio-magnetic resonance, and they are beginning to come to an understanding that we are all one, in that we are all part of Nature. No longer do we believe in the uniqueness of man (and woman) kind. Now we recognise that we inhabit a comparatively small planet that is infinitely fragile and precious. We see that the whole of Nature is interdependent and that the essence of the universe is infinite. And way beyond our comprehension.

I say this to demonstrate how much we, and thus the whole of Life, are affected by the constant alteration in our perception of energy and of the infinite.

No doubt my teaching will change too over the coming years, but, since I have been asked, I am about to set down the way I would approach teaching a Reiki 1 workshop in my present state of awareness and understanding.

I offer it as a framework for students and teachers alike. Take from it what resonates with you and chuck the rest out. Maybe you will come back to it another time, but maybe you won't. The important thing is to trust your own energy and to act accordingly.

I am not enlightened and I do not profess to be. I am simply someone who has walked along the Reiki path a little ahead of you. I offer guidance, but of course there is no need to accept it — most important is that you choose to walk your own way.

My hope and prayer is that amongst my words you will find something of value.

Namaste.

DAY ONE, MORNING.

1

Hello and Welcome

IT IS A great honour to be chosen as your Reiki Teacher, and I thank you for the privilege. You are giving yourself a wonderful gift by empowering your life with Reiki.

One of the lovely things about teaching Reiki is getting to know those people who choose to study with you, so thank you for taking this journey with me.

Because Reiki is energy, it has to be experienced, rather than taught. So I am asking you to come on a journey of experimentation with me. Use your body-mind as a laboratory and let's do some experimenting. There is no right or wrong. It is just how it is. Allow yourself to understand this, and relax.

Before we start, let us bring our energy into the room. Let us become present: letting go of all the getting here and all the things that are superfluous right at this moment.

So, let's all stand up! Take a silent inventory as to how you feel. Work from your feet up. Do you feel tense anywhere? Uncertain? Anxious? Wondering? Where in your body do you feel tension or pain? This is just for you. As I've just said, there is no right or wrong: and no reason to tell anyone, unless you want to.

Take a step backwards or sideways. Make sure you have room to move. Shake out any bits of you that are stiff, cramped or painful. If thoughts or aches and pains are making themselves awkward, take them off, shrug out of them as though they were a suit of armour (which indeed they are, in the energy sense). If you need help to unbuckle and release yourself, ask your neighbour to assist. Help each other. Then carry that energy to the window and toss it out into the greenness and wisdom of Nature where everything is recycled … more of that later.

Now come back to where you were. Ease your shoulders in a circle, pull them up to your ears and then backwards, feeling your shoulder blades drop down your back... see if you can make them meet...now circle your shoulders round to the front. Repeat a couple more times. Then circle them the other way round.

Now release your elbows by circling them, first one way for about ten revolutions — and then the other.

Do the same with your wrists.

Shake your hands at the wrist, feeling them loosen and relax. Open and close your hands, stretching the fingers as far as you can and then closing your fists. Do some mad piano-playing.

Now put your hands on your hips and circle at the waist: first one way, then the other.

Stand on one leg and circle the other at the knee. Ten times one way: then ten times the other. Then stand on the other leg and circle the first leg at the knee, ten times each way.

Repeat with the ankles, circling each of then ten times one way, and then ten times the other.

Next rock backwards and forwards on your feet, back on your heels, then on to your toes. Stand on tiptoes, if you like.

Now stand still, feet flat on the floor, close your eyes, take a deep breath in .... And let it out slowly. Take your awareness into your body and see how it feels now ... Again there is no right or wrong, but you may find that tension has relaxed, your mind is more relaxed, body and mind are connected ... you feel more present.

Share your experience with me and the others if you feel like it. Or make a note ... or not. This experience is yours to do with as you wish.

Opening Circle

Now that you have come into your body, into your own energy, let's form a Reiki circle. Turn your left hand palm upwards, and your right hand palm downwards, then place your right palm gently on the upturned hand of your neighbour. In this way, all hands should be meeting palm to palm.

The left palm is upturned because in most (right-handed) people this is the 'receiving hand' while the right palm is turned down because this is the 'giving hand'. Sometimes in left-handed people the energy runs the other way, so if more are left-handed in your circle change the direction of the palms accordingly.

Gently close your eyes.

Make sure your shoulders are relaxed … your elbows are relaxed … your hands are soft and resting gently against those of your neighbour on each side. Your hips are relaxed … and your knees. Become very aware of your feet and your connection with the floor and through the floor, with the Earth below. Spread your toes and wriggle your feet against the floor.

Breathe in deeply … and gently out, feeling centred in your body and connected with the earth.

Begin to allow energy to pass round the circle. Receive it with your left hand … imagine it passing up your left arm … through your heart centre in the middle of your chest … down your right arm … and out through your right palm. Watch the energy as it passes round the circle … imagine it like a beautiful ribbon of light, and greet each person at the heart centre, feeling your connection.

Now imagine a huge column of light — big enough to fill the entire room — coming up from the centre of the earth … through our circle … and watch as it rises, up, up, out into the universe. Here it joins up with the light network that surrounds our planet and with all other groups who are practising healing for the highest good of all concerned.

Now we ask that all those who work for our highest good — on all levels of existence, including the Reiki Masters who have gone before, the ascended Masters, the angels, archangels, beings of light and Reiki guides — to be with us and to help us as we start our Reiki journey. And we thank them for the gifts they bring and for their sacred presence.

Breathe in slowly ... breathe out slowly. And again, breathe in slowly ... and breathe out ... gently, calmly. Bring your consciousness back into the room.

And let's have a Reiki hug. Gently place your arms around your neighbours and feel aware of the change in the energy, a feeling of connection, of warmth and togetherness... Stay in silence. Feel the togetherness of silence.

Stay here for a minute or two, feeling the smile on your lips.

Then, keeping your awareness of the experience, slowly open your eyes, step back, and take a seat. Do not speak.

If you wish to make a note of what you have experienced, please do.

Confidentiality

For today, this room is a sacred space. I have prepared it to be a safe, comfortable space in which you can be your true selves.

For this reason, I ask that we honour the Reiki energy — that means me and each of you — by respecting each other's process, and, in particular, the confidentiality of any confidences, emotions or intimacies that occur over the next couple of days. So please ensure that anything that happens in this room stays in this room. If you really feel it is appropriate you may, of course, talk about your own feelings and processes, but not of anyone else's.

Ask Questions

Also, I would ask you to understand that I teach from the place that I have reached in my own spiritual path. Because you have chosen to come to this workshop, I imagine that you will find that we are in accord.

I speak what I believe to be the truth. But it may not be your truth, or you may not yet be ready to accept what I say. Therefore ALWAYS question, always ask. If I do or say anything which doesn't resonate with you, or which does not accord with your own beliefs and understanding, then do take issue with me. I would remind you, though, that it comes from my heart, not from my personal power.

If you still feel it's not acceptable, then just chuck it out. I am not enlightened — although I feel I am much closer to enlightenment than I was years ago — but I have spent years studying and practising metaphysical matters and holistic medicine, so I do have a great deal of experience. That said, I do not know everything, and you may well be able to give me a gift of knowledge; and of understanding, too.

I am not a guru. I am just your guide on this part of your spiritual path and I hope that we may travel together for a little while.

You are your own guru. All that you need to know is available to you, and indeed, you already have the knowledge deep inside. Your spirit, your body, have a deep and special wisdom. My task is to show you how to access that wisdom and to trust it.

You are special

First, I would like to remind you that you are unique and special. There is no one quite like you. Even identical twins have differences.

You have been born into this world at this time for a unique purpose ... and that purpose is simply to be you. Thus it is important that you take responsibility for who you are, and for your journey through life. Don't forget that the journey is actually life itself. Enjoy your travels and don't rush to the end ... because we all know what that will be.

Second, I'd like to point out that your spirit has incarnated into this body of yours, the one that is here, now. Thus, you are here on Earth and this is where you need to dwell. It is fine to wish to be 'spiritual' and it is good to learn to meditate, but if you spend much time out of your body in your thoughts and emotions, you will lose the richness of life. Concentrate on keeping your body flexible and healthy, so that you can make use of all its juice and power.

All this brings me neatly to my third point. Be present. Be here. Let go of all the other stuff in your life and give yourself the gift of going within, trusting, and learning from your own wisdom.

Comfort

Before we go any further ... I presume you all know where the bathroom is? If you need to go, just go. You don't need to ask permission. Leave the room quietly, and come back quietly. I will notice that you have gone, and will repeat anything of importance that you may have missed. If you still feel that you have missed something, tell me, and I will fill in any gaps.

You are responsible for your own comfort. If you would like a window opened ... if you have a headache ... if you need to go out of doors ... if you're hungry or can feel your blood sugar dropping ... honour that feeling and tell me. Bring it to the class. Some of them may be feeling the same. Do what you need and/or ask that something is done about it.

I would ask that if you are really uncomfortable you have a private word with me and we will see what we can do together to make it better.

Water

You each have a bottle of water and a glass. Please make sure that you drink all of the water, at least by the end of the day, and preferably before lunch.

When we are dealing with, and using energy, it is *really, really* important to be fully hydrated, because your nervous system relies on the water in your body to function.

You may not know that water has a memory and helps us to retain information. If you have any doubts about this, I suggest you read Emoto's book '*The Message of Water*'. If we have time later, I will go into this in more detail but simply looking at the images in Emoto's book will convince you, I'm sure.

During today and tomorrow you will be channelling Reiki energy. Those of your cells that are ready to heal themselves use water to do so. Similarly those cells that are past their 'sell-by' date (pun intended!) need water to enable them to ride out of the body.

So now, let's find out a little about each other.

All you need to say is your name, but if you would like to add a little more, that will be wonderful. I'm particularly interested in the reason that you have come to learn Reiki and what you would like to get out of it by the end of the workshop. Maybe this is an opportunity for you to go within and find the real reason — not just the one you have given others.

We'll go round the circle in a moment, but I'll start.

2

A little about me

My name, as you know, is Marion Eaton. I'm married with two grown-up daughters who are wonderfully independent.

In 1973 — aeons ago, it seems now — I qualified as a solicitor of the Supreme Court of Judicature of England and Wales. I was lucky enough to be employed in private practice in Rye. Then I fell pregnant, and things being very different in those days, I was delighted to think that I would be a stay-at-home mother. However, when I asked the local Bank Manager — in Lydd on Romney Marsh — for a loan to tide us over, he not only granted it, but suggested that I start a practice in the town so that he could send clients to me. In the end he not only sent me clients, but helped me by finding me a baby-minder, a secretary and office premises, in that order.

I was very happy running my own legal practice for nearly twenty years, but in the late nineteen-eighties, I reached a crunch time. Everything seemed to go wrong at once. Big things. My parents, who were living with us, died within six months of each other, and my mother-in-law three months later. While I was grieving, I lost two important members of my staff to illness and in addition there were big financial upheavals in the country and my business went through a very difficult patch. I found myself in an emotional abyss and my doctor diagnosed nervous exhaustion. Eventually I merged my firm with another: I continued to work in it for a few months, but my heart was no longer in the law. I needed time to mend.

During this time, I was seeing a homeopath, who helped me hugely. One day, while sitting in his waiting room, I saw an advertisement for a course in aromatherapy. My elder daughter was about to take her 'A' levels and intended to study physiotherapy at university after a gap year in Australia. I took details of the course home, thinking that she could take the aromatherapy course at weekends and that she would then have a skill to take to Australia. I even enrolled her. But, of course, it was too much for her to undertake with all her other studies. I rang up to cancel, but instead found myself saying; "But I'd love to do it."

I did love it, too. But the course revealed to me how much I, myself, still needed healing. Once again, serendipity, or fate, took a hand. Reading a local listings magazine in our lunch break, I came across an article on Reiki. As soon as I read that Reiki could be used for self-healing, I knew I had to learn it: and luckily enough, there happened to be a course arranged for the next weekend. Not only that, but the venue was very close to my home. I booked in straight away.

I would like to say that it was miraculous, but it wasn't. I found my common-sensical, rational, down-to-earth, legal self very resistant to the idea of energy in general and to the teachings of Dr Usui in particular. Nothing seemed to happen. No great light or sense of wonder. Instead I felt vaguely uneasy and rather let down. I had hoped for so much …

Fast forward to the next Aromatherapy weekend and the whole class was being disturbed by one person. You know the sort … the one who queries everything, who is not prepared to take part, whose hands are like claws. Receiving a massage from her was very uncomfortable. The sort of person who puts on a make-up mask in the morning and refuses to remove it even when she is learning to do a facial massage and has to practise on other members of the class. Something inside me recognised her mask as one of fear. I understood she felt so vulnerable that she didn't dare risk showing her true self.

I asked her whether I could practise my Reiki on her, and to my surprise she accepted with alacrity. Even more surprisingly, she dozed off as I worked on her. When she awoke, she was like a different person: kind, helpful and accommodating. Everyone else in the class wondered what I had done to her. The good news was that the change was permanent. Soon everyone in the class wanted Reiki over the lunch-hour.

And so, having moved my legal practice to a different place, my husband and I turned the old office premises into a Holistic Health Centre, letting out the front shop to a nutritionist. In our hey-day we had sixteen therapists (including me) working there. By that time I'd qualified as a professional aromatherapist and studied lots of different healing modalities as well as becoming an Usui Reiki Master and Teacher and a Karuna Reiki Master Practitioner and Teacher. I was also working part time as a lawyer.

Eventually, I retired ... but people still ask me to give treatments and to teach and so... here I am.

Reiki: my spiritual path

I have a huge love of, and interest in, all sorts of holistic, complementary and alternative medicine, which I have found to be incredibly effective. But I always come back to Reiki as the simplest, safest, most effective method of reminding the body-mind that it can heal itself. I have been teaching it for over twenty years and I hope I shall never stop.

- Reiki is simple.
- Reiki is safe.
- Reiki is easy ... you always have your hands with you, at the end of your arms.
- Reiki is profound.
- And Reiki is very effective.
- Quite simply, Reiki works.

I love everything about Reiki. Reiki has become part of my being, and my spiritual path. I hope you, too, will fall in love with it and that you will find it a wonderful addition to your life.

3

Understanding Subtle Energy

ALTHOUGH I HAVE learned a great deal about the subtle energy system as I've travelled my Reiki path, I well remember the bafflement I felt when it was first described to me. In those long-ago days, when I was a practising lawyer and used to rational ideas and explanations, I found the whole concept of energy difficult to understand.

Since then, of course, the internet has made information available as never before and the understanding of metaphysical concepts through the medium of quantum physics has blossomed. However, although there is a great deal of information available, it's not always understandable.

Before I teach you about Reiki, I need to make sure you understand the way that energy spins into matter, and of its interaction with the whole of creation. So I'm going to start by giving you a brief, crash course on the subtle energy body and its subtle energy channels.

Trust and Inner Knowing

The first step in understanding our subtle energy is to learn to trust our inner knowledge.

This can be difficult because we've been conditioned by society to trust only what we are taught by others and to hide all those parts of us which we believe to be unacceptable to society. So let's take a long hard look within, imagining we are seeing with the all-seeing Eye. This Eye sees everything within the compass of our body-mind-spirit — our hopes and fears, our happinesses and sadnesses, our kindnesses and cruelties, joys and griefs, wellness and illness, and everything else that we like to keep hidden.

The Eye sees without judging, but with compassion. It looks deeply within, seeing where we are lost, where we are selling ourselves short, where we are stuck in our thought processes, where we are clinging to a belief system that is harmful or weakening. Compassion sees: and, in seeing, understands.

From this understanding, we humans have a choice that comes from our free-will. We can stay as we are, or we can choose to change and take responsibility for all that we are — including our feelings, our beliefs and our judgements.

If we choose to change, the change occurs spontaneously.

If we choose to stay as we are, limited by our existing patterns, beliefs and thought forms, there is no judgement. But there is acceptance — and in that acceptance there is also compassion. And that is a kind of change.

Once we accept ourselves, exactly as we are, we can move on — if we want, there is no compulsion — to seeing what serves us and what does not. From there, it is only a short step to deciding what we would like to keep and what we would like to fall away.

This sounds easy, but can be uncomfortable, especially if we realise that the things we need to let go are things, beliefs or people to whom we are attached. For this reason we need to be gentle with ourselves, giving ourselves time and encouragement as well as understanding. If you find difficulty in letting go, try blessing each thought, idea or belief — with gratitude for what it has taught you — before releasing it.

The Macrocosm – the Cosmos

'In the beginning was the word. The word was with God and the word was God.'

'Om — the sound of the universe.'

'The Big Bang.'

It all began with sound, whether you take as your text the Bible, the ancient Indian scriptures, Chinese metaphysical thinking or modern science.

In the beginning there was a sound and that sound continues to reverberate throughout the cosmos. Sound is the great creator, its vibrations spread and gather and return to the beginning, only to be recreated: so the cycle continues.

Sound is vibration. Vibration is sound.

As the sound of the universe swelled and grew and created particles, those particles began to cling together, forming larger particles that in turn found a belonging together, and those particles found an affinity with other particles. Particles continued to join together until we have the cosmos that we know today.

Everything of which we are aware had its seed in that first vibration of sound.

But it did not stop there, with the Creation: for sound, the creator, is also the destroyer. As sound swells and dies, so do we humans grow and fade — as does everything else that has its being in the Cosmos. As particles cling together, so they part and return to the matrix from which all is created and re-created.

Change, movement and energy are the only constants.

We are limited by our human senses. Whilst we are aware

that our ears pick up certain sounds, we know that there are sounds of both higher and lower vibrations that our sense of hearing cannot discern. Thus we speak of 'ultra-sound' when we mean a sound that our human ears cannot hear. We accept that there are different levels of hearing: not only does human hearing vary from individual to individual, but we know that dogs, animals and insects are sensitive to different frequencies from those of which we humans are aware.

The sounds we hear with our ears are those that travel comparatively slowly, because we can only pick up sounds of certain frequencies. Very low sounds are beneath our perception. As the frequency speeds up, the sound moves beyond our human capacity to hear with our ears: at higher frequencies we see vibration as light.

Light is vibration. Vibration is light.

Light is sound speeded up, travelling faster than the human ear or eye can follow. For years it was thought that light was the fastest vibration in the cosmos, but now it has been proved that there is a faster dimension.

This dimension is one that we can seldom discern within our bodies, but of which our living being — our body-mind-spirit — is aware. Those things we see with our inner eyes when our physical eyes are closed, those vibrations we pick up from the world about us — vibrations of which our senses are unaware — these are reverberations of the 'First Sound' thrumming through our being.

There are faster dimensions still: many are just being discovered as scientists unravel 'the field' in which we all have our being. Now it is known that there is no single universe but a multiverse of different dimensions. Now scientist and quantum-physicist alike accept that we do not live in a world of three, or possibly four, dimensions as had been previously thought. We live in a multi-dimensional world, scientists now agreeing that there are eleven or twelve dimensions to our cosmos. This resonates with centuries-old Buddhist teachings. And long before the Buddha lived, the sages of ancient India comprehended this, although, since their wisdom was passed on orally, their masterful understanding was not written down for centuries.

For those of us who seek to find more than the physical world around us, who feel that Life is greater than a single life on earth, who seek answers to the many facets of Life of which we are aware, although we know not how — it is time to awaken and acknowledge our inner knowing.

The Microcosm – the Human

Sound is a form of energy. Light is a form of energy. The earth is a form of energy. Plants are a form of energy. Animals are a form of energy. We humans are a form of energy.

Although we seem to be individuals in our own right, solid flesh and warm blood, in fact we are pure energy. We can recognise our thoughts as energy because they have no physical form, but it is much more difficult to see our individual bodies as nothing but vibrating energy. However, this is a fact. A fact which has been recognised by metaphysical thinkers and knowers for millennia: and — perhaps more importantly to those of us who are alive here and now — a fact which modern scientists and physicists also proclaim.

In the beginning was the word — or the twinkle in your father's eye, or the immense longing of your mother for a child. In the beginning there was ENERGY. From this word, longing, or twinkle emanated a being in its own right. First, the new being was simply a cell. A cell that used its energy to divide itself into two, according to the energetic pattern set down in its DNA — and then to replicate its cells into ever larger and more elaborate patterns and organs: until, over the course of nine months or so, a baby is born that holds within its small person the blueprint and energy of the adult it will become.

The pattern is set down in an acid that is contained within the baby's cells. DNA (deoxyribonucleic acid, a self-replicating material which is present in nearly all living organisms as the main constituent of chromosomes) is the shortened name by which we know this amazing structure of genes, so small that it is impossible to perceive with the naked eye, so specific that there is less than one chance in a million that someone else will have the same DNA pattern as you: unless you are an identical twin, when the possibilities are much higher.

The mitochondrial DNA passed down by the mother of a child seldom alters over the centuries. For this reason it is possible to find descendants of a known woman millennia after she has lived. However, the paternal offering is different, varying from child to child. The fascinating result is that when both parts join, the combined DNA pattern is unique to each individual.

It is well known that DNA is a double helix, spiralling round and twisted in upon itself, confined within a tiny space in each cell. The amazing reality is that, when stretched out, a single DNA strand measures a little over a metre — yet it is contained within the tiny nucleus of a cell that itself is invisible to the human eye. The only way to store this information within a cell is to contain it within a spiralling structure. This remarkable discovery — which was only made (by a woman, Rosalind Franklin) in the middle of the twentieth century — is now common knowledge.

It is this common knowledge which makes it easier to understand that energy, and thus the information it contains, is constantly in motion, spiralling through every atom and nano-particle in the cosmos. As energy spirals into form it travels in an anti-clockwise direction — the constructive cycle — but as it dissipates and moves out of form its polarity is reversed and it spins clockwise — the destructive cycle.

This constant spiralling movement, as things spin into form and then out again into formless energy, is illustrated by what happens in Nature. Each year, a plant will put out shoots, grow, flower, fruit, seed, die back and decay. The length of the process is different for each living thing, but this is the inevitable way of energy — constantly giving and constantly taking away. If this did *not* happen, the world could not exist as it is today. It would be full of the things that had not decayed. And the bacteria and fungi that feed on dead matter would have no function and no life.

As the process of Life continues, other factors begin to have a bearing on our cells. The usual factors are our thoughts and emotions, but nutrients, air, water, accidents and other apparently random events have an effect as well. Slowly our cells themselves change. And this means that they produce slightly different cells that they reproduce before they die — a process called apoptosis.

But I digress. Let me take you back to the spiralling form of energy: the Goddess's spiral of construction. Energy spins anti-clockwise as it comes in from the cosmos and permeates every fibre, every cell, every tiny space within our cells. This energy is strong and loving, containing all the information in the universe.

In spinning into form, we have ceased to be creatures simply 'of Spirit'. We have taken the decision to come to Earth: and in order to do so it is essential to clothe our beautiful, spiritual soul-energy in a physical body.

The vibration of the physical body is comparatively dense and gross. To exist, live and move, this form requires a completely different set of attributes — skin, limbs, organs, skeleton etc — but also organs of knowledge and thought, spiritual senses and a range of intuitions and emotions to guide it through the maze of Life.

Energy

As science has now ascertained, we humans (and all other living things) are far more than a physical body and a thinking mind. We are all living beings with an individualised energy field which makes us distinct from the energies surrounding us. However, essentially we are not separate, since we are all part of the living energy matrix that surrounds the planet and envelops the whole cosmos.

Urbanised creatures that we have become, we may find it difficult to comprehend that we are essentially a full and functioning part of Nature. We are dependent on Nature for everything that we have. No matter how clever we become at manufacturing 'man-made' goods, every single substance from which those goods are constructed, comes from, and is a part of, the planet on which we live.

We are dependent on the atmosphere to protect us from the strength of the sun's rays, on gravity to keep us secure on the Earth's surface, and other living organisms for the ability to continue to live. These include the bacteria on our skin that keeps our epidermis healthy; the bacteria in our intestines that produce our B vitamins, and the plants that clean and oxygenate the air that we breathe.

We are dependent on the oceans for the weather, for food and for the water in our cells; on the animals that provide us with food and warmth and that keep the planet's ecosystem in balance. The whole of life is dependent on the whole of life: a truth which brings us back to the beginning, and to the life force energy that permeates all things.

When the 'Big Bang' occurred, energy began to spiral outwards and that spiralling has never stopped from that moment onward. All energy is vibrant. All particles spin and move and constantly change.

In truth, change and movement are the only two constants in existence. The rates of change and movement may vary, but the essential constants do not.

The ancients understood this property of energy. They looked at the clouds and saw them move, they watched the spiralling currents in water and the way the rivers zig-zagged along their courses, they watched the ever-changing night skies and understood the procession of the stars and planets and the changing course of the sun. They recognised these things so well that they were able to build huge monuments like Stonehenge in England, the round towers in Ireland and the Pyramids of Egypt, all of which act as almanacs for the sun and stars.

Most importantly of all, they recognised that we are of the stars, made of the same substance as all of Life. Today, science recognises the truth of these observations and adds its own interpretations of the subject matter.

Although energy is constantly in motion, because of the rotation of the Earth, it never moves in a straight line. Always there is some spiralling movement along a line's length. The Earth's energy spirals like a snake or dragon and for this reason the creatures themselves were, and in several cultures still are, honoured and considered sacred. Examples are the song lines of Australia, and the green hollow roads of England. The great labyrinths of the world from Nebraska to Chartres Cathedral, all move in a spiralling motion from the periphery to the centre and from the centre back to the periphery.

4

Energy pathways and the Chakras

The Aura

If all the energy-information in the cosmos were available to us, our senses would experience overload and would be unable to function. For this reason we have a range of filters that process this energy-information.

The first of these filters is known in poetic Sanskrit as 'the aura'. In modern 'scientific speak' it is called *the electro-magnetic sheath*, but I will use the term *aura* to describe it.

Both ancient wisdom and modern science agree that the aura is a roughly egg-shaped envelope of energy, of a fairly low electro-magnetic frequency, that surrounds the physical body. Many factors — such as the health of the person, her awareness, her emotional and spiritual state, the nature of her personality and mood and her physical surroundings — affect the aura's size and efficacy.

The Auric Membrane:

Surrounding and containing an individual's aura is a strong, fine membrane that protects the stepped-down energy layers within. This membrane's function is to prevent certain energy-information — usually energy that is either of too high or of too low a frequency for the individual to bear — from entering the individual's electro magnetic field.

As energy is filtered into the auric system, the body-mind-spirit is continually adjusting to the information that energy contains. (Please note that I use the term 'body-mind-spirit' because it is clear that we are more than a physical body. We have beliefs, thoughts, aspirations and emotions that, in their totality, are unique to us; and they are all contained within our individual auric field.)

If a person's auric membrane is damaged or distressed, he or she is likely to suffer from spiritual, mental, emotional or physical problems.

The Auric Layers/Bodies:

We have already seen that the aura itself is subject to change. So, too, are the several layers of energy within the aura. These layers (often known as *bodies*) are formed as the frequency of the energy is gradually lowered on its way into the physical body. This system of layers is often described as similar to a series of Russian dolls that nest inside each other, but this analogy is flawed because there are no finite boundaries surrounding the auric layers. Each energy-frequency interpenetrates the others and all interpenetrate the physical body.

The Spiritual Body:

The layer of the human aura that contains spiritual understanding vibrates the fastest and thus can be sensed further away from the physical body-mind-spirit than layers of lower frequencies. Remember, though, that its vibration interpenetrates the person's whole being.

The Mental Body:

Much more dense in vibration is the auric layer of the mind: our thoughts. Thoughts are strong energy: so strong, in fact, that they can bend and mark a person's whole being. In this form they are often referred to collectively as 'the ego'.

The Emotional Body:

Close to this mental layer, and intimately linked with it, is the layer of our emotions. Thoughts and emotions are so interconnected that they constantly affect each other. For this reason this auric layer/level of energy is often considered as being joined with the layer of mind: 'the mental-emotional field.'

The Etheric Body:

Last of the auric layers is 'the etheric body'. Often seen as a thin bluish haze around the physical body, this is the energy 'blueprint' for the physical body and the field most easily seen with our physical eyes.

Other energy pathways

The Ten Long Currents

Inside all these inter-connected auric layers, the energy is not still: it is a swirling, spiralling mass of information. But as it enters the physical body the energy becomes more cohesive, running in streams through the etheric body. The Indian sages realised that these streams of a high frequency energy run along ten channels that encircle the physical body. Five streams on each side of the physical body run through the head and trunk (including the main organs) as well as through the limbs, fingers and toes. On the left side of the body they pass up the front and down the back, while on the right side the flow is reversed, running down the front and up the back.

The Meridians:

As their frequency reduces, these streams become both more confined and more defined. In the physical body they can be mapped precisely, and were named 'meridians' by Chinese scholars and 'nadis' by Indian guru-philosophers.

The Sushumna:

At the same time, spiritual energy from the cosmos streams down from the crown of the head through a central channel along the line of the spine, to the pelvic floor. From there it descends into the earth. This channel is called the 'Sushumna'. Through it, the energy of the universe is earthed. When the energy of the Sushumna reaches the earth, its polarity is reversed, and runs from the earth up the spine and out into the universe.

The Ida and Pingala:

On either side of the Sushumna channel are two spiralling energy lines known as the 'Ida' and 'Pingala'. They run from the nostrils to the base of the spine, and from the base of the spine upward. The Pingala is masculine and hot: the Ida is feminine and cold. These spiralling energies cross at various points along the spinal matrix and in those places they also interconnect with the energy centres that are known as 'chakras'.

These are not the only energy paths in the human body-mind-spirit that have been mapped by physicists and meta-physicists alike, but to include reference to more than those given above is beyond the scope of this book.

Chakras

'***Chakra***' is a Sanskrit word and its meaning is usually translated as 'wheel'. This word indicates the continuously spiralling whirling nature of the energy at these centres; centres which are the energy interface between our body-mind-spirit and our surroundings. The chakras are the vehicles that collect, interpret and deal with the information and power that is available to us through the energy that is processed here.

We seldom give a thought to the fact that we possess information about the world around us long before we react to that information. When we are in conversation with someone else, the words that he speaks account only for approximately seven per cent of the information we pick up about him. Long before he has finished speaking, we have processed his size and shape, his emotional baggage, his intentions, his feelings about the matter, the truth of what he is saying, whether he is lying, what we intuit he really wishes to say and some understanding of how his words relate to his spiritual belief system.

The way that we process this information is through our chakras.

We might say: 'I have a gut feeling about this…' What we are implying is that we have an emotional reaction (Sacral chakra) to whatever it might be. Again, we might acknowledge that 'His heart is not in it,' (Heart chakra) meaning that we are aware that he is not truly happy or committed.

I will pay more attention to the individual chakras in the sections dedicated to them, but first we need to be aware that as energy slows it becomes denser. Thus the vibration of the bones in our bodies is much slower, and the frequency lower, than in the liver or the skin.

The highest vibrational energy (approximately 2,500 htz) has been measured, by scientists, in the crown chakra: the lowest (approximately 250 htz) in the base chakra. As energy is stepped down at each chakra, the vibration rate becomes slower, so that the fastest spiritual energy whirls at the Crown chakra while the densest, most physical energy is found in the Base chakra.

Specific frequencies above the frequency of the Crown chakra have also been measured by scientists. These are the frequencies of meditation and evolve as the meditator raises his consciousness towards the Infinite.

The wonderful truth is that we have power over our own energy: and that power is exercised by our intention — by simply making a choice.

MORE ABOUT CHAKRAS

So without more ado, let's look a little more closely at the whirling centres of energy known as chakras.

Many have written more eloquently than I about the individual chakras and I don't intend to go into great detail here: I only want to give you an understanding of them.

The chakras are invisible to all but a few people, but that does not mean that they are not powerful. Quite the reverse. They exercise a powerful pull and impact on our mental-emotional-physical selves.

We are seldom aware of a chakra's impact on our physical energy. Often the only thing we notice is that we are feeling 'out-of-sorts', or nervous, or apprehensive. Sometimes this feeling is reflected in part of the body. Sometimes we feel nauseated, or sick, or unable to eat. Perhaps we are tearful and 'choked'; maybe we feel dizzy, or have a headache. These symptoms can present themselves suddenly or appear over a period of time. All are indications that a chakra is out of balance. The way to find out which one is causing the problem is to pay attention to your feelings and emotions and track them into the body.

In my experience, it is by becoming aware of how a chakra feels when it is *in* balance and functioning well, that we are able to notice when that chakra is out of balance and that we need to pay it more attention. So I believe it important to gather a *feeling* for each individual chakra. There are meditations to help you do this. Amongst many others is my own meditation CD (and mp3s) entitled *Spinning into Form* which is available from www.cdbaby.com.

When a chakra is balanced it is spinning happily, giving and receiving information from the whole cosmos in general and from our own aura and our other chakras in particular.

All chakras have an affinity with the organs and endocrine glands that are close to them, but I do not intend to go deeply into these relationships.

Once you experience the feeling of the chakra the rest will follow naturally. You will find yourself the owner of personal wisdom and understanding that you had no idea was available to you because we actually have access to far more understanding, inner knowing and intuition than we think. Too often we are brought up to believe that we know nothing unless our knowledge is garnered from books.

But all knowledge that is contained in other people's writings — including these — is from the writer's own mind. Their own thoughts, in fact. Or the thoughts of others re-worded and re-distilled.

You are so much more than that.

You are the essence of all mankind. Each of us is aware and open to all the knowledge in the universe and beyond. Our physical body, our brains and our thinking mind can only hold a microscopic amount of the information and knowledge available to us. Beyond the little 'self' is a huge self that has access to the whole, to All-That-Is. We are here on Earth to use the gifts we are given in this earthly life to discern those things that will make our lives full, happy and contented, useful to the cosmos and a gift to all Beings.

First we must throw away the trappings of our education and the belief systems that we have inherited or taken on from others. Only then are we ready to experience life in all its richness exactly as we were designed to do, and in the way that was ordained for us when we clothed our spirits in flesh and came down to this Earth.

We are here to be ourselves, truly ourselves; and in doing so to raise the vibrational level of all Life, not only on this planet but everywhere.

So throw out all that you think you know — and experiment. Take yourself back to the day you were born: perfect, a blank canvas on which Life has yet to be written. Allow yourself to forget all that you have learned from books, people, your environment, your family, teachers and gurus. You are your own guru. You have the power to choose your own belief system. You have the power to experiment with all that the chakras, in their magnificent simplicity, have to offer, and to learn — whatever your wishes and needs — from the process.

I will give only the most basic information on the seven major chakras so that you know the area to which you should give your attention.

BASE CHAKRA

Seed syllable/mantra: LAM

Relates to issues of: Security, Basic survival, Trust

The ***base chakra*** is situated at the bottom of the energy channel known as the Sushumna near the base of the spine. It spills out from the pelvic floor between the sex organs and the anus. General wisdom has it that the chakra spins downwards towards the ground. The slowest of the seven major chakras, its frequency is close to the magnetic field of the Earth.

Thus, the element to which this chakra relates is Earth, and the sense connected with it is the sense of smell. Its main function is of elimination, but we should always remember that all the atoms of our being are made from substances that come from this planet; and that when we die, whether we are cremated or buried, our atoms will return to the Earth: "dust to dust, ashes to ashes," in the words used in Christian funerals.

When we excrete, whether faeces, urine, sweat, breath or

thoughts, our excretions return to the world around us. Our excrement and urine is needed to support other forms of life that, in turn, support us. The beetles and bacteria that live on our waste matter process it into forms available to other units of life, making it available to plants which use it to grow. From our waste matter, plants fashion cool, green cathedrals for our refreshment and food for us to eat, not to mention the oxygen on which our breath depends. Life supports Life.

SACRAL/HARA CHAKRA

Seed syllable/mantra: VAM

Relates to issues of: Sexuality, Family

The ***sacral chakra*** is situated about three finger widths below the navel, shining out from where the top of the sacrum or pelvic girdle meets the spine. This chakra spins out towards the front of the body although some clairvoyants see it also emanating from the back. It is the second slowest of the seven major chakras, its frequency so close to that of the base chakra that in some healing modalities they are considered one.

The element to which this chakra relates is Water, and the sense connected with it is the sense of taste. The senses of taste and smell are so intimately connected that one does not function well without the other. The watery secretions of the mouth are vital to the sense of taste. We recognise this when our mouth literally waters when the sense of taste is stimulated — most often by delicious smells emanating from the kitchen.

But water is also changeable and liquid just as our emotions tend to be, constantly changing from one moment to the next.

Thus it follows that this is a chakra where perpetual change is normal. Related to it are the kidneys, a paired organ, indicating that this chakra relates to twosomes and partnerships. Since the reproductive organs are also dependent on watery secretions, it follows that such partnerships are often of the emotional and/or romantic kind. It follows, too, that this chakra is concerned with reproduction and creativity as well as with the emotions.

When we 'go with the flow' we allow our emotions to settle of their own accord. This action also reflects our inner strength, for we cannot conquer our emotions by controlling or ignoring them. We need to allow the feeling of the emotion to show us the place in our bodies where we feel unsettled or uncomfortable. Then we can bring our attention to that part of ourselves and then — do nothing. Simply be, breathing into the part that feels out of balance. Usually the place feels tight and uncomfortable, or perhaps unsettled.

It is easy and familiar to judge the feeling and ourselves. Classic thoughts or words are: 'pull your socks up', 'how could you do that?', 'you should know better'. All of these reactions pull us away from the feeling itself and bring in a great deal of judgement.

Why should we judge ourselves? What is the benefit? To answer the second question first: there are no benefits. And judgement serves no purpose at all. What is the point of it? Better to be aware. If there are things that breed discontent, awareness of them allows us to see them for what they truly are and to take appropriate action.

Remember: feelings are one of the body's ways of showing where there is an imbalance. Once we know this we can help to rectify the situation.

I suggest that you sit with the feeling/emotion, no matter how raw it may feel. Simply allow it to be there within your body and your energy field. Then begin to 'give it space': imagine the feeling relaxing more and more with each breath. Allow it to dissipate and it will gradually fade.

Do not analyse your feelings. Just sit with them, feeling the feelings in your body and becoming aware of the emotions they contain or represent. Like the tide, emotions ebb and flow, changing constantly.

Emotions and feelings are what give our lives light and shade. Without them, life would be bland. With them, we are open to new experiences and understanding. Celebrate your ability to feel, remembering that sadness is just the other side of happiness. All emotions are just that — emotions — they are not who we are, but they can be powerful if we allow them to be so, holding us within a straight-jacket of 'shoulds', 'musts' and 'oughts.' Just for a while, let go of any conditioning — no matter how much it is shrieking for attention — and simply breathe.

SOLAR PLEXUS CHAKRA

Seed syllable/mantra: RAM

Relates to issues of: Immortality, Authenticity, Fame, Will

The ***solar plexus chakra*** is situated above the diaphragm at the point where the sternum ends and the ribs part, shining out like the sun for which it is named. This chakra spins out from the front of the body and less so from the back. This is the centre of our being and the frequency is faster than those of the base and sacral chakras.

The element to which this chakra relates is Fire, and the sense connected with it is the sense of sight. It is the centre of our being, our personal sun, the place from which we shine our light and the chakra of our own personal will and our sense of self. A fire burns brightly, illuminating all before it. But it can also burn too fast, burning itself out. Or it can burn too slowly, easily dowsed by the water of emotion. Sometimes it burns too fiercely, without concern for others or their surroundings; or too weakly, when it is at the mercy of any enemy.

The Solar Plexus Chakra's main function is digestion — the digestion of food, certainly, but also the digestion of ideas, events, happenings, problems, difficulties, etcetera. The nature of fire is unpredictability. While we know that fire can be a sudden explosion that spreads fast like the bush fires in Australia, it is helpful to remember that even a slowly burning fuse can ignite a whole barrel of gunpowder. If we allow our fire to go out or to burn too low, we will have no energy for ourselves, no energy to do those things we wish to do, and we will be at the mercy of those who wish to take our power and have us do their bidding. Too often, this can be seen in controlling situations or partnerships where one person strips away the power of another, slowly, (or not so slowly) dowsing their fire.

We need to nurture and feed our personal fire, letting its flames burn away all the dross within us. We need to own our fire and tend it carefully, as we digest all the life experiences through which we pass.

Like water, fire is changeable but it is vital we keep it alight and glowing. It gives us our energy, our juice and our power.

It is deeply connected to the breath. Air fans the embers of a dying fire or cools a fire that has burned too hot. When our fire is out of control, we can experience anger, a need to control, nervousness, anxiety, a fierce possessiveness, a sense of powerlessness, or a red rage.

Again, allow space for the fire to burn. Sit with the feelings and emotions in your body, those feelings and emotions that are connected to the solar plexus and relate to our personal space and our sense of will and of simply being. Allow the fire to be there, accept it and breathe ...

HEART CHAKRA

Seed syllable/mantra: YAM

Relates to issues of: Love, Faith, Duty, Devotion

The ***heart chakra*** is situated in the centre of the chest at the level of the heart and the fifth of the twelve thoracic vertebrae. Sometimes, tongue in cheek, I call this the 'bra-strap' level. This chakra spins out towards the front of the body although some clairvoyants see it also emanating from the back.

It is the gateway between the three lower chakras — which are mostly concerned with our earthly, emotional, physical body and our connection to Earth — and the three upper chakras, which are our connection to the Universe and Spirit. As such, the Heart Chakra holds the key to the merging of our physical, emotional, earthly selves (The Goddess, the Earth Mother) with the energy of the universe (God, the Heavenly Father)

The element to which the Heart chakra relates is Air, and the sense connected with it is Touch. Its main physical function is concerned with the breath and breathing, the only unconscious action that we can also do consciously. But its main purpose is to allow us to feel, understand, and become aware of the nature of unconditional love.

This unconditional love must start with ourselves. Only if we can accept every part of ourselves — exactly as we are in each moment — can we offer unconditional love to other beings, both conscious and unconscious, on this planet and beyond. When we link in to the nature of the love — which surrounds us, and which is the unifying force of All-That-Is, the cosmos and the million universes that are present in every tiny speck of dust — only then can we be fully conscious and fully functioning spiritual beings within the temple of our earthly bodies.

Love is in the air. Love is carried on the air that we breathe. We breathe the cosmos's love into our souls and bodies with each in-breath; and with each out-breath we send out our own unconditional love to the cosmos and all that has its being in the magnificence of the world around us.

THROAT CHAKRA

Seed syllable/mantra: HAM

Relates to issues of: Creativity, Knowledge, Abundance

The ***throat chakra*** is situated at the base of the neck, in the hollow below the epiglottis or Adam's apple. It is the centre of our creativity and the place from where we speak *our* truth, no matter what that truth may be.

This centre spins outwards, its frequency higher than the Heart Chakra. Now we are moving into the realms of the spiritual, for it is the throat chakra through which we communicate, not only through words on the physical level, but through communication with all levels of being, including angels, arch-angels, nature spirits and the Earth itself. This list is not exclusive as there are many other levels of communication.

The throat chakra is connected to the ears as well as to the voice. It therefore relates to true hearing, listening, and understanding, as well as to speech. Because of this, it is also the centre of creativity. When we really listen to higher understanding and directions we are able to create wonderful things of which our rational selves may be completely ignorant.

Sometimes inspiration comes to us in dreams. This is the centre through which other realms communicate with us and is often easier — because there is less interference from our rational minds — when we are in a semi-conscious state. Many famous inventors, Tesler and Eddison amongst them, have found the answer to conundrums in lucid dreams given to them by this centre; dreams which they have remembered in a conscious state and put to good use.

Our rational mind can block the urgings of the higher intelligence that brings us this information. Sometimes we deny the very possibility of receiving important messages 'through the ether'. Funnily enough, the element of this chakra is Ether. Here I use the Ayurvedic term for this amazing energy which is of a substance finer than the gaseous air that we breathe. Ether is space: the space between our joints, inside our sinuses, that is part of each cell in our body. It is the substance in which all the vibrating atoms in our cells move and 'have their being'.

Ether is fine, but it is strong. It is the substance that

conveys our thoughts and directions to the autonomic nervous system — the system of which we are not consciously aware, but which controls all aspects of the living life force within us. Bringing awareness to the functioning of this element within our very being allows us to communicate with unseen, unknown realms and to bring their wisdom to our daily lives.

So, once again, I urge you to breathe and to take your full awareness and consciousness to this chakra and this aspect of your being.

BROW CHAKRA

Seed syllable/mantra: SHAM

Relates to issues of: Intuition, Insight, Realisation

From the ***throat chakra*** we move upwards on the ether towards the ***brow or Third Eye Chakra*** which lies in the centre of the head: its energy emanates from between the eyebrows. If we close our eyes we can sense this place, a place where a 'third eye' would be if we possessed one.

This centre spins outwards. Its frequency is very high because it is the centre through which we experience our intuition or inner knowing. This is also the chakra of 'mind'.

At the Brow chakra all communication is through the medium of light, vibrating at a speed which makes it almost impossible for the human body to detect. Instead, we understand and interpret it as colour, dreams or visions — and it is interesting that even people who have been blind from birth often experience these phenomena. Sometimes we even say: 'the light dawned' when we receive some information which makes all other things as 'plain as day'.

The Brow Chakra pierces the space between the two

hemispheres of the brain, the rational left brain and the intuitive right brain. When we allow a balance here between the two halves of our brain, we allow light to inform each of our cells at a vibrational level far higher than our conscious minds can even imagine. Luckily we have no need to understand or perceive this light — all we need to do is to take our awareness to this centre and meditate on the purest form of light.

Light shines from the oily membrane that surrounds and contains each of our cells. Kirlian and other scientific photography confirm that our energy field is a field of light. This is the chakra through which we experience that light, allowing it to make us whole — healing us at a spiritual level before the energy is stepped down in vibration to serve the lower chakras.

'To those who seek, it shall be given'. If we come to the Light of the brow chakra with trust, humility and openness, the Light itself will reveal to each of us the truth of our being and the joy of existence. Light is a true blessing to those who are prepared to trust in the highest good and the highest realms of communication and vibration.

CROWN CHAKRA

Seed syllable/mantra: OM

Relates to issues of: Union, Unbounded Awareness

The ***crown chakra***, known in Sanskrit as the 'thousand petalled lotus', is different from all the other chakras. Situated on the crown of the head in the place which is open longest before the fontanels finally close together, this 'soft spot' can be easily seen in new-born babies. Often it is pulsing slightly;

for it does not close completely until a child is nearing five years of age.

From this spot, a myriad sparkling filaments of energy expand and rise towards the heavens, reaching out into the cosmos like a thousand pulsating sensors — which indeed, they are. This is the centre into which the energy of the universe pours, filtered by the aura and these filaments into a form which we can absorb, interpret with our physical senses, and use with our physical body.

This is the centre through which our spiritual self, our soul, enters our body and makes us alive. It is not to be confused with the artificial way that the life force can be kept within the body by machines. This spiritual self, this light body, is the Truth of who we are, being of a much finer energetic substance than the denser energy of the mind and intuition at the Brow Chakra level.

While the Brow Centre seeks to balance our rational mind 'the ego' with our spacial mind 'the intuition', the Crown Chakra is the funnel for the life force which is known as compassion or supreme love. This is love that asks nothing more than to exist. Even though we may deny it, seeking to use our mind to bring about those things and events we seek — and even though we may be very successful at this during our lifetime — at the end of our time here on Earth within the temple of our spiritual body, it is to Love that we return. For love is the energy of the universe. And spirit is the vehicle for that love to enter our being, the body-mind-spirit that is the physical experience of our presence on Earth.

And so, to Spirit, and through Spirit, we will always return to All-That-Is, the Oneness from which all creation springs.

It can be tempting to abide here at the Crown Chakra, so

that we can dismiss the trials of everyday life. But everyday life, with its challenges and rewards are what we are here to experience on this planet. We sell ourselves short if we do not embrace human life and the human condition to the full. Only by doing so can we rise beyond joy and sorrow, into the wonder of 'The One'.

CHAKRAS IN BRIEF

BASE CHAKRA
Seed syllable/mantra: LAM
Relates to issues of: Security, Basic survival, Trust

HARA/SACRAL CHAKRA
Seed syllable/mantra: VAM
Relates to issues of: Sexuality, Family

SOLAR PLEXUS CHAKRA
Seed syllable/mantra: RAM
Relates to issues of: Immortality, Authenticity, Fame, Will

HEART CHAKRA
Seed syllable/mantra: YAM
Relates to issues of: Love, Faith, Duty, Devotion

THROAT CHAKRA
Seed syllable/mantra: HAM
Relates to issues of: Creativity, Knowledge, Abundance

BROW CHAKRA
Seed syllable/mantra: SHAM
Relates to issues of: Intuition, Insight, Realisation

CROWN CHAKRA
Seed syllable/mantra: OM
Relates to issues of: Union, Unbounded Awareness

5

What is Reiki?

Ah, this is an interesting question. Words are paltry things when it comes to defining Reiki, because, in general, language relates to the physical world while Reiki, like all energy, exists in the land beyond the senses. A land I call 'the place of inner knowing'.

So, having said that it's impossible to define Reiki, I will do my best to do precisely that.

Although Reiki is described variously as *universal life force energy, a natural healing modality*, or *a form of spiritual healing*, the truth is that Reiki, while encompassing all these, is yet something far more.

Most people come to Reiki because they are interested in healing. And they are usually interested in healing others rather than themselves. In true Reiki, healing is a by-product. Healing is an 'extra' that one experiences as part of the practice of Reiki.

In its truest and simplest form, Reiki is a spiritual path: a way of connecting to the inner wisdom that runs deep in the core of each of us. This inner wisdom is the God-spark, the divine essence, that is connected to All-That-Is, to the Divine, to the Life Force that permeates every cell of your body.

I should say here that Reiki has nothing to do with religion, or religious dogma. The Divine I mention here is the highest good, whatever you perceive that to be. What the words '***the Divine***' mean to you may be completely different from what they mean to me. That is absolutely fine and how it should be.

We are each a tiny but essential part of the wonderful creation that is the web of Life on this planet. We are made from the Earth. Thus, we are each connected to the sun, the stars, the universe, the twelve or more dimensions, the multiverse. Reiki is our connection to all of this.

When we allow ourselves to merge with the ultimate wisdom, the energy of creation, then we are experiencing Reiki. As we become aware of this wonderful light, bright energy, we make ourselves into a vessel, and allow the energy to fill us to overflowing. Soon we can use our conscious self to channel Reiki from the outermost reach of the universe into our lives, for our benefit, and the benefit of all Beings, everywhere, in all forms.

Meditation is the key. As we quiet our mind and bring our attention to the breath, we learn to allow Reiki to guide us spiritually; then we can choose consciously to walk the Reiki path to enlightenment, when all troubles fade, all problems cease to be. In the light, with Reiki, we meld into the universal consciousness: we cease to strive. We become one with All-That-Is.

This is a natural process. It is our birthright: it is part of who we are. So we do not have to do anything to be in Reiki, we simply accept it, simply allow ourselves to become a channel between the Light of the Universe and the Darkness of the Earth.

As Reiki is natural, so is healing. We are all natural healers. It is what we are, what we do. If you cut your finger, it heals by itself. You might wash it to make sure it is clean, you might cover it to keep it so, but the healing is done by your own body. You do not have to think about it. The body's own intelligence knows what needs to be done and supplies all that is needed.

Meaning of Reiki Kanji

The Reiki Kanji

To explain this in a profound but simple way, let us look at the old-fashioned kanji for Reiki. This is the 'picture writing' of China, also known as Chinese characters, and used in Japan up to the second World War. After WW2 the Japanese eschewed Chinese characters and developed their own script. And so, for some time, a lot of Reiki scripts became unreadable and apparently lost. Luckily for us, they have been re-discovered and translated during the past fifteen years or so.

Actually, the Japanese have no sound in their language that equates with 'r', so they would pronounce the word 'Leiki'. However, Reiki has travelled round the world during the past seventy years or so as 'Reiki'. That is the word we use for it in the West, so that is how I teach it.

Now let's look more deeply into the Rei-ki Kanji. Two Chinese characters that are put together to give a particular sense and an extra dimension to the word. The upper character stands for *Rei*: the lower one for *Ki*.

Ki is the Japanese word for life force energy that is known as Qi or Chi in China, as Prana in India, and as the Vital Force in Europe. It is the spark, the energy that makes us alive. All healing modalities, and most spiritual paths, make use of this marvellous energy within us. The Chinese Kanji for 'Ki' shows the starlike character for 'rice' within the more flowing character meaning 'a vehicle'. Thus we have both the vital force and energy that is rice, the basic food stuff of the East, and a container that moves and is made for such movement. Such is *Ki*.

Rei is a much more subtle concept: one that is difficult to convey. A Japanese student of mine once covered nearly two sides of A4 lined paper with meanings for *Rei*. They ranged from 'tomb' to 'universe'. So let us now look at the *Rei* kanji in more depth.

The first, upper part indicates a precipitation, something coming down from heaven. It might be snow, or rain, or manna, or light or blessings.

Beneath this precipitation are three small squares in a line. One such small square indicates a mouth: two squares therefore indicate speech; and three, as here, indicate prayer.

Next there is a line which indicates heaven, a lower line that signifies 'earth' and a vertical line in the centre that represents the connection between the two. On either side of this line is a small 'h' — the kanji for a person, in this case a shaman. One 'h' would indicate a man, two mean both men and women. Thus we have an indication that humankind form an energetic and physical connection between the universe and the planet.

So, if we put all this together, we see that humankind is the bridge between Heaven and Earth, communicating through prayers (of gratitude and with healing intent) with the divine element of the universe which showers down upon us all that we need (blessings).

The universe does not discriminate. The energy that

comes from the universe is 'universal' in all meanings and implications of the word, continually pouring gifts upon us all, equally: gracing us with blessings that are abundant: limitless: endless.

Thus heavenly *'Rei'* informs and permeates the earthly *'Ki'*, in an energy that incorporates the spiritual with the physical.

As Reiki brings us into balance, our heavenly, spiritual abundance informs our earthly existence and makes us whole. This is healing: for the word 'heal' comes from the same root as the word 'whole'. They are the same.

Maybe we should speak of 'wholing' rather than of 'healing'?

ENERGY: EXERCISE

Right. That's enough chat for now. Let's have some fun with energy.

Stand up. Have a shake to loosen all those muscles. Circle your shoulders again, and your knees. And your ankles. Now circle your elbows and wrists. Shake your hands from side to side ... and up and down. Open and close your fingers ... mad piano playing.

Okay, now relax your hands and slowly bring the palms towards each other until you feel the slightest resistance. Separate your hands again and repeat. Gradually allow yourself to build a ball of energy between your hands. To me it feels very fine but quite definite. I always think of it as candy floss. Light and sweet, almost not there, and yet very sticky.

Some people may find that it takes a little longer for them to sense this than it does for others. That's fine. People sense energy differently. Much of your sense of energy will depend on when, and how often, knowingly or not, you use it.

If you feel nothing, that's fine too. Keep practising and eventually it will happen. I have never yet found someone who could not sense energy this way. For now, just pretend.

When you're holding this energy ball, play with it. Take it above your head … down to your feet. Balance it on one hand … then the other. Divide it in two. Take one ball up and the other down. Move them apart … and back together.

When you've had enough, either guide the energy ball into your solar plexus, or gently push it down to the floor for use by the Earth.

Take notice of your hands. How do they feel? They may be warmer, softer, lighter, colder, fizzy, or anything else. Mine usually feel slightly fizzy. Be open to the whole range of possibilities including ones I haven't mentioned. Be aware that you have sensitised your hands by taking your awareness to them, and also by energising them.

Now that your hands are sensitised, let's see what else we can sense.

Hold your dominant hand, palm down, a little way out in front of you. Raise your non-dominant hand, palm down, as high as you can comfortably reach. Now close your eyes. Bring the upper hand slowly down towards the back of the lower one. Stop when you sense energy. Maybe warmth, perhaps coolness, a slight sense of resistance in either hand, a tingle, perhaps.

Open your eyes and see how far apart your hands are. You will have come into contact with one of the layers in your aura. Usually people stop a couple of inches or so above the lower hand. This is the layer of the etheric body, which is the energetic blueprint for your physical body, it is often sensed as being slightly blue, too.

I always find this exciting, no matter how often I do it. Maybe it's just that I realise I can sense energy even though I don't see it.

Anyway, now you can play. I suggest you keep your eyes shut, because I, personally, find it easier to sense energy without the distraction of sight. But you may be different. You may like to discover whether you can actually see a pale blue mist around your limbs … your whole body, in fact.

Move your upper hand. First along the arm. See whether you can sense the energy with both your palm and your arm.

Then, using both hands, gently sweep your hands over other parts of your body. See what you sense. Write it down, if you like.

When you feel happy with this exercise, try the same 'sensing' exercise with another member of the class. You need permission, of course, as you are about to enter that person's personal space. If you, or anyone else, don't want to take part, that's fine. Take responsibility for your own personal comfort in this situation. But it is interesting, especially if you see whether you can sense a change in the person's energy. From warm to cold perhaps … or from fizzy to nothing.

Have fun together. Experiment. Enjoy. Make notes of what you have experienced.

When you feel you have completed this exercise, simply sit down and relax.

Now, perhaps you would like to share your experience? No pressure. If you prefer to stay quiet, that's fine.

If you find that you have not been able to sense anything, just keep on trying. Not now, exactly, but from time to time over the next few days. It *will* happen, I assure you.

What have we learned?

From this exercise, I hope you have learned, if you didn't

already know, that we can all feel energy, or at least be aware of it.

That energy is part of our electromagnetic field, also known as the aura. This field is not simply a concept. It is a fact: demonstrated by the MRI scans that use our Magnetic Resonance to discover what is happening inside our physical bodies. At last science and physicists in particular, are catching up with the metaphysical knowledge of the ancients.

In Reiki we work with this energy field. We simply allow the Reiki energy to flow through our hands. In doing so, Reiki assists the recipient's subtle energy to readjust to the perfection of its energetic blue-print.

6

The Body-Mind-Spirit

I am sure that you all know that we are more than just a physical body.

After all, each of us has a mind that thinks.

Each of us has emotions that feel.

Each of us has a psychic sense, or intuition, that informs us.

Most of us know that we have a spirit that is more than all these things: the part that does not die when we cease to breathe, or even when our body dissolves back into the elements from which it was formed. This is the part that all religions mention: the eternal soul, or spirit.

Reiki does not belong to any one religion or philosophy. Reiki is pure energy, and so these concepts are simply unimportant.

But Reiki does work on all these different aspects of our being, so it is important to understand their relevance.

We have played with the etheric field that surrounds and permeates our bodies. In the same way, the other vibrational energies I have mentioned actually exist in earth time and on the earth plane — even though we find it difficult to comprehend them with our senses. They exist just the same, and the function of Reiki is to bring them all into balance.

Reiki works in perfect right order and in perfect right time. Miracles are natural. They happen all the time. But only about one per cent of miracles are instantaneous.

All healing modalities have to work with the full person: body, mind and spirit, and Reiki is no exception.

Reiki requires the consent of the person receiving the Reiki energy before it can bring all parts into balance. And remember that, even if they do consent on all levels of their being, their healing must be for the highest good of all concerned with the process.

Dowsing the Aura

If you like, I'll demonstrate the layers of the aura with my dowsing rods. Do I have a volunteer?

Please stand at the other side of the room. Turn your side towards me so that you do not feel invaded by the energy from my rods.

Watch as my rods find the edge of each level of energy. When they do they will cross.

- This is the membrane of your aura.
- This is the edge of your spiritual body… the highest in vibration although, like the other vibrations it permeates the whole of the aura and the physical body.
- This is the edge of your emotional body…
- This is the edge of your mental body…
- You will see that they are very close together and intermingled. Sometimes the mental body stretches further, sometimes the emotional one…
- This is the etheric body … the blueprint for the physical body
- And this is the physical body itself. (Touching it)

Isn't it amazing how far out the aura stretches? And the light bodies, or layers?

Can you see how each aura overlaps everyone else's?

That is how we obtain information about them. Our thoughts and emotions affect others as well as ourselves, as you can see. Thought is a very strong energy. So strong that most other energy follows it. 'I think, therefore I am' is a very powerful concept — and a truth.

Garner your thoughts.

If you are a 'lazy thinker' — by this I mean that you allow your thoughts, and thus your ego-mind, to rule your energy — this is a good time to learn what you can achieve by controlling your thoughts and turning them towards a happy, healthy objective.

7

The Reiki Ethic

As you can imagine, there is a huge amount you can learn about Reiki, but, although it's all interesting, and intriguing, it's not actually necessary.

There are four things that are absolutely vital for you to take away from Reiki 1. Anything else can wait until you are absolutely conversant with these:

1. The Reiki Ethic
2. The Reiki Principles (sometimes called The Reiki Precepts)
3. The hand positions for self-healing
4. The hand positions for healing others.

Let's start with: **THE REIKI ETHIC**

***This healing is for the highest good of all concerned*.**

First, I must emphasise that it's essential to use these words in every healing you do, whether it's for others or for yourself. No cheating … use the exact words. You can say it inwardly or out loud. I personally prefer to say it internally. The other important thing is to turn your mind to the full meaning of the words as you repeat them.

Let me explain:

'This healing

The meaning here is quite straightforward, but let me just add a couple of points.

'This'

This particular repetition of the words is in respect of this one-off event. *This* healing only.

'Healing'

The word 'heal' comes from the same Anglo-Saxon root as the word 'whole'. Thus our intention here is that the object of the healing is made 'whole'. I don't think 'whole-ing' is a word, but perhaps you can think of it this way.

Remember: You don't know what is needed to make this person whole. All you can do is to have the intention to lay before the person's energy a smorgasbord of possibilities. It is for the person's own inner knowing to choose what is required and when.

'...Is for the highest good.'

'Highest'

Your intention is that the energy and healing offered to the person is appropriate for that person at that time. Again, we cannot know what that is, so we leave it to the Reiki energy and the receiver to interpret.

'Good'

It is important to state that the intention is for 'good', not good as opposed to evil, but good in all senses of the word. 'Good' is simple and easy. It is not for power over the person, or self-aggrandisement of the Reiki healer, or even what you think of as 'good'. You do not know. If you flavour these words with your own intention, wishes, or even thoughts of what is required, then you take on the spiritual responsibility for being correct.

'Of all concerned.'

Again these words have a deeper meaning. Of course, they include two people: you — the Reiki healer — and the recipient of the Reiki. But to show how they mean so much more than that, let me remind you of some quantum theory.

Quantum Theory

We know (we think!) that the universe began in a 'Big Bang' and then exploded to its current dimensions. It is still expanding. Within it, light and other things move. These are the 'elementary particles' — you know them as electrons, photons, quarks and gluons — that are the components of everything that sways in space around us. There is no such thing as a real void, a place that is completely empty. The fields that form the world are constantly in motion, even if only in minute fluctuations. These fields are continually created and destroyed by these movements.

I cannot explain this completely in the time we have, but what I am basically saying is that every thought, every action, every emotion by one person affects every other person in the world.

If you would like to know more about quantum physics, I suggest that you obtain a copy of Carlo Rovelli's very readable little book *Seven Brief Lessons on Physics.*

To go back to what I was saying before I started on quantum physics — when we use the word 'all concerned' we are, in effect, including the whole of creation and all the possibilities it contains.

How can one little person like me comprehend what is best for this person who needs healing? How can I possibly see the whole picture? To start with, I only have my own limited knowledge and experience to call on.

I need to call on the highest good, the Divine, who sees all things. As I have said earlier, what *the Divine* is to *you* is unlikely to be the same as it is to me. It does not matter. All that matters is that we have understood that we cannot know the answer, because we don't even know the question.

All we can do is to act from a state of compassionate love and to allow our energy field to be the vehicle for the divine energy that is Reiki. As Reiki flows, we take our human self out of the picture entirely. We are in a state of trust. In this state all things are possible. We allow the Reiki recipient the opportunity to choose what is appropriate in this precise moment.

That is all we have to do.

How to Use the Ethic

The lovely thing about having this formula is that it allows you to take yourself, or in my case, myself — me, with all my own hopes and fears, worries and wishes, concerns for the recipient, my desire to make them well, to free them from pain, and whatever else — out of the whole situation.

Before I start a healing, whether for myself or anyone else, I stand with my hands in the gassho — the prayer position at my heart centre — and repeat these words.

'This healing is for the highest good of all concerned.'

Then I take a step to one side. Now I have stepped out of me, myself — and into Marion, Reiki channeller.

Now it's easy to let the Reiki flow through me and into the recipient, even if *I am* the recipient. I know that the Reiki will have a flavour of my energy but it will be free of all the other things I mentioned.

8

About Reiki 1

Reiki 1 can be challenging because it may be the first time you recognise your own personal vibrational level. And it may also be the first time you become aware of the differences a Reiki attunement can make to your vibrational energy.

You may think you are bobbing along quite happily in a sea of energy. Everything is literally going 'swimmingly'. You are well, happy and healthy in all aspects of your life. Or you may feel that you are drowning under the weight of life's expectations and troubles.

Either way, Reiki will make a difference. Receiving an attunement (or, as in the case of Reiki 1) four attunements, will allow you to channel a higher vibration of the Life Force energy. Some Reiki Masters say that your ability to receive the higher vibrations of energy means that your personal energy is squared, that is, multiplied by itself. I do not know that this is always the case, but I do know that people are able to perceive and channel a much higher vibration of energy than is their norm before being attuned to the Reiki 1 energy.

Even so, the energy you can channel at this stage is of a lower vibration than that of a Reiki Master or of an adept in another energy tradition.

Reiki 1 is the energy of self-healing and of healing physical ills and disturbances.

I'll repeat that as it is very important.

Reiki 1 level Reiki is for:

1. *Yourself,* and
2. The *physical* body.

In this workshop we will concentrate on these two areas of healing. I will go into these aspects in more detail later, but for now, I would like to tell you a little about how I teach this class.

The Reiki 1 class

I divide the two whole days we have together into four half days.

In each of these segments we will:

- ✓ Spend some time learning and discussing the basis of Reiki
- ✓ Do some form of exercise
- ✓ A meditation — which may be either active or passive
- ✓ Receive an attunement to the Reiki energy
- ✓ Do some practical 'hands-on' work.

I intend, and hope, that by the end of the workshop you will have a thorough understanding of Reiki and be able to use it for yourself and for others.

From what I have just said, you will realise that there are four attunements to Reiki 1. The reason for this is that it is beneficial for the student if the Reiki energy is brought in slowly. Of course, we all channel energy all the time. The great life force which keeps us alive is … just energy, after all.

However, there will be a great difference in the amount of energy and the vibration of that energy which you will be able to channel after this workshop. If it comes in too fast it can cause a shock to your existing energy, particularly if your personal energy is at all depleted. Thus:

The ***first*** attunement is to bring the Reiki energy down into your aura.

The ***second*** attunement pulls the energy through your crown, third eye, heart, solar plexus and palm chakras.

The ***third*** attunement separates you — the student — from me — the Reiki Master.

The ***fourth*** attunement is simply a blessing that you will always use Reiki for the highest good.

9

Looking After Your Energy

You need to keep your own inner energy high in order to be able to access the Reiki energy because Reiki is of much higher vibration than we are accustomed to. If we want to fully experience Reiki we have to be vibrating at as high a frequency as we can.

So how do you keep your energy high? The answer is within. Be aware of your own body and you will know.

Sleep

Quality sleep is vital. The length of time you sleep is less so. Sometimes it can be beneficial to have two sleeps, one at night and one during the day. In medieval times, the night was divided into two halves: the first sleep, and the second sleep. In between the two, people would wake, make love, 'go to the bathroom', often dress, eat and even go out to visit friends. Of course, in the winter, especially in the northern hemisphere, the nights were long and cold and a break in sleep allowed for such things as stoking the fire and exercising.

Exercise

Exercise is more about moving the body than anything else. While it may suit some people to jog every morning there are many other ways. Personally, I feel that some gentle yoga, pilates or simple stretches are as good as half an hour at the gym. The important thing is to move with your body. Link in and see how it wants to move. Allow the moving to happen organically. You'll be amazed at the contortions you can do quite easily. Shaking is another exercise that clears loads of stress from the body.

In fact, let's do some now. It's simple and very effective.

Stand up and have a good long stretch. Now take your awareness into your body and see if you can become aware of the places where you are holding tension of any sort, aches, pains, or tightness. Don't try and change anything, just take an inventory of how it is for you right now.

Now I'll put on some music. I like the first part of Osho's Kundalini meditation which has been composed for this very purpose. But you can try anything with a beat that feels right.

Okay. Close your eyes, and go within. Now start to shake. Start at the top.

- Loosen your jaw and your shoulders.
- Shake out your arms, wrists and hands.
- Let the movement carry on down to your hips ... and your legs ... your knees ... your ankles ... your feet. You can stand on one foot to shake the other. You can lie on the floor and shake both arms and legs.
- Really get into it. Feel the loosening that is happening all over your body.
- Go back and check that your jaw is loose.
- Keep shaking.

Keep shaking for at least five minutes. Keep your eyes closed the better to shut out the outside world and go within. Enjoy. Enjoy the freedom from all cultural constraints against freedom of movement; from all taboos, self-imposed or otherwise.

Then stop. Keep your eyes closed. Take another internal inventory. How do you feel now?

Doing this in the morning clears the mind and emotions. You will find you are more relaxed and more able to cope with whatever your day brings. Shaking in the evening, before bed, helps to remove tension and to promote good, healthy and restful sleep.

WATER

Diet. By this, I simply mean what you eat and drink. Let's deal with the 'drink' bit first. The single most important thing is to drink plenty of … WATER.

As you probably already know, water makes up about 70 per cent of your body. The brain is about 80 per cent water.

Water has a memory and it is now thought that most communication between cells is done by means of water memory. Chemical communication (especially between glands by way of the chemical messengers known as hormones) certainly happens; but this, by itself, without water, would not be instant. It simply takes too long.

So each thought that you have happens by way of water.

Each movement you make depends on there being enough water in your muscles to enable them to move and slide over one another.

Water is needed by each sinew. Water is needed in each of your joints to allow them to function: cartilage gliding across cartilage.

Your digestive system needs water to move the food you eat through your intestines and colon, which is in effect a long tube.

Your blood needs water. How else would it flow around your body taking nutrients and removing toxins?

Your lymph (immune system) needs water.

Water is needed to remove waste products from the body.

The list goes on and on, but I'm not going to. Or at least, not at this precise moment.

Just be aware. Your body NEEDS water. It does not need any other liquid, good as others may taste and pleasurable as their effects may be.

We each need to drink about ***two whole litres*** of water a day. And no … no other liquid counts as water. To the body anything else is seen as a food and therefore needs to be digested. Digestion takes energy and water.

A word of caution. If you are unaccustomed to drinking two litres of water a day, begin gently. Start by increasing the amount by, say, a small glass each day. A good trick is to have a glass of water before you have any other drink. It will quench your thirst so you will be able to taste the coffee, tea, wine or other drink that you've been looking forward to.

Try to keep away from sweet drinks, even — in fact, particularly — from those that have no calories. They usually contain a number of artificial sweeteners, like aspartame, which affects our nervous system badly. So much so that, in my own case, I find they give me a nervous feeling in my abdomen and make me tremble all over, especially my hands. They are also linked to Attention Deficit Disorder and autism.

As a quick aside, I have found that putting children who suffer from such symptoms on a completely organic diet — obviously with lots of water. — can have an amazing effect. Withdrawn children will begin to relate: overactive children will become calmer: overthinking, nervous children will settle.

So drink water before any other drink and your body will respond very quickly. I have clients who have told me that the best advice I ever gave them was to drink more water. Drinking more water:

- ✓ Relieves pain caused by too much toxicity in the system;
- ✓ Allows the brain to function more efficiently;
- ✓ Assists in the assimilation and elimination of food;
- ✓ Calms the emotions and anxieties
- ✓ Helps the joints to function smoothly
- ✓ Thins the blood, which helps to reduce high blood pressure and to increase low blood pressure.
- ✓ Assists the working of the lungs
- ✓ And generally increases well-being and happiness.

Gradually, you will find that you are less dependent on other substances to raise your mood and revitalise you.

BUT, and it's a big but, you need to make sure that the water you drink is of the highest quality. Reiki can be used to raise its vibrational level — and improve its taste — but even so, it is best to make sure that you are drinking water that is not filled with chemicals. Eschew tap water, unless it is filtered. Water filter jugs can be purchased inexpensively, or you can obtain a model that goes under the sink and leads to a separate tap for filtered water.

Water naturally spirals and is full of life-force. It hates being confined in pipes. There are gadgets you can buy to raise the vibration again and to swirl water through before you drink it. All are very helpful and increase the life-energy of the water exponentially.

My grandfather always insisted that when you poured water from the kettle into a teapot, you should hold the kettle up as high as possible and alter the height while pouring. Mind you, he always said that tap water was 'dead' and we used to have to cross several fields to obtain water from a natural spring to make his tea! Sometimes the 'oldies' have a lot of wisdom which is only now being rediscovered.

If you buy bottled water, try to ensure that it is in a glass bottle. Similarly, always carry water in glass. Plastic bottles degrade very quickly, especially under artificial light and release harmful chemicals, including oestrogen, into the water. Do not leave a plastic bottle of water in sunlight. Sometimes it is tempting to keep a bottle of water in the car. If you do this, make sure it is a glass bottle and that you change the water often. It also helps to keep a small clear quartz crystal in the bottle to keep the water sweet and imbue it with life-giving energy. Even this should not be left for too long, however.

The relationship of crystals and water is fascinating, but if I go into it here we will never get to the end of this class. There are many good books on crystals. I suggest you invest in one. My favourite is 'The Crystal Bible' by Judy Hall.

Finally, a word of warning. Most other drinks are dehydrating, and many (tea, coffee, alcohol, fruit juices, canned drinks) also contain a lot of useless calories which tend to increase the perception of hunger. Guess what? Drinking them often puts on the pounds/kilos. If you find yourself feeling this way, guess what you do? That's right. You drink a glass of water.

Why? Because the body feels fuller and you realise you don't need to eat. It's just that your perception of the difference between hunger and thirst has been blurred.

If your body is used to being dehydrated, whether slightly or a great deal, it will confuse hunger and thirst. My theory is that this is a defence system for times of drought when the waterholes were dry and the only way of obtaining liquid was through eating. Those were the days when we ate our prey raw, of course, not dried up after cooking it over a fire.

Food

That brings us easily to the subject of food. From what I have already said, you will probably have guessed something of what I am going to say, but maybe you will be surprised that I do not advocate a vegetarian or vegan diet. If this is your persuasion, that is absolutely fine, but you must make sure that you have adequate protein (from beans, peas, pulses) and iron (from spinach, broccoli and other green vegetables).

However, a vegetarian diet does not suit everyone. In particular pre-menopausal women, at all times of the month, require sufficient iron in a digestible form — and often these are precisely the people who don't eat meat, particularly red meat. Since every month they lose iron-laden blood, they need to make sure they have an adequate intake of iron. It's the same case in pregnancy, because, although you are not menstruating, the developing baby takes iron from your blood.

There is no doubt that we humans have a lot to answer for when it comes to our enslavement and treatment of animals, but nonetheless, we are a hunting animal, and like other hunters, we need prey.

I have tried various diets for various reasons over my life and have come to the conclusion that the most important part of eating is to honour your food.

Bless it and thank it for nourishing your body.

Be grateful that another being's life force is energising your own.

This is the same whatever you are eating. A vegetable is just as alive as an animal: its life force has the same vivifying effect on your own. But it cannot energise your body if we eat it mechanically and unthinkingly, because we like the taste or texture, or just because we feel the need to eat.

These days, in our culture, we rarely feel real hunger. Instead we feel empty, or bored, or unsatisfied or sad. What I am actually saying here is that for most people, eating is a result of feeling an emotion. If we take the time to honour our food, to bless it and to feel it nourishing our bodies, then eating becomes an act of grace rather than a simple emotional response.

Again, a simple way to test whether the food you are eating will do you good — or simply be a prop for your emotions — is to ask your body.

Ask Your Body

Shall we try that now? I know it's nearly lunchtime and you must all be hungry so here's an organic banana … Bananas are usually okay for most people but if you know they don't suit you, then choose another piece of fruit from the fruit bowl.

Gently close your eyes and go within, by which I mean

take your consciousness inside your body. If you find this difficult, concentrate on the feeling inside your abdomen.

Hold the piece of fruit, feel its texture, maybe smell it (smell is a wonderful sense for testing the edibility of food). Now ask yourself: "Will this banana nourish me?" or "Shall I eat this banana?"

Be aware of your body's reaction. It can be very swift, or it may take a while if you are used to ignoring your body in favour of your mind or emotions. Just trust your body to tell you and it will.

Sometimes the reaction will be almost violent, or a sound may come like 'Ugh.' or 'Yum.' Everybody is different, but the more you tune in to yours, the more it will be able to communicate with you.

Isn't that amazing? If your body said 'yes' to you, then do eat the banana. If it said 'ugh' then choose something else and try the same test.

Muscle Testing

There is another simple way to choose and/or decide what food will be good for you. This is very helpful in the supermarket when you are buying packaged food that may or may not have ingredients that don't agree with you.

It's a simple form of muscle-testing. Let's try it first.

On each hand, touch the tips of the first finger and thumb together to form a ring. Interlink those rings so you have a figure of eight or infinity symbol. Tell yourself that if the answer from your body is 'yes' you will be unable to pull the rings apart, but if it is 'no' they will part easily.

Now test. Use something simple to which you know the answer. "Is my name ..." can be a good question. Try it with your correct name first and then with someone else's.

See? I'm sure you could pull the fingers apart when you asked with the incorrect name and vice versa.

If for some reason, it didn't work, then it might be that you are switched and have decided to have the opposite reaction from what I have suggested to you… there's nearly always a rebel somewhere! Funnily enough, they are usually left-handed people. Try again with another question. If you are switched, just accept that is how it is for you — the fingers part for 'yes' and stay strong for 'no'.

If you find this all just too confusing, just go back to asking your body.

High Vibration Foods

As I have said, we are all different, and the foods we eat have different effects on different people. Rejoice in your own uniqueness.

Having said that, I find that the higher our vibration becomes, the more we need to eat high vibration foods. These are organic, natural foods that have not been over-packaged or processed. The good old 'stone-age diet' can be very useful.

You may also like to look at the Blood Group diet which suggests that different foods are appropriate for different blood groups.

- Thus, if you are of 'O' group, you are a hunter-gatherer and need to eat meat.
- If you are an 'A' group you are an agrarian, and it is suggested that you would be happy either being vegetarian or eating lots of vegetables.
- The 'B' group comes from those tribes who kept animals so they can eat anything including milk products.
- The AB group is a mixture of A and B, so milk and vegetables suit them best.

As with all diets these are guidelines. Interesting, but not gospel. Find out more if you're interested.

As an aside, my blood group is 'B' but I am not good with fatless milk products. I can drink cream. Cheese is okay in moderation. More than that and I find myself full of catarrh. So treat this idea with caution.

Ayurveda

Even more intriguing is the Ayurvedic system of India which has been developed over millennia. Here there are three main body-types: Vata, Pitta and Kapha, but we are all a mixture of the three types. I do encourage you to find out more yourself. My favourite book on the subject is *Perfect Health* by Deepak Chopra. According to one reviewer:

Chopra has an interesting, quantum view of the body. Instead of considering it as something solid, he sees the body as interweaving systems of energies that are constantly being consumed and renewed. Ayurvedic medicine gives us the tools to intervene at the quantum level where we are being recreated every day.

This book provides an exhaustive step-by-step programme of mind-body medicine adapted to individual needs, based on the person's mind-body type. This typology forms the basis of a focused Ayurvedic program of stress reduction, diet, neuromuscular integration, exercise and daily routines.

Part I, A Place Called Perfect Health, explains these various body types. Part II, The Quantum Mechanical Body, explains the channels of healing via meditation, healing sounds, mantra, music and aromatherapy. Part III, Living In Tune With Nature, deals with diet, exercise and a seasonal routine that fits your type.

The book concludes with an appendix, glossary, bibliography and index.

IN BRIEF

- ✓ Eat well, at regular times and not too late at night
- ✓ Eat organic food that has not travelled long distances
- ✓ Eat according to the seasons
- ✓ Ask your body if you are unsure about anything you intend to eat
- ✓ Eat consciously: honour and bless your food
- ✓ Eat with gratitude for the life-force that is nourishing yours.

10

Let's Dance!

We've been sitting and listening for a long time, so let's change the energy before we all go to sleep.

Were going to dance. Actually, when I say 'dance', I mean 'move to music'.

This is a really important way to make sure your energy is moving easily through your body. As we have seen, energy needs to flow. It needs to be in constant movement to keep your body healthy and whole. And not just your body, of course, your mind and emotions need to flow too.

When we get stuck in our thoughts, our beliefs, or our emotions, our body too, becomes stiff and sore. Then it hurts to move and so we stay 'stuck.' Again we may adopt others' beliefs as our own, or worry about what others may think ...

Well, I have news for you. Nobody really cares how you act; or if you make a fool of yourself. Everyone else is too worried about what others are thinking of *them*, to care about you. Of course, that is provided you do nothing to hurt or upset anyone else. You are in charge of your own body-mind. You can use it however you like.

When you realise this, and bring it into manifestation by moving your body in the way it wants and needs to move, you will find an amazing sense of freedom, not only in your body, but in your feelings and thoughts, too.

First of all, stand up. Close your eyes and take an inventory of how your body feels. This is just for you. There's no prize. Just see how you feel. Do you feel sore anywhere? Are you in pain? Do you have headache? Or a stomach ache? Do you feel stiff? Tight? Uncomfortable? Stuck?

Just take an inventory. Nothing more.

Have you all done that?
Well done. Let's dance.

To dance the Reiki way, you close your eyes and keep them closed. You do not look at anyone else. This is about YOU. You go within *your* body and give everyone else in the room freedom to do the same.

A word of warning. It's really important to move, even if you don't feel like it. Everyone is giving off energy. So if you stand still, or only move a little, you are inviting all that 'stuff' to settle on you. *Move.* Experiment. Enjoy!

As you take your attention inward, you begin to move to the music. This is not about looking good, or not making a spectacle of yourself. This is about rejoicing in your body-mind and letting it get away from all the self-imposed restrictions under which it usually operates.

I'm going to use a track from *Sacred Spirit Drums* by David and Steve Gordon, but any authentic ethnic music with a strong beat would do.

It starts slowly ... so move gently. Stretch out your arms to the tips of your fingers ... lift up your chin ... smile. Stretch out your legs ... your feet ... your toes ....

Ah. Now the music is hotting up a little ... MOVE to it.

- Feel your feet ... be aware of your feet on the ground. Feel your connection to the earth down below the floor.
- Move your KNEES ... go with your body, not against it.
- Feel your connection to your legs and your knees. Enjoy.
- Shake your HIPS. Really get into your hips ... move them round ... do the hippy-hippy-shake-shake, feel the punchiness of your hips.
- Move up to your shoulders. Shake your shoulders

free. Move your arms ... right down to your wrists, your hands. Shake out your hands.

- Move your head. Let your Jaw hang loose.
- Be aware of your body. Feel every part of it.
- Go within, feel the music, let your body move.
- Move every part of your body.
- You can jump and shake or bounce or dance or clap your hands ... you can shout or sing if that feels right ...whatever you feel your body wants to do.
- Rejoice.
- Rejoice in LIFE
- Rejoice in freedom

Experiment.
How does it feel to move your body in this way?
Do you feel silly? Or clumsy? Or cross?
Chuck it out. Take yourself back to your body. Let go.
ENJOY.

Music stops after about 5 minutes.

Keeping your eyes closed, let your breath settle and come back to normal.

Keep your eyes closed.

Now take another inventory of your body. How do you feel now? Check out any places where any of the things I mentioned applied. How do they feel now?

Again, this is just for you. But if you would like to share anything you have experienced, I'm sure the rest of us would like to hear it.

When you're ready, take a deep breath, gently open your eyes, and slowly come back into the room.

Did you enjoy your dance?

11

Meditation: Flowing Energy

Now that your energy is flowing, close your eyes. Let your breath settle and come back to normal.

Now take your awareness inside. Let anything that you no longer need drop down … any feeling or energy or pain or discomfort that you no longer need … let it all drop down.

Start at your head … Let everything you no longer need float down.

…through your throat. Gathering everything else that you don't need on the way, let it all drift down …

through your chest…

though your diaphragm…

through your abdomen…

through your buttocks,

If anything is stuck and doesn't want to move, that's fine. Just accept it. But let everything else you no longer need, float down …

through your thighs …

through your knees …

down through your lower legs and into your feet.

Just encourage it, let it all flow … down.

Now put out strong roots … from the centres of the soles of your feet … let them dig deep down into the Earth, our mother, going further and further … down, down into the crystalline layer of the Earth.

Allow all that no longer serves you, that you no longer need, to float down into Mother Earth …

For transformation … transmutation … transfiguration.

Let it flow down

Let anything that remains in your upper body or your arms flow down through your arms and drip off your fingertips into the earth and into your roots.

The Earth accepts all our dross and transforms it into life in another form. Just as she takes the manure from our bodies and uses it to fertilise wonderful plants, turning it into the beauty of flowers, so everything is recyclable.

There is far more life below the crust of the Earth than there is above it. Bacteria and viruses thrive on the energy that we throw off, just as we breathe the oxygen that is given out by the leaves of plants ... the waste product of photosynthesis, a process that uses the carbon-dioxide we breathe out to feed the plant. Everything works together. All life is dependent on another form or forms of life.

So give away your waste with joy.

When you feel that you have let go of all that is ready to go at this time, begin to draw up the wonderful, nourishing, nurturing energy from Mother Earth. She is our true mother. She provides all that we need. Every cell of our body is made from a substance which comes from her.

Allow that energy to rise up through your feet, through your ankles, filling each part of the foot, the toes, the nails, the ankle joint.

On up ... and up ... this nourishing energy fountains, up through your lower legs, your knees ... filling every part ... spiralling up through your thighs... your abdomen ... your buttocks...

On up through your diaphragm, through your lower chest, filling and nourishing each of your organs, nurturing you, loving you.

Feel that lovely warm, delicious, energy fountaining up and filling your heart.

Feel warm, nourished, nurtured. Feel anchored to Mother

Earth by the roots from your feet.

Now imagine a wonderful, bright, white light from the heart of the Father, Father Sky, coming down to fill a reservoir about twelve inches above your head. This is the vitality and joy of the Father, the Life Force of the universe.

Let it flow in through the crown of your head, bringing with it vitality and positivity ... allow it to fill the whole of your head, your neck, your throat.

Feel it filling your head completely with its strong dynamic energy, let it flow on down through your chest, filling every part of your chest, until it flows into your heart ...

Here it meets the loving Energy of Mother Earth in a wonderful vortex of delight, of joy. The two mix and meld in a celebration of life, of vivacity. Together they form the Christ-child that we are.

Together they flow out from the heart ... together they flow down your arms ... filling the upper arm, the elbows, the lower arms ... the wrists, the palms, the backs of your hands ... on and on into each finger and thumb, each fingernail and thumbnail.

And as you feel that wonderful melded energy flow into your hands, put them on any part of your body that feels appropriate.

As you stand there ... feel the energy fountaining up from Mother Earth, warm, nurturing, nourishing, understanding ...

Feel the wonderful energy of the Father, the universe, flowing down through the crown of your head, light, bright, positive, full of vivacity,...

Feel the two energies mixing and twirling and whirling together in your heart centre.

Feel that wonderful joined energy flowing down your arms, into your hands and back into your body.

Really bring your awareness to this wonderful flow of energy. There is nothing else to do, or be, or think. You are perfect in this moment as you receive this loving nurturing energy.

But now it's time to come back, knowing that you can do this meditation and have this experience at any time you choose …

First, thank the Universe, the Father, for the light, his gift. See your crown chakra closing, keeping that energy within. Seal it with any symbol that has meaning for you … a flower, the ankh, a cross, or any other symbol that has a special significance for you.

Now thank Mother Earth for her gift of nourishing, nurturing energy … draw your roots up … back into your feet … and close your feet chakras, sealing them in the same way as the crown chakra, with a symbol that has significance for you…

Stay still for a moment or two longer … feeling filled with the love of the Mother and the Father … of Earth and Universe.

Then, when you are ready, and only when you are ready, let your hands drop.

Take a deep breath. As you breathe out, gently open your eyes and come back into the room.

Welcome Back.

Okay, do take a seat. Stretch.

It's lovely to see you all smiling.

If you'd like to share anything that you experienced, we'd all love to hear it. But there is absolutely no need … no pressure. If you want to keep your experiences to yourself that is absolutely fine.

Just a reminder though … if there is anything that didn't

feel right, or if you feel uncomfortable in any way, it is important to let me know so that I can help. You can do this privately if you prefer, or you can tell me now.

How was that meditation?
Did you enjoy it?
How do you feel now?

Remember that you can do this at any time on your own.

12

The First Attunement

Any questions on anything we have covered so far?

Are you all comfortable with what I have said?

If not, do tell me.

All okay? Right, let's talk about attunements.

The purpose of an attunement is to bring the Reiki energy through the energy field (aura) of the person who is being attuned.

It's a simple process which relies on the energy of the Reiki Master and his/her ability to process and pass on that energy. In effect, the Reiki Master uses his/her own energy field to step down the Reiki energy to a level where it can resonate at the same frequency as the energy field of the student.

This afternoon, I will talk in more detail about the history of Reiki, but you have probably guessed that the natural healing system we are learning, Usui Reiki, was founded by a man of that name: Dr. Mikao Usui.

Dr. Usui had no specific attunement process. He taught Reiki in a very different way from 'Western' Reiki Masters. He considered Reiki to be a spiritual path, with healing as a bi-product. A Reiki student in Japan in the 1920s would agree to spend several hours a week meditating and imbibing the Reiki energy.

When Dr Usui considered a student ready, with the student's consent, he would attune him to the next level of Reiki. To do this, he used his intention allied to the breath. He would hold the student's hands and concentrate until the energy in the student's palms reached a certain vibratory level.

After Dr Usui's death, his successor, Dr Hayashi, developed the attunement system we use today. He did this in order to make it easier for the grandmother of Reiki in the West, Hawayo Takata, to take Reiki to the United States shortly before the second World War. I believe that he realised that Reiki needed to spread far and wide. Maybe he foresaw the outcome of the War and of Japan's defeat — who knows? But we owe him a debt because the attunement system is the means by which the Reiki energy is passed on from Reiki generation to Reiki generation in the West.

As I have said, Dr Hayashi's system forms the basis for all the Reiki attunement processes currently in use. Some Reiki Masters have added 'bells and whistles' but it is essentially the same.

While a current-day Reiki Master could attune a student to Reiki in a similar way to Dr Usui, a ceremony makes the whole process more sacred and memorable. In addition, a ceremony that is often repeated develops its own sacred energy. You may well have experienced this if you have received holy communion. When he blesses the 'host', the priest is using his own energy to transfer and enhance the energy of the bread and wine.

So ... An attunement is simply a ceremony, a ritual — and like all rituals it has acquired an energy of its own. In this case a sacred energy, a sacred effect.

Ritual is important, too, because it brings us closer to our own spirit as well as to the Spirit of Reiki, including a connection to all those who have been attuned to Reiki in the past and who will be attuned in the future — for Time is just a construct of the brain to allow us to function on this planet. In bringing us closer to Spirit, it purifies our desires so that we melt into the whole — All That Is.

Preparation

Now it's time to get ready for your attunement. Each attunement is similar and the preparation is similar too.

I will have to pass from the front to the back of you more than once, so we need to make sure we have sufficient space around each chair. If the room were large enough, it would be good to place the chairs in a circle, looking inwards, but that's not possible here, so we'll place them in a line. I will pass along the back of the row and then come round to the front.

So, do take a seat. Any one you like.

It's important, in my opinion anyway, to be comfortable. I have been very uncomfortable when I've received attunements, and I found that it distracted me from what was going on …

Oh yes. We had to sit on the floor, keep absolutely still and breathe through our mouths …

I have found it completely unnecessary to make students comply with these rules.

Talking of attunement experiences, I must just say that you may experience absolutely nothing. That is perfectly okay. Everyone is different and reacts to each attunement in their own way. Each attunement is a different experience.

On the other hand, you may experience any of these:

- Heat,
- Cold,
- Inner shaking,
- A feeling of peace,
- Intense feeling of any kind,
- Visions,
- Colours,
- Fragrances,
- Voices,

- A message of some kind in any way,
- Or something unique to you.

So make yourself as comfortable as you can. Put a cushion in your back and/or under your feet. If you would like a throw or blanket around you or over your lap, arrange it comfortably. Just remember that I will need to be able to move your hands, so don't snuggle them away. Also, please keep them relaxed so that I can move them.

It *is* important to sit in a comfortable upright position so that your energy can flow freely up and down you spine. Adjust your position so that your back is straight, your shoulders in line with your hips and your nose is in line with your navel.

Take a breath and relax your shoulders. If you find it relaxing, breathe in through your nose and out through your mouth, but that is not compulsory. Being comfortable is, though.

Now gently close your eyes and bring your hands to the prayer position (gassho, namaste) at your heart centre, in the middle of your chest. The reason we close our eyes is that it makes it easier to 'go within'. Without the distraction of sight, we are able to enter fully into the experience. The attunement process, while not secret, is sacred. Experiencing the process on an energy level means that your mind is disengaged. You are not constantly parsing what is going on and trying to make rational sense of it.

Energy is not rational. It is experiential.

Relax. Just allow this to be an experiment. Allow yourself to experience whatever happens.

Are you all comfortable? If not, let me know and I'll try to help, or perhaps you only need to adjust your position.

I'm going to put on some music. Allow it to move through

every one of your cells … Is that all right? Is everyone comfortable with this music? Yes? Good.

Let's begin.

Beginning

Take another deep breath and relax. This is for your unique self. Remind yourself that you are a magnificent being and capable of anything.

Take your attention to your breath. If you would like to invite your personal guides — or your angels or any other being who works for the highest good of all — to be with you, now is the time to do so.

This is the first of four attunements to Reiki 1. The purpose of the attunement is to bring the Reiki energy down into your aura. If your mind wanders, bring it gently back to this intention.

At the end of the attunement, keep your eyes closed until I ring the Ting-Sha three times.

Ending

Sound of Ting-sha: three rings. Silence for a few moments.

The first attunement to Reiki 1 is now complete.

Take as long as you need to open your eyes and come back in the room.

Now I would like you all, please, to spend a little while in your own energy, not speaking to anyone else — just until I come back into the room and ring the ting-sha again.

This is a special time for you to do exactly what seems right for you. There is no one who can tell you what that is … Maybe you would like to stay exactly where you are … maybe you would like to take a little walk outside in the garden … or to snuggle up in a blanket on the settee. You may like to make a few notes of your experiences.

Do whatever feels right for you.

Do, also, drink some water.

I am going to leave the room now and will return in a few minutes.

Afterwards

I return to the room and sound the ting-sha once.

Without speaking, I spend a little while putting the room back in order, being as quiet as possible as I tidy away chairs and cushions.

Okay, now it is time to come back into the circle. Make yourself comfortable in the same place … or perhaps you would like to choose a different one?

Is everyone okay?

Would anyone like to share what they experienced?

There is no pressure. If you would prefer to keep your experience to yourself, that is absolutely fine.

If you have any questions, please ask them.

Is there anything in your experience about which you would like to ask me? If so, ask away.

If you feel you would like to keep things to yourself for the moment that is fine.

13

Self healing

THE MOST IMPORTANT thing to do now is to get your Reiki hands working. You can probably feel a difference in your palms? A bit tingly or hot perhaps? Well, if not, they soon will be!

We'll start with learning the hand positions for healing yourself. There are photos in your hand-out and at the back of this book, but for now I'll just talk you through them.

First of all, you need to know a little about how to use your hands.

The Reiki energy comes through your palm chakras. If you look closely at your palms you may notice a lighter coloured circle in the centre. Reiki is light.

Now, slowly bring your palms together, until you can feel the energy between them. I think you will be surprised at how easily you feel it, and from what a distance. If you feel nothing, no problem. It will come a little later.

Some people, me included, take a little while to open to the energy. We are all different after all, and the Reiki energy works with our own energy. Everything happens in perfect right time and in perfect right order.

This is the way we hold our hands when we are giving Reiki, including when we are giving it to ourselves:

Keep your hands soft, with fingers and thumb together — as one little girl said, as if you were wearing socks on your hands — and slightly curled, as if you were cradling a baby bird.

Float them in towards you. Don't plonk them on. Lay them gently on your body, keeping the pressure light. Remember that it is the energy from your hands that does the work, not your hands themselves. That energy needs a little space.

The Hand Positions for Self-Healing

1. Eyes.

Gland: Pineal

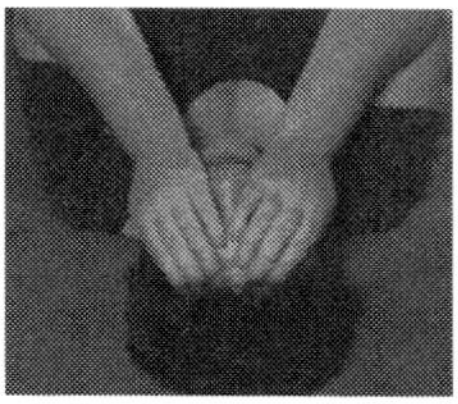

We start by gently covering our eyes. Because they are *your* eyes, your hands will fit over them perfectly. Keep your hands soft and pliable. You can decide how much pressure feels right for you, but usually it is best to err on the light side. Experiment a little.

We start with the eyes because they need to rest and also because as we close our eyes, we relax more easily. We *feel* more, too as we withdraw from the 'monopoly' of sight. Think how much you use your eyes during the day, each and every day.

The eyes take in light for the rest of our body. Each of our three trillion cells needs light to heal, grow and, eventually, to recreate itself. Each cell has a very short lifetime.

Apopsis is the term given to the way that cells create a new version of themselves before they die. Think how much energy that takes. Cells take a lot of their energy from light. Reiki is concentrated light.

2. Ears.

Glands: Pineal and Pituitary

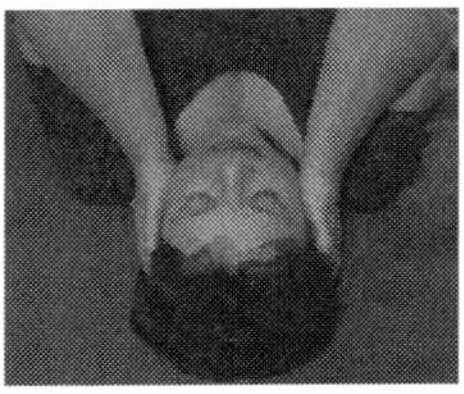

Now move your hands over your ears. Reiki here helps with all problems with hearing and balance: tinnitus and dizziness to name but two common ones.

The ears are also a hologram for the whole body. Basically, the curve of the ear represents the foetus in the womb with the head downwards. Any good book on Chinese acupressure will show you the specific points that relate to the organs in the body, but by covering the whole ear we can treat them all.

This hand position also shuts out a lot of extraneous noise. Thus, we are less distracted, so again it is easier to concentrate on the inner self.

3. Temples.

Gland: Pituitary

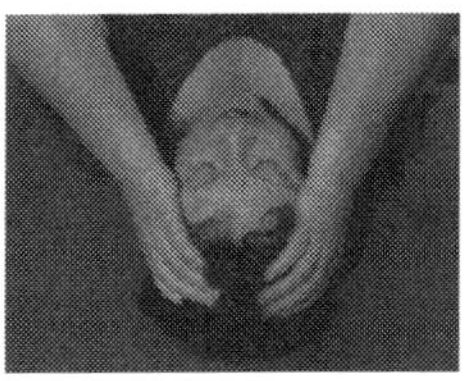

Now move your hands to your temples. You will find that letting the Reiki flow here is very calming, helping our consciousness move towards the centre of our being. Again, this is a key place for holding tension and stress. Often this is where headaches hang out. If you are feeling tight or tense in this area, allow the tension to melt away under your hands. Often a light headache will fade away.

However, a word of warning. If you have a strong headache in this area, miss out this hand position. When there is a lot of tension in one place, a great deal of energy is being used. Sometimes it is the excess of energy that is the main cause of the headache. If this is the case, and you add more Reiki energy, it can make the headache worse rather than better.

In such a case, I find a better technique is to use the 'dustpan and brush'. Use one hand (the brush) to sweep the excess energy lightly towards the other hand (the dustpan). Keep the action light. Your hand can come close to your head or not — it's your choice. Go with where you feel the headache to be: you will be correct. And do whatever seems best for you.

You can repeat this action as often as needed. But when the 'dustpan' is full, it needs to be emptied. Either go out into the garden and allow the 'dust' to fall into the earth, or imagine a violet flame — the violet flame of St Germain has been given to us as a swift method of purification and transformation. Empty the contents of the dustpan into the violet flame and watch as they are consumed by it.

N. B. You can do this at any time or in any place (and for any part of the body).

4. Back of head.

Gland: Pituitary

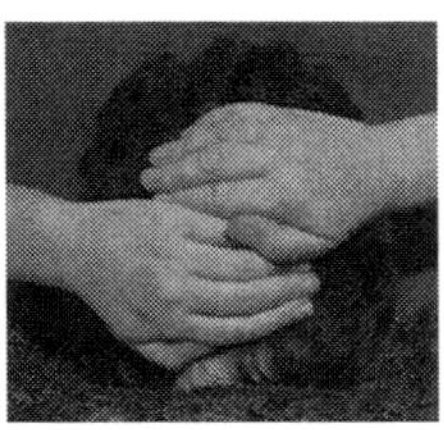

Make sure your hands overlap slightly. You can do this in any way that feels comfortable for you. For me, I find it most comfortable when my hands are parallel to the floor, but, as I have said, your hands will fit you perfectly. Do whatever is most comfortable. Your lower thumb will be in contact with your occiput, the brain stem, and thus with the fluid that bathes the brain and the spinal cord. This has a very slow pulse — usually much slower than the breath.

See whether you can feel it. Some people can sense it easily, others find it more difficult. It doesn't matter which sort you are.

In any case, this contact allows you to send a message of healing down the whole spine. You might feel the Reiki energy gently adjusting the nervous impulses in the spine. Be aware and simply allow.

Reiki energy has its own intelligence and will go to any place that is in need of healing. Whether we know it or not does not matter. We just need to keep an open, relaxed mind.

Again, if you can't feel anything, just be aware that it is happening, and imagine it as clearly as possible.

5. Throat.

Gland: Thyroid

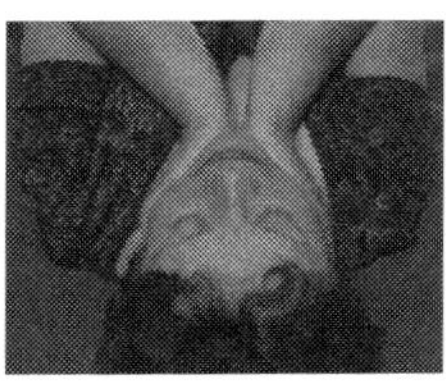

Your hands will fit your own throat perfectly. Bring the heels of the hands together and let your fingers curl round either side of your neck. If this feels restrictive, bring the hands a little away from the throat. Find the distance which seems comfortable.

This is usually a very reassuring and comforting position. Not only is it good for the voice, and helpful for sore throats, but it also stimulates the throat chakra. You will remember that this is the centre of our creativity, and also the place from where we communicate with all levels of existence, both speaking (even on the inner plane) and listening/hearing.

The gland connected with this centre, and thus this position, is the thyroid. This gland is often overstressed and is very grateful for some extra energy and soothing assistance.

6. The heart centre.

Gland: thymus

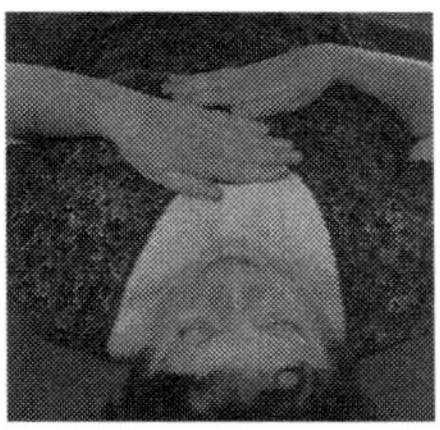

Next we move on to the heart centre. This is in the centre of the chest, *not* exactly over the heart. Put your hands one above the other, overlapping a little, and feel the Reiki energy entering the heart space. This is the place of compassion for all things, of empathy and unconditional love.

Recently science has discovered what meta-physicists have always known. The heart has a brain. The heart brain has to do with ... wait for it ... love. This is our connection to all that we love, and again, on all levels of existence.

I have come across a couple of stories — they are often dismissed as 'only' anecdotal evidence — of people who have had heart transplants discovering that they have a love for something that they never liked, but that the donor of the heart did. For instance, one young woman discovered a passion for football, and later found out that the donor of her heart had been a footballer.

On the physical level, here is the place to treat the heart and circulatory problems connected with it. Also the lungs and the respiratory system. The lungs hold joy and sadness. The heart holds love.

The thymus gland is the gland connected with our immune system. If you do not love and honour yourself, you may well find problems with immunity.

7. The Solar Plexus.

Gland: pancreas.

Move your hands so that the tips of your fingers meet at the hollow below your breastbone, and the palms rest along your lower ribs.

The Solar Plexus is the place of your inner fire: your will. Energy is often lacking here, particularly if we are inclined to doubt ourselves.

On the physical level it is our digestion, and on the emotional level it is how we deal with problems and life events. Can we use them as fuel? Or are we going to allow them to overwhelm us?

Here is the place of sweetness in life … or sourness. The pancreas is often overworked because we pour in too much sugar. As always, we need a balance in our lives.

We need to take back the power we have given to others. We need to use it for ourselves. How can we be the best we can be — for ourselves and everyone else in our lives — if we don't have enough oomph? How does it help to let others, or

Life itself, overwhelm us?

8. Hara, abdomen.
Glands: ovaries and gonads

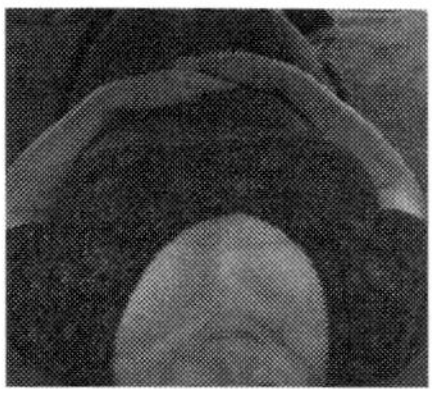

When you are ready, move your hands down so that they rest in the centre of the abdomen, one above the other. The lower hand's thumb rests gently over the umbilicus, or tummy button.

Like the heart, the intestines also have a brain. How often do we talk about a 'gut feeling'? How often do we pay attention to it?

As you may have guessed, or already know, the abdominal chakra (often referred to as the sacral chakra or the hara) has to do with our relationships with others. This is where we connect with the emotions that others are feeling.

This is where our own emotions sit. This is where we nurture ourselves. If we act only in accordance with what this centre tells us, we will always be in harmony with ourselves.

It is also the place of the womb and the ovaries, where new life grows within and is nourished by its mother's body. For this reason, in men it relates also to the gonads.

Let the Reiki flow into the centre and feel its comforting warmth.

9. Base, pubic bone.

Glands: adrenals

Place your hands gently on your hips, with the fingers pointing inwards and down. Then gently move your hands towards the pubic bone, until their fingers meet. Rest here. It is your body, and this is a very supportive and comforting position.

The base chakra relates to all our basic needs, and whether or not they are met. It is a place, often, of fear ... and in particular, the fear of lack.

Reiki here helps us to realise that we are able to supply all our own needs. We do not have to rely on anyone else. Events which have scarred us, are simply that — past events. We need to look to the future with hope and determination. But most of all we need to be fully present in the here and now.

Here we live. Here. On this Earth. In this time zone.

Feel the simplicity of it. There is nothing else more profound. In this moment everything is perfect. Now you can move on to the next perfect moment.

The adrenals are the glands which regulate the fight, flight or freeze response. Each of those is our reaction to a current event. The adrenals will become easily overworked if we spend a lot of time stressed and anxious. So take a deep breath and breath it out silently, softly; taking as long as possible.

10. Legs.

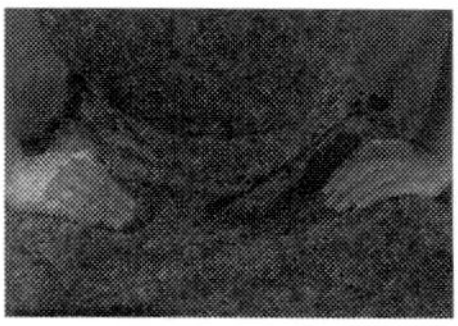

Many Reiki Masters don't teach any hand positions for the legs, but I have found that they are vital. I will tell you why in a moment, but right now, let's try putting a hand on the front of each of our thighs. Make sure your hands are comfortable. Try and point them down towards the knees and imagine the Reiki energy running from your hands into your thighs and on down to your knees.

Feel your thighs letting go of all the tension they hold. These thigh muscles are the strongest in the body. They have to do with running: flight. Yet they can hold us immobile, or help us climb — a ladder, a mountain.

Okay, now tell me: do your legs feel exactly the same as your upper body?

Yes? Great.

No? Interesting, isn't it?

Many people, through extreme or constant emotion, often grief, seem to 'cut off' their legs. Their energy no longer runs all the way down to the earth for grounding and transformation. No longer do they have access to the Earth's wonderful healing energy. They wear shoes with manmade soles, or walk on artificial fibres, or journey in cars, rather than walking. They become divorced from the Earth's energy. All their energy comes from their food, and that is often denatured. No wonder they feel out of balance.

I have already mentioned the wonderful flow of natural energy through us: from the universe it flows down through the body and into the earth. From the earth it flows the other way. It is like the breath. We are the breath and the universe is breathing us.

But when we cut off that flow, we can get stuck in our heads, particularly in our minds, so the lower brains of the heart and the hara receive no energy. We live a half-life of rationalisation. To make ourselves whole again, we need to re-connect with the earth and that wonderful flow of energy.

Feel your thighs becoming warm and responsive under your hands. Feel the energy beginning to flow again. Now you can move on with your life.

11. Knees.

Let's move our hands down to our knees. You can put one hand on each knee, or bend the knee slightly and make it the filling in a sandwich between your two hands. Imagine this area, perfect, beautifully oiled and easily moved.

The knees hold our fear. We know this because they tremble when we are frightened. We even talk about knees knocking. No wonder they often crumple and let us down, or hurt or creak. Often the fear of death — our own or another's — is held here.

We expect a lot of our knees, but we seldom give them any thought. We might give them the occasional rub, but what is that when they work for us all the time? Concentrate on seeing the joint moving easily and smoothly and they will bear you easily and smoothly through life.

12. Shins.

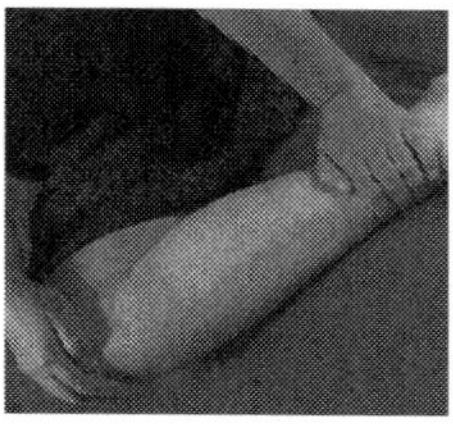

The shins are not often considered in Reiki or other healing modalities, but I have found them to be very responsive to Reiki, and, consequently, I have learned how often they need some tender, loving care.

My own shins often used to feel cold right through to the bone. In fact the bones felt like shards of ice. Cold travelled right up my body. Sometimes it was even difficult to walk because my shins felt so icy, so rigid and lifeless. Reiki soon puts paid to that.

A client of mine found that when she was depressed (and here I mean, really depressed) and almost suicidal her shins would itch as if there were pins and needles just under the skin. Reiki helped immensely.

I believe that the reason for these feelings (and I am sure other people have similar but different experiences) is that we have lost our connection to the earth energy, probably because we spend so much of our time sitting down. This causes a bottle neck of energy around our knees. Consequently we are walking around in a toxic field of energy and emotions that would normally be discharged through our feet.

We need to bring our attention to this and do anything that feels appropriate to get our energy moving again. Feel that wonderful flow from crown to feet, and back again from feet to crown.

Walking, running, shaking, dancing, and exercising generally, all help with the flow, but they are more effective still if you bring your attention to your lower legs.

When you are sitting down, put your feet up and give your shins Reiki just like you are doing now. If it feels right you can move your Reiki hands and give your shins a massage, or just smooth and stroke them, using as much, or as little, pressure as you like.

13. Ankles.

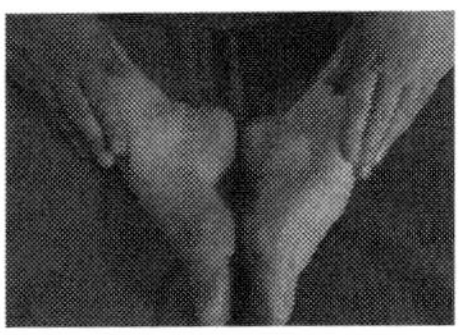

Wrap both your hands round one ankle or one hand round the outside of each ankle. Make sure that your thumbs are parallel to your fingers. Let the Reiki flow.

The ankles are about flexibility. If your ankles are locked, walking becomes almost impossible and certainly very painful. Each time you walk, your ankle rocks back and forth. Imagine how it would feel if the joint were static. You would certainly lose the spring in your step!

We need flexibility in our lives because the only constant in life is change. We need to be able to move with that change both mentally and physically, so keep Reiki-ing your ankles.

14. Feet.

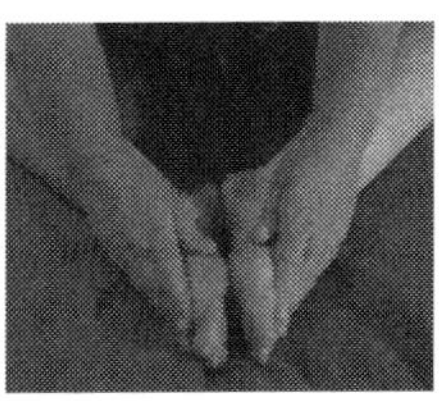

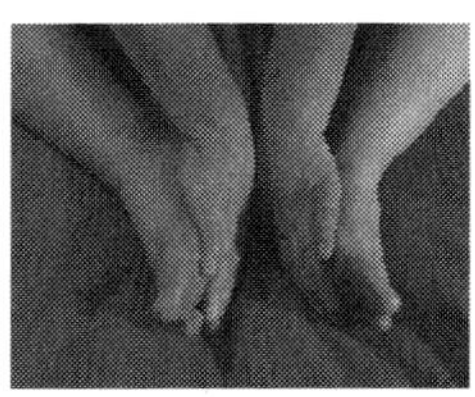

Ah! Feet. Such important parts of our anatomy and so

neglected.

Again, you can choose which way is easiest for you to give Reiki to your feet. You can put a hand on the top of each foot for a minute or two, and then move on to put a hand on the sole of each foot, but this can prove to be a bit of a contortion. The easiest way is to bring one foot up onto your knee and then to make a 'foot sandwich' of it with one hand on the top of your foot and the other on the sole. Relax as much as you are able.

So what is special about feet? Not only are they our support, and the means by which we move from place to place, but they are also our connection to the earth. Through them we are able to discharge 'disqualified' energy into the earth, but, even more importantly, we are also able to draw up the earth energy which gives us our 'oomph', or vital force.

There are other special points about the feet:

a. they are a holograph for the whole body, so you can treat the whole of you by treating the feet. Simple. *And* effective.
b. If you have issues with a particular organ or part of your anatomy, do make sure you're aware of where the reflex is, and then put your palm chakra over it. Any good reflexology book will tell you exactly where the reflex is for a specific part of the body.
c. the feet are also the negative pole for the body. In Polarity therapy, Dr Stone always recommends that you clear the feet first. When this is done, it clears the way to the rest of the anatomy. Try it. Perhaps not now, because we need to move on. Try it tonight and/or tomorrow morning.

The feet are often quite cold. This is because all your energy is traditionally placed in the upper torso, leaving only a little to trickle down to the feet. Now they are warming up, feel your gratitude to your feet and the grounding they do.

Finishing

Now just bring your hands together into the prayer position and give a swift prayer of thanks to the Reiki energy.

And that's it. You have completed your first session of self-Reiki. Congratulations.

Not that hard, though, was it?

Zen the Room

Now, you must be famished. Let's go and have some lunch. But before you go, let's zen the room — by which I mean tidy up a little. Just make sure that you put your possessions together and put cushions and chairs back where they belong.

One last thing: before you eat your food, hold your Reiki hands over it to bless it with Reiki. And, as you eat it, give thanks for the life force in it which nourishes yours. Eat slowly and with awareness.

If you'd like to take a little while by yourself afterwards, that's absolutely fine. You're welcome to wander into the garden or down the road but make sure that you're back in time for 2.00 pm as we have a lot to get through this afternoon.

Thank you.

DAY ONE, AFTERNOON

14

Movement: Hollow Bamboo

Hello, welcome back.

I expect you were hungry after your busy morning? You may think you have just been sitting quietly listening to me chattering away — but you don't realise how much energy you are using, do you? In a good way, of course.

Okay, now before you settle down, let's have a little gentle exercise. I'll just put on some music …

Stand tall. Be aware of your feet on the ground, and feel as though you are being drawn upwards by the angels fishing from their clouds. The fishing line gently draws you up by the crown of your head until you feel perfectly balanced on your feet.

Now cup one palm inside the other, thumbs touching. Let your arms hang low, between your base and sacral chakras. Gently close your eyes if you wish.

Begin to sway gently from side to side, backward and forward, as if you were a hollow bamboo rustling in the wind. Stay aware of your feet. Just let your body guide your movement. Feel relaxed … and comfortable … and easy.

Take a deep breath in ….and let it out … slowly.

Just sway.

Back and forth.

Side to side.

Feel the connection with your breath and your movement.

Right at this moment, nothing else matters.

Just breathe and sway.

Back and forth.

Side to side.

As you sway, feel the Reiki energy gently entering your crown and descending slowly and gently down your hollow tube, filling you with gentleness and ease, grace and calmness.

Right at this moment, nothing else matters.

If your eyes are open, gently close them now, the better to experience the ease and grace of this moment … these moments.

If your mind wanders, let the thoughts float by … like clouds in a perfect blue sky … and softly bring your attention back to your breathing … and your swaying ….

Feel the connection *you are* between the earth and the universe.

As you sway, allow any aches … pains … or discomforts to disperse into the air around you. Feel them dissolve … permit yourself to feel comfortable in your body … but if some remain, that is fine. Let them be.

Again, feel the connection *you are* between the earth and the universe….

Now gently bring your attention back to this room. Allow your swaying to continue until you are able to find the perfect balance again. Take a breath … in and, as you breathe out, gently open your eyes.

If you need a stretch … S.. T.. R.. E.. T.. C.. H.

How lovely to see you all smiling.

Starting with Ourselves

Before lunch you gave yourself a Reiki treatment. Of course, you actually put your hands on your body.

How did that feel?

Yes, most people find it warm and reassuring. Some say that it validates looking after themselves. Have you felt that? Giving themselves Reiki through their hands makes others feel secure and that it's all right to do something like this for themselves.

When it comes to healing, most people say they want to learn so that they can help others. When I say that it starts with healing yourself, they can find the idea quite challenging. Our society makes us feel selfish and self-indulgent if we do anything so beautiful — in fact, so spiritual — for ourselves.

But, as I have said before, and will no doubt say again, we need to start with ourselves. We need to fill ourselves up so that we run over ... we need to put on our own oxygen mask first. If we don't, despite our very good intentions we will end up depleting ourselves when we heal, with disastrous results for us and our dear ones ... and a lot of guilt for the person we were intending to heal.

But now, I want to turn to another side of this. We can use Reiki on or off the body. When you learn Reiki 2 you will be able to heal from a distance of many miles from the person you are healing.

So which is best?

To touch or not to touch?

That is the question.

Let's discuss touch for a moment. Touch is a human need. Touch is natural. When a baby is born, a mother's first instinct and need is to cuddle her baby. Without touch, babies do not thrive. They become withdrawn and ill, and sometimes die.

If you burn yourself, or bump into something, what is your first reaction? Touch. A burned finger flies to your mouth automatically. You bend to rub a bruised shin immediately.

A mother soothes her child to sleep by stroking his hair. You hold the hand of someone who is ill or badly hurt. That human contact has a healing quality all by itself. I have African friends who touch your arm in sympathy, or to include you in a conversation or joke. That is how we used to act, too.

And yet, sadly, for us, in our culture touch has become a difficult area. Something natural has become seen as something dingy, something unnatural. We expect the worst. If a man touches a woman, it is too often read as sexual assault. Nowadays, with the blurring of genders, any sort of touch can be read as sexual or inappropriate. Saddest of all is the fact that a teacher cannot touch, let alone cuddle, a child who runs to her for comfort when hurt or upset. Even a wound has to be dressed by another child. This is becoming ridiculous and breeds distrust, which, in itself, is sad.

One day, my husband and I took our daughters swimming. We were enjoying playing in the pool when another little girl started joining in our games. She said her name was Sarah. The three girls struck up a conversation from which we learned that the little girl was six and was at the pool with her elder sister who was nine. Her sister decided to go to the pier, but our little friend had wanted to stay in the pool, so she did. Her mother was out at work and there was no-one at home to care for her. We were ready to go home, but before we did we bought the three girls a sandwich and a drink while we tried to work out what to do. In the end we decided we had no choice but to take her along to the police station. We were all sad that we couldn't take her home with us and give her a good meal and a good time, but we knew we would be opening ourselves up to all sorts of charges if we did. My husband even said he would not have dared to buy her a drink if I had not been there.

What are we coming to, when we see danger everywhere?

Compare that experience to our holiday in a village on a Greek island. Admittedly, my husband and I had stayed in the village before, and we knew a few people, but before we had taken more than a few steps from the little ferry, a group of older people called over to us. One of them, an older woman, ran her fingers affectionately through my younger daughter's curls, and smiled.

"You need never be worried about your children. We will all be looking out for them," she said.

Surely, that is how community works? If we all look out for each other, then evil has little opportunity to fester.

Anyway, we have moved beyond that scenario in our society. Now we have to be careful not to act 'inappropriately'. Nonetheless, out bodies have not moved on. We still need human touch.

Reiki is all about touch. Obviously not inappropriate touch, but compassionate touch. How seldom this happens nowadays. Nearly always touch has its own agenda — sex, violence, warning. What differentiates healing touch from any of the others is the intention of the giver and the acceptance of the recipient. Healing touch is — well, healing. Often it brings a person back in contact with their own body: even more often, it will release emotions that have been dammed up inside. Repressed emotions lead to illness, both physical and mental.

In Reiki, touch is the way that we reassure and comfort, soothe and heal. Yes, it is possible to heal with Reiki without touching the body, but the Reiki touch has a magic of its own.

Reiki touch is gentle, non-invasive, warm and comforting. Or occasionally cold and powerful. But it is always healing.

One more word about healing. I emphasise that putting

your Reiki hands on someone does not heal them. Oh no. They heal themselves.

Your hands allow energy to flow towards the person, but their inner being makes the choice as to whether or not to open to, and use that energy. Their inner being also has the choice as to where the healing energy is directed. For instance, you may be thinking that you would like to make their painful knee better, but the person's unconscious mind decides to use the energy to heal their phobia of spiders!

15

The Reiki Precepts/Principles

As I mentioned this morning, there are four important parts to Reiki 1:

1. the Reiki ethic,
2. the Reiki Principles (or Precepts),
3. the hand positions for self healing and
4. the hand positions for healing others.

We have already covered the Reiki Ethic and the hand positions for healing the self. We will work tomorrow on healing others. I will teach you how to do a Reiki healing whether the recipient is lying prone (face down) or supine (face up).

But now it is time to learn the Reiki Principles or, as they are also known, the Reiki Precepts.

The Reiki Principles have been compared to the Ten Commandments in that they prescribe a good way of living. However, there the similarity ends. The Commandments command, whereas the precepts suggest. With repetition, they will merge into your energy field so that you live your life to the full, enjoying each day.

The precepts are both simple and complicated. Obviously, they have had to be translated from the Japanese ... a difficult task in view of the varying meanings of Japanese kanjis. For this reason, the original precepts handed down by Mrs Takata related more to her Japanese understanding and traditions than to those of the West.

Various versions can be found online and in books about

Reiki. The one thing that they have in common is that they all commence with the words "Today only" or "Just for today". Like many other systems that seek to provide a simple and repeatable formula for living happily in the present moment, when you have Reiki you will find that the precepts have most effect when you repeat them twice a day. Each precept is repeated three times.

There is a magic to the repetition of words: the brain is lulled into a neutral state, allowing the person to become truly conscious of the present moment. As the ego calms into insignificance, the underlying soul shines through the personality, allowing in peace, clarity and inner knowledge. Repetition is the reason why mantras are so effective in manifesting what is needed in a person's life.

The original Reiki precepts that I was taught are:

Today only,
Do not anger,
Do not worry,
Be grateful
Work hard
Be kind to others.

Or, in Japanese:

Kyo take wa,
Okolu-na
Shinpa-suna
Kansha shite
Go'o Hage me
Hito ne shinsetsu ni.

You will probably come across lots of other versions.

Some years ago, a student of mine had learned the art of

Neuro Linguistic Programming (NLP). He explained to me that the brain does not understand a negative. If you say to someone *"Don't think of a pink elephant,"* what does the other person (and probably you too) immediately think of? You've got it in one: a pink elephant.

I instantly realised that by saying: *don't worry* and *don't get angry*, I was actually encouraging myself to worry and get angry. I am grateful to that student because I understood that for me, and my students, 'to achieve the calm mind of the ancients' as Dr Usui put it, I needed to change the wording of the Precepts that I taught.

For years afterwards, I taught the following:

Just for today, I live in gratitude
Just for today, I let go of worry
Just for today, I allow anger to dissipate
Just for today, I do my work honestly
Just for today, I am kind to myself and every living thing.

However, in 2015, my inner guidance suggested that I rephrase these precepts to make them simpler, easier and shorter. I thought this was for one particular class, but when I requested clarification, I was told that the words still had negative connotations. The brain is apparently hardwired into the negative, rather than the positive — so using the word '*worry*' overrode all the positive action of '*letting go*'.

These are the precepts that my inner guidance suggested to me:

Just for today:
I am gratitude;
I trust;
I understand;
I am honest;
I am compassion.

The next day, I gave both versions to my Reiki 1 class, and suggested they choose whichever version they felt better suited their own needs. Without exception, they chose the second version. When I explored their reasons, they generally found the second version simpler, easier to learn and to repeat, and more profound. Since then, my students have agreed that the second version resonates more quickly with their own energy and forms a pattern that brings the Reiki energy instantly to the forefront. This allows them to relax into the Reiki energy and allow it to guide their lives and thus, their actions.

I'll go into this effect in more detail later, when we discuss the optimum way to use the Reiki Precepts in your life.

For now, let's go into the Precepts themselves in a little more detail.

Just for Today

Let's start with the first three words: ***just for today***.

It is important to live in the present moment. If we do this, we do not fall into worry — which is usually about the future, although often based on past events. Nor are we so likely to become angry — which is usually to do with the past, or past experience.

These words, *just for today*, are more profound than they appear, for if we live in the present moment we live in a state of joy and excitement. For who knows what the next minute, the next hour, the evening may bring? If we are *present* then there is nothing to fear, nothing to hope for. We live in a state of bliss, happy and content with whatever is happening in the moment. We know the moment will pass. It is ephemeral. What is the point of allowing one minute more importance than the next minute?

In any case, time is relative, as Einstein proved. Time bends round large objects. We are only slaves to Time because we live on this planet. We are slaves to Time only because this planet spins on its axis, giving us hours of light and hours of darkness, and travels round the sun, giving us the seasons. If we had nothing with which to mark the passing of time, how long then would a minute be? … a moment be? For millennia, before trains needed to run to a timetable and so the clocks in this country had to be synchronised, we relied on the relative times of dawn, noon (when the sun was directly overhead) and sunset. In fact, each of those times still varies across the country, being earlier in the East (because that is the direction in which the sun rises) and a little later the further West you travel.

I AM GRATITUDE

WE START THE Reiki Precepts with these words. Just saying them reminds you that you have a lot to be thankful for, but it takes it much deeper than that. You become gratitude. You live in gratitude. You give thanks at every moment for all that you have, all that you experience and all that is yet to appear in your lives.

Some of the things for which you are grateful will be in manifested form; others will never manifest. Love, for instance, joy, happiness. In fact all the emotions are a gift, whether we perceive them as such or not.

From our own limited viewpoint we cannot see the whole of life, nor the patterns and colours of it. In this state of duality in which we have chosen to live our lives, there are two sides to everything. We tend to feel that we must always live in the light, that the darkness is something to fear, and yet we were first conceived in the darkness of our mother's womb.

A light shines brightest in the dark. The dark is also the void from which everything manifests, a beautiful velvet darkness which bears the seeds of all possibilities.

We start 'in the dark': only later does 'the light dawn'. What would that dawning be without the darkness? Doesn't something we love seem even more precious when there is the possibility of losing it?

So we need to be accepting of all that comes to us, and to accept whatever that might be, with gratitude. For the more gratitude we express in our lives, the more we encourage the flow of all that serves us best. Even in adversity, we can find something for which to be grateful.

I'll give you a simple, personal example. Recently, I was

taking my usual morning walk in the valley near my home. Because it was Spring, the birds were carolling in trees that were beginning to leaf. Wild flowers carpeted the ground, and a stream sang as it ran beside the path. Overhead, clouds scattered across a blue, blue sky and a gentle, scented breeze kissed my cheek. I felt an overwhelming connection with Nature and to the countryside around me. The feeling of gratitude was so strong that it took over my whole body. For weeks afterwards, whenever my mind drifted back to that moment, I was aware of a wonderful warm feeling in my chest. As I recount this, I feel it now, just as strongly.

The more gratitude we express in our lives, the more we encourage the flow of all that serves us best. And feeling gratitude is a lovely way to stay in the flow. The more gratitude we feel, the more it becomes part of who we are, and the more happens in our life for which we are grateful.

Simply: gratitude is the easiest way to manifest all that we desire for ourselves, others, and the whole universe.

I TRUST

YOU WILL REMEMBER that originally this precept was 'don't worry', or 'let go of worry'.

Worry is a problem for most of us. It is what society expects us to do. But worry is a very pernicious evil. It keeps us living in the past, but it also allows the past to influence the future.

In talking of gratitude, we have seen how that on which you put your attention manifests in your life. If you are grateful, you receive more for which to be grateful.

It follows that if you worry, you will receive more of those things about which you worry.

I am sure that we have all experienced this. Even in a small thing like worrying that we will be late for an appointment. It's amazing how many times, even with the best will in the world, and careful arrangements, something happens to make us late. Of course, we knew it would.

Worry is also a state that is self-perpetuating. This means that it consumes a lot of energy, mental, emotional and physical. It can literally make you ill. How often have you heard someone say 'I was sick with worry'?

The opposite of worry is trust. Instead of worrying about something that may never happen (but probably will if you worry about it!) simply trust that everything is, and will be, fine; that everything will happen in perfect right order and perfect right time. You will be amazed how often this works. The more you use it, the more you believe it, the better the results.

In any case, what good has worrying done? Has it helped you? Or anyone else whom you have worried about? Think about it. I cannot think of one instant when it has helped in my lifetime.

I used to worry all the time. I would wake up every morning with my heart fluttering, full of fear as to what would go wrong during the day, unable to speak sometimes, definitely unable to eat breakfast. Sometimes it was even hard to smile. What was I worrying about? I was worrying that something (usually unnameable) would go wrong during the day, that everyone would blame me, that no-one would like me.

You name it, I worried about it.

Then I learned Reiki and discovered what a waste I had made of the beautiful mornings of my life. I vowed not to worry, ever again. Of course, there have been times since when I've worried, but now I call it concern.

Concern is easier than worry. Worry never stops. Allow it, and it will consume you. Concern lasts until you know what has happened. Then it disappears.

Again, I'd like to give you an example of my own. When my daughter went off to university I was delighted for her. I thought of the wonderful friends she would make, the fun she would have, how independent she'd become, how interested she would be in her work, etc.

And then it seemed that everyone I met, everyone I knew started saying things like;

"Aren't you worried about her?"

"What about drugs?"

"Date rape?"

"Alcohol?"

"Will she work? My son's just dropped out."

"There's meningitis going round there, you know."

Suddenly it seemed I was a very inconsiderate, irresponsible mother. I began to worry. Then I was passing my bookshelf one day and a book flew off the shelves and landed at my feet, open at a page. I'm sure you can guess what that page was saying…?

Exactly. It reminded me that worry is a very heavy energy to send to someone. It takes a lot of their energy to overcome that thought form, so you are sending your loved one the reverse of the love and help you thought you were.

Instead, the writer suggested that you trusted that the person would be perfectly fine. In short, I was being advised to go back to my previous way of thinking about her.

I must admit it worked for both of us. She had a whale of a time, and I felt as though a load had been lifted off my shoulders. Of course, you can ask someone's angels to look after them, just to absolve you of that last bit of worry.

When my daughter came home at the end of term, she gave me a huge hug and told me what a wonderful time she'd had and how well she was doing academically. The icing on the cake for me, was when she told me how good it was to be trusted and how it stopped her from doing things that she knew would harm her. Besides, she said, it meant that she didn't have to worry about *me*.

I UNDERSTAND

I CAN SEE that perhaps you find it difficult to trace the way in which the original precept of "Don't be angry" became "I understand".

I know ... at first sight it appears rather a leap, even from the half-way house of "I allow anger to dissipate."

Before we discuss this further, I'd just like to point out that there's nothing wrong with anger. It's just an emotion, like joy, sadness and happiness. Our emotions are constantly changing and that's one of their purposes: to be in a state of constant flux.

If you watch a young child, of two or three, you will see that he moves easily between emotions. One moment he's laughing, the next he's stubborn, then moved quickly to frustration and on to tears, but another moment and he's back to smiling. A child has not yet learned to control his emotions. He allows them to run freely. As he does this, energy is quickly freed for more important tasks like growing and learning.

As we grow older we are taught to control ourselves and particularly our emotions. The reason is that we then fit into a mould ... the one of the society in which we are living.

I once read an account of an amazing discovery in India, of a little girl who had been brought up by wolves and believed herself to be one. She had never learned to stand on her feet, or to speak, but she had a wide range of wolf noises and behaviour. She had fitted in to the culture around her. When she was 'rescued' and expected to become a human being, she reacted with all the emotions and behaviour that a wolf would display. She had control over her emotions, but only in a way that fitted her for wolf culture.

As I have said, our emotions, left to themselves and expressed, will change of their own accord. Try this sometimes when you feel stuck in a certain feeling. Give it space. Allow the emotion to be there. Feel it fully. Keep allowing ... without restriction or conscious thought. I guarantee that you will find its hold on you relaxing, the emotion itself receding and beginning to change .... This was what is meant in the Reiki precept "Allow your anger to dissipate."

This technique is much easier when you are on your own, and in a place where you cannot be disturbed. It is much harder when you are faced by someone who is angry with you. One of the reasons is that, as soon as someone attacks us, either verbally or emotionally, we defend by attacking *them*. Before long, we are involved in a game of emotional ping-pong: one person attacks, the other defends by attacking, and the first attacks again. In each case the emotional intensity increases until we have a full blown argument. Sometimes you might find yourself literally shaking with anger. Personally, I often burst into tears. These are not the tears that need comfort. These are tears of utter rage.

Anger is wonderful in many ways. It is totally energising. It is clearing and cleansing. The trick is to let it out in some physical way. Shout, yell, dance, jump up and down, go for a run, or a swim, throw something. Do whatever you need to do to express the anger inside you. Sometimes it can really make the housework go with a swing — and gets it done in half the usual time.

This is a brilliant technique in the right time and place. But what about that argument? Someone attacks you — what do you do then? If you throw something, it's not going to lessen your anger and it might increase the other person's.

The main problem with anger is suppressing it. We feel it is 'not nice'. Sometimes our own anger can frighten us. We feel we must contain it. We must put it down and keep it there.

But if we do that, we are laying down serious physical and mental health problems. Anger that is unexpressed and/or unowned will have a serious deleterious affect on the liver, spleen and digestion in particular. It can lead to clinical depression and other manic behaviour.

No. Anger needs space. It needs to be expressed, or it needs to dissipate. The easiest way to dissipate it is to understand the cause.

Osho, the guru whom I love, always states that it is possible to defuse anger by pausing, taking a breath and letting it out very slowly. If at this moment you can step into the shoes of the person who you believe to be attacking you, you will find that your understanding of him or her lessens your anger.

That breath gives you pause: time to look more deeply into what lawyers call 'causation'. What has caused the other's behaviour? Is s/he unwell? Upset? Grieving? Have they made a mistake about the situation? Heard something from another?

The breath gives you time to go within and to see whether you are judging the situation wrongly. Maybe you need to question whether it's necessary to judge at all.

Little that is lasting can be attained by using anger. Anger is intended as a quick release of energy. Good if someone thumps you, or aims a spear at you. You have the energy to retaliate or to run away. It is intended to be quickly used and then to drain away.

So allow this to happen.

Even in worldly events over which it would appear you have no control, anger is not the answer, unless it stirs you to do something positive. And by that I do not mean retaliating. If you can use your anger to fuel a way to help orphaned children, or save a battered wife, or challenge someone in authority, it has done its job.

But if you allow it to simmer away, you are simply adding your negative energy to the negative energy that makes you angry. It is self-defeating. Instead, understand the situation if you can. When your anger lessens, that is the time to send Reiki and love to the situation. Love is the strongest energy there is. No wonder Christ said: "Love thine enemies." In doing so, you are blessing them, blessing yourself and blessing the world.

The key to finding it in your heart to give love in place of anger, is by taking time to understand.

I hope this makes the Precept 'I understand' more understandable? If not, I suggest you simply try the strategy anyway. It's the only way to experience its power.

I AM HONEST

THE ORIGINAL JAPANESE precept was 'work hard' and the more modern version was 'I do my work honestly.' Now I have honed these down to 'I am honest.' Let me explain.

Dr Usui taught that the word *work* included *inner work*, or meditation. This, he claimed, was the true work of the Reiki practitioner: to make oneself the best one can be.

'Work hard' also included the more usual meaning. Work hard at whatever you do: do it to the best of your ability. Give your full attention to your work. If you do this, you will do it honestly, and if you do that, you will achieve a state of fulfilment and purpose, even in the most menial of tasks.

If you bring your full awareness into washing a floor, for instance, it becomes a form of meditation. You can take it further, by imagining that the floor is simply a part of the earth and you are washing it clean of negativity. Each time you wring the dirt from the cloth, you clear some horrible act, or the propensity for some horrible act, from the world. Now you see the deeper purpose in washing the floor. As you have cleaned the house, so your action has resonated out into the wider world.

Doing anything with a sense of awareness helps to transform the act itself: it becomes an act of celebration and of oneness with the Divine.

Of course, when you bring the totality of yourself into your work, you also lose any idea you may have had of making use of your working environment, or the work itself, for your own benefit. It is easy to thieve from one's employers. In the old days, it might have been taking the odd stamp or making unauthorised personal photocopies — even photocopying your buttocks is theft, after all! You are making use of machinery and paper that is not yours.

Nowadays it is more likely that you 'thieve' from your employer by spending time on social media when you should be working. We have become so dishonest as a nation that we don't even see such actions as theft. Instead we have almost come to believe we have a right to look at our Facebook page or personal email during time for which our employer is paying.

What we don't always see, is that we are, in fact, thieving from ourselves. Slowly, slowly, our honesty is leached away. Similarly, when we are always promising ourselves that we will meditate, look after ourselves, eat the right food, and yet never actually get round to doing whatever it is, we are, in fact and in deed, stealing from ourselves. We are being dishonest.

If you do not want to meditate, even though you know it would be beneficial, then don't do it. What good will it do to meditate if your mind is busy thinking of other things? No. Go out and give your whole heart to whatever you want to do. Do it with the whole of your being.

If, when you are dancing you think 'I should be meditating in silence', what happens? You set up a conflict in your mind and in your body. You are not giving attention either to dancing or to meditating. Your body will be uncomfortable: your mind will be uncomfortable. You will obtain no benefit from the dancing or from the meditating.

You have two choices.

The first is to make the whole dance a meditation. Go within, feel the music in your body, feel how your body wants to move. Take your full attention inside. Allow the exercise to throw off all negative states of mind, all pain in the body.

Become the dance. Now you are being honest with yourself. Now you are meditating — and meditation will have the effect you desire.

The second, is to rejoice in the dance. Give yourself up to it fully. Express through the dance all that needs to be expressed. Maybe you have thoughts or worries that are stuck in your body. Release them. Afterwards, you will find yourself falling into a meditative state. Then meditation will have the effect you desire.

Meditation is natural. Meditation is easy. Meditation is merely an altered state of consciousness, similar to how you feel when you are driving your car on 'autopilot'.

Being honest is listening to the voice of your true self, the self within, not the self that society has imposed.

Going back to dancing ... do we not admire the freedom of expression of children who jump for joy? Do we not wish that we could be true to our feelings in such a simple, ingenuous way?

To be truly honest, we must go beyond the mind, which is always rationalising, into the body. For the body is the temple of the soul and if we go deep enough into the body, we listen to our soul. Your body-soul will always guide you in the right direction. Trust it.

Let whatever you do, think or say, be done with inner honesty.

Okay, I know that we fear what people will think if we are truly honest. There is no need, take it from me. Honesty does not mean being brutally frank, but it does mean speaking the truth from your heart centre. If you engage this centre before you open your mouth, you will offend no-one and you will be fully understood. Don't take my word for it. Try it. Experiment.

Enjoy.

If you do this life becomes easy. If you do this, you become happy. When you are happy with yourself, you spread that happiness to others. By your example, you allow others to do the same. You live a life of authenticity and inner truth.

'I am honest.'

I AM COMPASSION

THE ORIGINAL TRANSLATION of the fifth precept from the Japanese was 'be kind to others'. This translation missed out much of the meaning contained within the Japanese kanji, so it was lengthened to 'I am kind to every living thing, including myself'.

In Japan, the old Shinto religion informs all others practised in the country. Shinto is a belief system which sees us all as part of Nature, and that everything, including inanimate objects like rocks and stones, is alive.

Thus, the word 'others' included the whole of Nature. Similarly, in Japan there is a strong sense of each person being an indivisible part of the groups to which they belong. Indeed, I understand that the Japanese language contains no personal pronouns. For this reason 'others' would naturally include the self.

This, I hope, explains the extension of this precept, but my translation still did not give a complete picture of the 'kindness' which was intended. The very word 'kind' can be used to suggest someone or something of a similar nature, so it would seem we should be kind to animals say, but not to insects. 'Kind' also smacks of patronising, a sort of looking down from a height.

Compassion is altogether different. The 'strong feeling' of 'passion' is preceded by 'com' meaning 'together, or jointly'. The metaphysical meaning of the 'passion' contained in the word compassion, comprises empathy, sympathy and concern while 'com' states that all things are interlocking and interconnected. So, if we hurt another, we hurt ourselves: if we help another living thing, we help ourselves.

Compassion is truth and freedom. If we feel and contain compassion within us, then we love, help and protect the whole of creation.

If we do this from our deepest core, then nothing else is needed. If we become true compassion then all the previous precepts become unnecessary because we treat ourselves with grace and kindness in the same way that we treat all of life.

"But I can't be compassionate to slugs or mosquitoes." I hear you cry.

Yes, you can. You can understand that they are doing exactly what they're made to do. The mosquito who bites you is just slaking her hunger. You can recognise this, but you do not have to submit to being bitten. You can use a mosquito net or an insect repellent spray.

Slugs are actually very useful. They dine on rotting material and their excrement makes a wonderful feed for vegetables and flowers. Put them in your compost bin. They have a ready-made source of food and you will have wonderful compost. Or you can explain to them that they can have the first lettuce in each row.

I expect you have heard of the wonderful gardens of the Findhorn community? If not, let me tell you a little about them. Findhorn was founded as a community in the early 1960s on a sandy, cold, windswept site in the north of Scotland. One of its founder members had a wonderful relationship with the devas (nature spirits) and they agreed that if the Findhorn community was started, the nature spirits would work with them to produce wonderful plants, so they did not starve and so that the community would grow. For seven years, as they had agreed, the nature spirits made sure that the produce from the garden scratched out of poor sandy soil was amazingly luxuriant. In fact, most people could not believe the size and health of their vegetables. Even after those seven years were over, the garden remained abundantly fruitful. Many people were attracted by its fame, and stayed on to become part of the community.

In fact, it is so to this day. Of course, the community continues to work with the devas and to apply organic and bio-dynamic garden techniques as well, I believe. Today, although all the founders have now passed away, the Community continues to flourish and attracts thousands of visitors each year. They come for workshops, retreats, and to help with the running of the place. Findhorn also has its own publishing arm for spiritual and alternative books.

One of my favourite authors and spiritual workers, Caroline Myss, often holds workshops there.

"I eat meat — how can that be compassionate?" I hear someone else ask.

My answer, again, is that the whole of this natural world is organised so that, in nature everything eats everything else. Of course, there are prey species and hunter species. Those who are prey, proliferate. Those who are hunters, keep the prey species numbers down sufficiently for nature to be balanced. It is only when things are unbalanced that there are problems. If you shoot lions and tigers because they take sheep, then you will soon find that your fields are overrun by the small animals which are the hunters' normal prey.

Humans are omnivorous by nature. We can, of course, be vegetarian or vegan, but we are still eating living things — vegetables are just as much alive as animals. The short answer is that compassion begins with understanding and gratitude.

We are what we eat. Our food makes our cells, becomes part of the fabric of our bodies. If we honour our bodies by feeding them healthy and nutritious food and with thankfulness, we change the energy of what we eat. It transforms into part of us. So make sure that, if you are eating meat, it is organic or at least free-range, that the life it has led has been a good one. Offer a libation, such as a prayer to the animal's life force.

Give thanks for all that you eat. Bless the life force that nourishes your own life-force. In so doing you bless All-That-Is and you exercise compassion.

When you exercise compassion, differences fall away. When you exercise compassion, you come to realise that we are all one, that all things are one.Then anxieties and worries fade away. You can find peace.

And in giving thanks, you feel gratitude. This takes you back to the first precept. Compassion and gratitude are interlinked.

And remember, whatever you give energy to, is returned to you a thousand fold. If you worry, it seems that is what you want, so you will have more to worry about. If you are grateful for everything good in your life, you will receive more of those good things.

"I am compassion"

16

Time to Move

Once again, we've been sitting and listening for a long time, so let's change the energy before we all go to sleep.

First of all, stand up. Close your eyes and take an inventory of how your body feels. This is just for you. There's no prize. Just see how you feel.

Do you feel sore anywhere?

Are you in pain?

Do you have headache? Or a stomach ache?

Do you feel stiff? Tight? Uncomfortable? Stuck?

Just take an inventory. Nothing more.

Have you all done that?

Well done. Let's shake!

To shake the Reiki way you close your eyes and keep them closed. You do not look at anyone else. This is about YOU. You go within to *your* body and give everyone else in the room freedom to do the same.

A word of warning. It's really important to shake, even if you don't feel like it. I know I've said this before, so this is just a reminder. Everyone else will be giving off energy. So if you stand still or only move a little you are inviting all that 'stuff' to settle on you.

Move.

Experiment.

Enjoy.

Osho's Kundalini Meditation

I'm using music from Osho's Kundalini meditation. In this meditation you shake for fifteen minutes, but we will only do it for five or six minutes. The music is perfect for shaking to. I'll turn it up a little ...

And all you have to do is ***shake.***

Let your whole body shake. Imagine you are shaking out all the creases in your muscles just as you shake out the laundry. Start at the top. Let your shoulders shake.

Shake out all the tension they hold.

Shake off all the burdens and troubles you carry.

Shake your arms, your hands.

Shake out all the tightness in your elbows, your wrists, your fingers ... let it drop onto the floor, to go through the floor into the earth. The earth receives all our dross and turns it into golden energy.

Shake your hips, your buttocks.

Let go of all the tension you carry in your abdomen. Let your belly soften. Let it all hang out — as they used to say in my young days. Feel the tension dissipate. Let yourself breathe deep, deep down.

Shake down your legs. Release the tension in your thighs and calves.

Shake your ankles and feet. You can lie on your back to do this if you like.

Just shake all tension out of your body. In doing so you will relieve it of all sorts of emotional and mental rubbish that no longer serves you.

Go back up to your head. Loosen your jaw. Shake it from side to side. Shake your head from side to side ... up and down ... whatever helps you to loosen the ties of tension and fear.

If you feel like it ... whoop and shout. I do. Nothing moves energy better than sound. And for you, your own sound is the most healing sound of all.

Enjoy the feeling of freedom. You are in a safe place. You can let yourself go.

When you free yourself you encourage others to free themselves, so you do a great service to them, and to the world, as well as to yourself.

REJOICE.
Rejoice in LIFE
Rejoice in freedom
Experiment.
How does it feel to move your body in this way?

Do you feel silly? Or clumsy? Or cross?
Chuck it out. Take yourself back to your body. Let go.
ENJOY.
I'll stop talking for a while to let you experience your inner world for yourself.

Music stops after about 5 minutes.
Keeping your eyes closed, let your breath settle and come back to normal.
Okay, do take a seat. Stretch.
It's lovely to see you all smiling.

17

History

I AM TEACHING you Usui Reiki. This is the basis for all other sorts of Reiki that are taught in the West today.

I am only going to go briefly into the history of Reiki, mostly because it's a system of healing that is constantly changing and evolving. As such, the history is not of great importance. Not to my mind anyway.

When I first learned Reiki it was considered to be an oral tradition. There were no books on the subject and its origins were lost in myth. This seemed appropriate to me. We each grow through our own experience and practice of Reiki and because it is an energy source it is almost impossible to define exactly what Reiki is, or to encapsulate it in words. At that time I thought that Dr Usui had lived hundreds of years previously, and that his teachings had been handed down like those of the Buddha and Christ.

In fact, Dr. Usui 'discovered' Usui Reiki Ryoho in the early nineteen-twenties and died only in 1926. To explain how he and his teaching came to be shrouded in myth, I need to tell you a story...

How Reiki came to the West

This is the story of how Reiki came to the West from Japan not long before the outbreak of World War Two.

It all starts with Hawayo Takata, a Japanese-American lady who, as custom required, returned to Japan to inform her parents of her sister's death in America. While she was staying in Japan, she fell ill and was taken to the local hospital where she was told that she was suffering from gallstones, a tumour, appendicitis and asthma. Advised that she should have an immediate and urgent operation, she declined in view of the risks. Instead she opted to attend the Reiki clinic nearby.

After a period of four months she was completely healed. Amazed by the power of Reiki, she asked to be taught it; and in the spring of 1936 she was initiated into the First Degree. She worked with her Reiki Master, Dr. Hayashi for a year and then received the Second Degree, returning to America in 1937. That same year Dr Hayashi made her a Reiki Master, following her to America and helping her to establish Reiki as a healing modality in the United States.

Mrs Takata was a powerful healer and set up Reiki clinics in Hawaii and other places, travelling to many parts of the United States. By her death in 1972 she had initiated twenty-two Reiki Masters to carry on the Reiki tradition in the West.

Reiki evolved under her leadership. She refined the attunements and also developed her own system of hand positions for giving Reiki. In addition she founded the system of Reiki that we learn today.

This was vital, because as a result of the American occupation of Japan after WW2, Reiki practitioners there decided to keep their healing modality secret. Reiki no longer spread in Japan. We owe Mrs Takata a debt of gratitude for bringing Reiki to the West and having the courage to share it with so many people at a time when Japanese nationals in

America faced immense difficulties.

Immediately after World War Two, anything Japanese was anathema to most people in the West. Viewed in a similar light to Nazi Germany, their actions, and morals were incomprehensible to the Allies who had fought against them. Their cruelty, too, was legendary, as was the fact that they were prepared to commit suicide rather than surrender.

Reiki itself was likely to be viewed with suspicion as it came from the same people who had abused prisoners of war, particularly those who had been forced to build the Burma railway.

On a personal note, my father and my father-in-law both fought in Burma, and one of my schoolfriend's father had been their prisoner and a labourer on that dreadful railway. None of them had any sympathy for the Japanese. On the contrary, they considered them the embodiment of evil. I believe that Mts Takata decided that Reiki's history should be massaged to present it in the best light possible in the circumstances.

However, let's go back to the beginning. Reiki Ryoho (Reiki treatments) were known in Japan in the early twentieth century. There seems to have been a number of different schools before Dr Usui founded his own system.

As a result of many years of study, culminating in a long, twenty-one day meditation on Mount Kurama, the holiest and most sacred mountain in Japan according to the Shinto tradition, Dr Usui felt the great Reiki energy on the crown of his head. Originally, he believed this was part of his spiritual practice, but eventually he found that it was also a way of healing on all levels. He spent some time working, meditating and calibrating this wonderful energy. Not long after his experience on the mountain a great earthquake occurred near where he lived and he took this system to the locality to assist those who has suffered.

His fame spread far and wide and he started to travel, setting up clinics and teaching others how to use the energy for the highest good. After his death in 1926, a great memorial stone was erected and one of his students was deputed to write Dr Usui's obituary on it. But before he died, Dr Usui had asked one of his students, Chujiro Hayashi, to open his own clinic and use his experience as a medical doctor to continue to develop and expand Reiki. This Dr Hayashi did, and it was to his clinic that Hawayo Takata resorted in 1936.

This is a very short history of Reiki and, if you are interested to enquire further, I suggest you go to the website (www.reiki.org) which is run by William Rand. William has also written a useful book entitled *Reiki, The Healing Touch*, in which he goes into the history of Reiki in some detail. Another good book is Frank Arjava Petter's book *Reiki Fire* which catalogues his research into the origin of Reiki, and includes a translation of the long inscription on Dr Usui's memorial stone.

18

Meditation: By the Ocean

We will go straight into the second attunement after this meditation. Just as we did this morning for the first attunement, after the Flowing Energy Meditation.

- Let's prepare by putting the chairs in a row.
- Now choose your place and put a cushion in your back and/or under your feet.
- Are you warm enough? If not, grab a cardigan, throw or blanket and have it nearby or put it around your shoulders or over your lap.
- Have your glass of water handy, and your notebook and pen in case you want to make notes about your experience.
- Make sure you are really comfortable as you will be sitting for quite a while. Wriggle around a little, if you need to, or have a stretch. Having said that, if you need to move, or cough or swallow or anything similar, allow yourself to do so, but try not to disturb the others.

Gently close your eyes. Become aware of where you are sitting. Feel the floor beneath your feet … feel your sitting bones on the chair. Let your shoulders be relaxed and in line with your hips. Feel a silver thread running from the top of your head up into the clouds and adjust your position until your nose is in line with your umbilicus. Take your awareness to your body …

Now, breathe out … all your breath. And take a long slow breath in … expanding your ribs and softening your tummy.

Great. Let the breath escape though your mouth and feel yourself relaxing and letting go of all that you do not need right at this moment. Breathe in through your nose, softly, silently ... and out through your mouth, softly, silently ....

And now you find yourself walking along a beautiful, deserted beach ... the temperature is perfect, neither too warm nor too cold ... the sand beneath your feet is firm but soft ... the sky is the blue of high summer ... and beneath the green trees that come down to the edge of the sand ... wild flowers bloom ... their fragrance is borne to you on a fragrant breeze ...

The breeze ruffles your hair ... you feel the sun on your face, your arms, your legs ... the clothes on your body.

Gentle waves wash against the shore ... you walk at the edge of the sea ... feel the water caressing your feet.

You become aware of the salt smell of the sea combined with the fragrance of wild flowers and the green scent of the trees at the edge of the beach.

Taste the freshness of the air and the slightly dry salt on your lips.

A seagull swoops away over the sea, giving a sense of freedom and you hear its inimitable cry ... let the swish of the waves against the shore fill your ears and lull you ... feel the smile on your lips.

As you look around, you take in the perfect harmony of the scene, the blue sky reflected in the smooth water ... the golden-white sand of the beach ... the contrasting darkness of the trees behind ...

The peacefulness of this beach ... the comfortable aloneness ... allows you to reflect, without effort, on the interconnectedness of all things ... you and the beach are one

... you and nature are one...

Now you turn to face the water and are seized with a great desire to feel its freshness all over your body. You strip off any clothes you may be wearing, and leave them above the water line ... Now you walk, skip or run into the sea ... you can bask in the shallows ... go a little deeper ... or dive in for a long swim ...

Take some time to play in the water. Maybe fishes nibble at your toes ... or a dolphin comes to take you for a ride ... or a seagull lands on the water, bobbing up and down just out of reach, as though to tease you ...

Then take a little time to luxuriate in the feeling of the water ... its freshness ... its coolness ... its saltiness ... its exhilarating quality ... its cleanliness. Allow your body to float, feeling the gentle waves uplifting you, feeling the water's support.

Be aware that the water is cleansing you of anything you no longer need, on all levels ... spiritual, mental, emotional ... particularly emotional ... and physical. Feel how there is no gap between you and the water, it embraces you completely.

Accept its support, and allow all troubles or pain to disperse into the sea. Let the water take all negativity from you ... Feel how all the sea creatures rejoice in all that you give them ... let the sea cleanse and transform you.

As you feel your troubles and pain float away, you give grateful thanks to the water ... you call down a blessing on the water that brings life to the Earth ... to the sea that encompasses such a great proportion of the life force on this planet ... for giving us the food that we eat ... that nourishes our body ... We give thanks to the sea and all it contains ...

Now it's time to leave the water ... You allow yourself to

float towards the shore and as you find your feet, you notice how refreshed, invigorated ... clear and clean you feel ... you are washed clean of all the mental constructs and belief systems that limit your amazing creativity...

Smiling, you walk up the beach to where you left your clothes ... and ... they are gone. In their place lies a huge fluffy white towel. Pick it up and dry yourself ... perhaps you give yourself a brisk rub, perhaps you dab gently at the places where water still lurks, or maybe you spread it out on the sand and lie on it so that the sun can dry and energise you.

When you are dry, you see that your old clothes have been replaced by shining new white garments perfectly designed for you. You put them on ...if you wish ... or you may prefer to stay naked...

Whichever you choose, you give thanks again for the feeling of purity which encompasses you and start to walk back along the beach the way that you came...

As you go, you notice again the smells, the tastes, the sounds, the sights and the feelings all around you ... You acknowledge that you are part of Nature ...and you realise that all that you do or think or feel emotionally has an effect on All-That-Is.

You are unique, you are special ... you are you.

Bring this knowledge with you as you walk back the way you have come ... until you find yourself walking back into this room ... you become aware of where you are, sitting in the chair. Again you take your attention back to your breath, feeling yourself softly breathing in and out.

Wiggle your fingers and toes ... have a good stretch and when you are ready ... and only when you are ready ... gently open your eyes and come back into the room.

19

The Second Attunement

Now we'll move into the second attunement to Reiki 1.

It *is* important to sit with your back straight with your shoulders in line with your hips. Take a breath and relax your shoulders. Make sure your nose is in line with your navel. If you find it relaxing, breathe in through your nose and out through your mouth, but that is not compulsory. Being comfortable is, though!

Now gently close your eyes and bring your hands to the prayer position (gassho, namaste) at your heart centre, in the middle of your chest. You will remember that the reason we close our eyes is that it makes it easier to 'go within'. Without the distraction of sight, we are able to enter fully into the experience. I'll just remind you, too, that the attunement process, while not secret, is sacred.

Relax. Just allow this to be an experiment. Allow yourself to experience whatever happens. Just remember that I will need to be able to move your hands, so don't snuggle them away.

I'm going to put on some music. Allow it to move through every one of your cells ... Let's begin ...

Beginning

Take another deep breath and relax. This is for your unique self. Remind yourself that you are a magnificent being and capable of anything.

Take your attention to your breath. If you would like to invite your personal guides — or your angels or any other being who works for the highest good of all — to be with you, now is the time to do so.

This is the second of the four attunements to Reiki 1. The purpose of the attunement is to bring the Reiki energy down through your chakras. Starting with the crown, it falls like a waterfall down through all your energy centres and out through your palm chakras in the centre of your hands.

If your mind wanders, bring it gently back to this intention.

At the end of the attunement, keep your eyes closed until I ring the Ting-Sha three times.

Ending

Sound of Ting-sha: three rings.

Silence for a few moments.

The second attunement to Reiki 1 is now complete.

Take as long as you need to open your eyes and come back in the room.

Now I would like you all, please, to spend a little while in your own energy, not speaking to anyone else — just until I come back into the room and ring the ting-sha again.

This is a special time for you to do exactly what seems right for you. There is no one who can tell you what that is … Maybe you would like to stay exactly where you are … maybe you would like to take a little walk outside in the garden … or to snuggle up in a blanket on the settee. You may like to make a few notes of your experiences.

Do whatever feels right for you.

Do, also, drink some water.

I am going to leave the room now and will return in a few minutes.

Sharing

If you'd like to share anything that you experienced, we'd all love to hear it. But there is absolutely no need … no pressure. If you want to keep your experiences to yourself that is absolutely fine.

Just a reminder though … if there is anything that didn't feel right, or if you feel uncomfortable in any way, it is important to let me know so that I can help. You can do this privately if you prefer, or you can tell me now.

How was the meditation?

How was the attunement?

Did you enjoy it?

How do you feel now?

20

Chakra balance

Now that you've received the second attunement to Reiki 1, it's important that we get the energy moving through you again, particularly through your hands. I'm going to show you a simple Chakra Balance that you can do with Reiki.

This is easy and doesn't take long, but it's very effective for bringing you to your centre. It's so easy to be thrown off-balance by the events of the day — or the week, or month — but this short exercise will soon sort that out.

For this exercise, we forget the crown chakra. We forget it because its primary purpose is to connect us with the energy of the universe, just as our foot chakras connect us to the earth energy.

When we do this, your dominant hand is placed on the lower chakras in turn, and your non-dominant hand covers the upper chakras in turn. Do you know why?

That's right. It's because of polarity. The dominant hand has a positive charge and the non-dominant hand a negative one. The positive poles are at the top of the body, the negative ones lower down. And the middle has a much more neutral charge.

You may find it helpful to close your eyes.

We start by balancing the two poles, positive and negative:

1. Your non-dominant hand covers the third eye in the middle of the forehead. Your dominant hand covers your base chakra. I'll just remind you that the base chakra is

right underneath your body, on the perineum in front of the anus. Make sure you cover it. Your body is your own so there is no need for shyness. You will feel when you are covering the correct part.

All you need to do is to concentrate on feeling when the Reiki energy in your palms equalises and comes into balance. Concentrate on your palms, not on your chakras. It's easier and more effective.

It doesn't take long … perhaps a minute or two. You can stay in that position for as long as you like. You may feel the energy in your hands start to decrease. That's a sign that it's time to move on. If you stay in the same position you may find your hands warm up or tingle (or both) again and you start another round of healing. If so, wait for the heat or tingling to ebb before you move on.

This position is very good for grounding and bringing you back to your centre.

2. Now bring your upper, non-dominant hand to your throat chakra and move your lower, dominant hand up to your sacral chakra. This is situated about two fingers' width below your belly button.

   Again, hold this position until you feel the equalisation of the Reiki energy in your palm chakras.

   This position is very good for helping you to express your emotions, and is particularly good for your creativity.

3. And finally bring the two hands closer together still. The top one comes down to cover the heart centre in the middle of your chest, and the lower one comes up to your solar plexus — that little indent at the bottom of the breast bone which is the source of your 'fire'.

Again, hold this position until you feel the equalisation of the Reiki energy in your palm chakras.

This is a very useful position. It is very good to use for shock of any sort, or when you are feeling anxious or worried.

There. That's it. A quick, simple Reiki chakra balance that you can use whenever you feel in need.

21

Ending day 1

Well done. You've all worked really hard today. I hope you've enjoyed it?

Any questions on anything? If you can't think of one now, you may find that you get home and suddenly have a load. If so, write them down and bring them into class tomorrow. I'll do my best to answer them.

Don't be shy. I know that others will want to know the answers too. Just because they haven't asked the question, doesn't matter. They probably haven't thought about it.

Speaking to Others

Here is one thing I would ask you.

Please don't chat about Reiki and what you have done today with anyone. Reiki needs to settle into your energy field. At the moment we have brought a huge amount of high vibrational energy through your aura and through your chakras. A little time is required for your own energy to adjust.

If you start chatting about what has happened today — even with your nearest and dearest — they will make comments and ask questions that you are not yet equipped to answer. Often, I have found, it only takes one disparaging comment to throw the whole process into disarray and to make you feel inadequate or silly.

Just say that you will tell them all about it when the workshop is over and you are ready. In this way, you keep your own counsel and do not give your power away.

Also you may be very tired tonight, and you may have a headache. Try to get plenty of rest and drink lots of water. The

Reiki energy is healing, but sometimes it comes in fast and, if you have not been following a pure diet for a few days, it can release toxins into the bloodstream. That is why you need to drink *buckets* of water!

Try to resist painkillers. Do put your Reiki hands on yourself. It doesn't matter where, as long as you feel comfortable. This will help Reiki to flow. Flowing is good.

Closing circle

Let's form a Reiki circle.

I wonder how different this will be from this morning's circle?

Turn your left hand palm upwards, and your right hand palm downwards, then place your right palm gently on the upturned hand of your neighbour. In this way, all hands should be meeting palm to palm.

Gently close your eyes.

Make sure your shoulders are relaxed ... your elbows are relaxed ... your hands are soft and resting gently against those of your neighbour on each side. Your hips are relaxed ... and your knees. Become very aware of your feet and your connection with the floor and through the floor, with the Earth below. Spread your toes and wriggle your feet against the floor.

Breathe in deeply and gently out, feeling centred in your body and connected with the earth.

Begin to allow energy to pass round the circle. Receive it with your left hand ... imagine it passing up your left arm ... through your heart centre in the middle of your chest ... down your right arm ... and out through your right palm. Watch the energy as it passes round the circle ... imagine it like a beautiful ribbon of light, and meet each other at the heart centre, feeling your connection.

You will remember that we have created a huge column of

light big enough to fill the entire room, coming up from the centre of the earth, through our circle and out into the universe to join up with the light network that surrounds our planet. We will leave this column of light here. If anything comes up for you, on any level — that is physical, mental, emotional or spiritual — send it into this column of light for healing.

Now we thank all those who work for our highest good, on all levels of existence, — including the Reiki Masters who have gone before, the ascended Masters, the angels, archangels, beings of light and Reiki guides — who have been with us to help us on our Reiki journey.

It is always a great honour to be chosen as your Reiki Master, so I thank you all for coming and lending your special energy to this workshop. I hope you have enjoyed this day. Remember to take special care of yourself tonight.

Breathe in slowly… breathe out slowly. And again, breathe in slowly and breathe out … gently, calmly, bring your consciousness back into the room.

And let us have another Reiki hug. As you place your arms around your neighbours let yourself relax, 'blissing out' as one of my teacher's used to say. Become aware of any change in the energy between us all: a feeling of connection, of warmth and togetherness…

Stay in silence. Feel the togetherness of silence.

Thank you all.

See you tomorrow at ten o'clock. Have a safe journey home, and sleep well.

DAY TWO, MORNING

22

Welcome and Reiki Circle

GOOD MORNING, ALL.

Welcome back. Take a seat in the circle. It doesn't have to be where you were sitting yesterday. Try somewhere else if you like. It's good to have a change and to be flexible.

I hope you all slept well? I did. I always do when I'm teaching Reiki.

Did anything — thoughts, worries, feelings, emotional stuff — come into your awareness after you left here?

Let's go round the circle and you can let us know if there's anything you'd like to share. But it's not compulsory: there's no reason to say anything unless you want to.

Let's start the day proper with a Reiki circle. So let's all stand up and connect our hands. Left hand up to receive: right hand down to pass on.

If it's easier there's a little trick to this. Put your hands together, turn your joined thumbs to the left ... and slide them apart. They should be in the right position now. Does that help? Sometimes it does, sometimes it doesn't. But as long as we all have the left palm facing upwards and the right hand facing down, we're fine.

Gently close your eyes and go within. Feel your connection to the floor and the Earth through the soles of your feet. Soften your knees ... and your elbows. Feel your body nicely balanced, and relaxed right down to your fingertips.

Now, once again feel the Reiki energy passing round the circle, receiving it with your left hand and passing it on with your right. If you can't feel it, no problem. Just be aware that it's happening and imagine that it is flowing round to your right. Follow it round the circle, greeting each person in turn at their heart centre, so that once again it seems we have a rainbow-coloured ribbon of blessing joining us together as it runs through our palms and our hearts.

You will remember that we left a wonderful column of light here from yesterday. It is still here: still available to transform any heavy or strong energy that no longer serves you. If any problems, pains or worries come up, send them into this column of light for transformation.

We also ask that any higher energy that works for the highest good for all, and who would like to be here to help us on this journey, joins us now. We thank them and bless them.

And I thank and bless all of you for coming back again today and for dedicating your energy to healing and wholing everything with which you come into contact. The world is direly in need of healers, so thank you all.

Now let's step into this column of light and have our lovely Reiki hug. Feel the connection between us, and its power for good.

Let's enjoy that for a minute or two …

Okay, let's go back to our seats.

It's a good time for a comfort break if you need one … any questions about anything that we covered yesterday? In fact, do you have any questions about anything? I'll do my best to answer.

What We Did Yesterday and What We'll Do Today

We have a lot to cover today, but first, let's recall about what we did yesterday.

- ✓ We spent some time beginning to understand that, in Reiki, we work with the subtle energy that emanates from every living thing:
- ✓ We learned what Reiki is and what the Reiki kanji means.

- ✓ We learned the Reiki ethic.
- ✓ We learned to begin to feel the energy swirling within and around us.
- ✓ You received the first attunement to Reiki which brought the Reiki energy down into your aura
- ✓ Then we learned the hand positions for treating the self including how to 'switch on' the Reiki energy.
- ✓ After lunch we went on to learn the Reiki Precepts or Principles and then a little about Reiki history.
- ✓ You then received the second attunement to Reiki 1 which brought the Reiki energy through your chakras and into your palms.
- ✓ We finished by learning the Reiki Chakra balance.

Today will follow a similar pattern. We'll do a little brain work, then some movement, a meditation and an attunement, after which I'll teach you how to give Reiki treatment to someone else. Before lunch we'll concentrate on the front of the body.

The afternoon will be very similar, but we'll learn the hand positions for treating the back of the body.

So there's a lot to get through. We'd better get on with it.

23

The Reiki Degrees

Let me tell you about the degrees (or levels) in Usui Reiki Ryoho.

I have already told you a little about Reiki 1, so now I will remind you that this is the energy of self healing, and of healing physical ills and disturbances.

I'll repeat that, as it is very important.

Reiki 1 level Reiki is for:

- ✓ **yourself,** and
- ✓ the **physical** body

1. Yourself

You may think that healing is a way that you can help other people. This is true. But unless you are healthy and your energy is running smoothly, you will not be able to access the Reiki energy. Instead, you will be giving away your own energy.

We all know how often we have been to see someone who is ill or depressed, or both. Sometimes we even dread going to see them. The reason is that, quite unintentionally, people with low personal energy will try to obtain it from someone else.

These people often perk up considerably while you are there: they say something along the lines of "S/he does me so much good. I always feel better after s/he has visited." On the other hand, *you* leave feeling quite exhausted and often mentally and emotionally tired too.

I am reminded of the story of the aboriginal people in Tasmania. Because Tasmania had been separated from the

Australian mainline for millennia, somehow the Tasmanian aboriginals had managed to lose the ability to make fire. Being nomadic, this caused great problems. Each tribe carried a coal from the previous fire with them and used that to light the next. But if a coal died, they had no option other than to go cold and hungry — and Tasmania is a cold island, particularly in the winter — unless they could obtain fire, in some form, from another tribe. Many and vicious were the fights that ensued, as you can imagine.

The situation would have been very different if they had retained the knowledge of how to make fire.

In this scientific world in which we live, we have embraced the mechanical idea of the body: as a machine, rather than a living entity. We believe all our energy comes from our food. We have forgotten the way to garner our energy and to keep it alive and healthy. So when our energy becomes so low that we cannot reach all that is provided by the Universe, we have to take it from someone else. Often we don't realise that we are stealing our 'fire' from others and seldom does the person from who it is stolen really understand what is happening. They simply feel tired while we feel much more lively.

So your own energy is … yours. It is *your* responsibility to keep it high. Thus your mind and body will be healthy and your emotions more balanced. In this state of being — of grace — it is easy to share our energy and a delight to do so. Nonetheless, if we give away too much, without taking time and effort to look after ourselves, we can still end up depleted, and depressed and unhealthy to boot.

Now just imagine the difference if we each took responsibility for our own health, on all levels — mind, body, emotions, spirit. Life would be so much easier for everyone.

But there is another important reason to keep your own

energy high. The Reiki energy is of a very high vibration and unless you are yourself vibrating at a high level, you will find it impossible to channel Reiki either for yourself or for others.

2. Physical healing

Physical healing is about healing the body. The body itself may be your own, or it may be someone else's.

First, since Reiki 1 is about self-healing, we will start with healing yourself. As I have already said, the physical body is the densest of the vibratory levels. It therefore responds very well to touch.

Touch is a vital part of our well-being. Babies who are not picked up and cuddled simply do not thrive. Often they die. The same thing happens in other species, too. If you watch a bitch with puppies, she is constantly licking and cleaning them, sometimes cuffing them when they hurt her or misbehave in some other way. If the sound of her growl has no effect, she will nip them. They soon learn what is acceptable and what is not.

The instinct to touch in order to comfort or reassure is hardwired into the animal system (including humans). How often do we 'kiss it better' when a child is bruised or hurt? I even find I do this to myself. How often do we cuddle or hug someone to comfort them? How often do we reach out to ruffle a child's hair by way of endearment?

Unfortunately, because of the way 'political correctness' has entered into all walks of life — often because of over-reported cases of abuse — it is much more difficult to touch or caress a child without incurring some form of penalty. I have heard that some teachers cannot even bathe a child's scraped knee or apply a dressing to it. Instead, another child is deputed to go and help the injured one.

What harm we are doing to relationships of all kinds. No wonder children are becoming more withdrawn from life itself, less able to communicate, and less able to express emotion through the physical body. Instead, all those emotions are dammed up inside the physical body, causing physical pain and discomfort. We need to respond with loving touch, just as our instincts suggest.

Reiki is a beautiful way of using touch to heal. Reiki touch is compassion itself. We all need compassion and reassurance in our lives. We also need love. The love that is the Reiki energy is pure compassion and empathy. There is no ulterior motive of any kind. We simply allow the Reiki energy to flow from our hands into the body, knowing that its built-in intelligence will guide the body's own energy to heal whatever is necessary to heal.

Remember, we do not heal, nor does the Reiki energy. The body heals itself, but sometimes its energy is too depleted to do more than keep the 'status quo'. In other words, by giving Reiki, it is as if we plugged the body's electrical circuit into the mains. Now the body has sufficient energy to heal itself and sufficient intelligence to know which parts of the body require energy to heal themselves, and the most beneficial order for that healing to take place.

We heal ourselves by putting our hands on our body and letting the Reiki energy flow. We heal others by doing precisely the same. There is a little more to it than that — we will go into this aspect in more depth later — but not much.

Although Reiki 1 is primarily about the self, you also learn the hand positions for treating others, because you will soon want to share your skills with your friends and family. At this stage it is imperative to ask for their consent, and perhaps, an exchange of some kind, or a donation. However, you cannot obtain insurance until you have completed the Reiki 2 workshop, so you should not practice Reiki professionally (i.e. for money). Having said that, if you are already qualified in another therapy, you may well find Reiki flows unbidden through your hands when you are working. This is fine.

The only other thing to remember is that Reiki always has an effect, even if it is not precisely what you wanted, or expected. Maybe someone has a painful back. You give it Reiki, thinking it will soon be back to normal, but alas! the pain is still there when you've finished the treatment. You feel dismayed — but then you hear that their anxiety has faded away.

Reiki knows what needs to be healed and the most beneficial order for that healing to take place. All you need is a large dose of trust. And you will be amazed by the results.

After Reiki1: Perception

Whilst the attunement process means that your energy is immediately raised in vibration and you are able to channel Reiki immediately, it takes about three months for the Reiki 1 energy to 'bed in' so that it becomes so much of your own vibration that you hardly notice it.

This is a wonderful time for self-watching. See what you notice about the change in yourself on all levels: physical, mental, emotional and spiritual. I'm sure you will notice all sorts of little alterations.

It's also a lovely time to 'play' with the energy. Become aware of your own energy. See how much you can perceive, not only with your hands, but also with your intuition. Maybe you 'see' more things on an energy level, maybe you 'hear' — this is a strange phenomenon because it's not really like hearing, words just appear in your mind. They may seem quite surreal, but pay no attention to that, test by asking an open question of yourself or the other person. (e.g. 'Does ...mean anything to you?) Nearly always your 'hearing' will be very accurate. Some people 'taste' or 'smell' appropriately.

I remember the vivid smell of burning rubber when I was treating someone. At the time, I was newly attuned to Reiki 1 and wasn't sure whether I should mention it. Luckily my client said: "Can you smell it?"

"What?" I asked.

"Burning rubber."

"Yes, I can. I don't think it's anything inside the house, though. Maybe it's something outside…"

"No, it's my brother. He died in a motorcycle accident when he was nineteen. His body reeked of it."

"So … do you find it uncomfortable?"

"Oh no. It's his way of reassuring me; telling me all is well."

I felt myself relax.

"Good."

"But this time he's telling me something else. Only I can't quite hear what it is."

The words popped into my head.

"Tell her to take the main road when she drives home. There'll be a heavy fog and if she goes through the lanes she'll meet a lorry head-on."

"Something about driving, I think," my client said.

"Yes," I agreed. "He wants you to take the main road home."

"Then I will," she said with a sigh. The next moment she seemed asleep, and I continued with the Reiki treatment.

Of course, the following morning I couldn't resist checking about the fog and the lorry. And, of course, there had been fog and a lorry had come off the road down that very lane. I phoned my client. She sounded very perky and said she had driven home along the main road and the conditions had been unexceptional. In fact, the road seemed clearer than usual. And she felt wonderful. Of course.

Reiki 2

Now we come to Reiki 2.

Reiki 1 was about healing yourself and healing the physical body.

In Reiki 2 we move up a level of vibration. This is where we learn to treat emotional, mental and spiritual illness.

Whereas Reiki 1 was about the self, Reiki 2 is about healing others as well as yourself.

There are three symbols to learn at Reiki 2 level.

- ✓ The first is a 'power button' which makes all Reiki energy you use 'more'.
- ✓ The second is about mental and emotional healing.
- ✓ And the third is about healing on a spiritual level and also is the key to distant healing.

There is a lot more to it than these three symbols, but between them, they encompass a myriad possibilities.

Once again, after the Reiki 2 attunements there will be a huge shift in your energy as the amount of Reiki energy you can channel increases exponentially. You will also become aware of higher levels of energy, vibrating so fast that before Reiki 1 it is unlikely that you were aware of them at all.

Again, it takes about 3 months of practising — especially distant healing — before you become fully comfortable with Reiki 2.

Advanced Reiki

The advanced Reiki workshop is not part of the original system set out by the mother of Western Reiki, Hawayo Takata, but I have found that there is a need for it.

When I had completed my Reiki 2 training, I worked with Reiki often, but I still didn't feel ready to move on the Master's Degree. Of course, twenty years ago, the custom was to stop at Reiki 2 unless you wanted to teach Reiki, in which case you took the Reiki Master degree.

Fascinated with the amazing results from Reiki, not to mention the enjoyment of learning that I could channel Reiki, I felt I wanted to know more about this amazing energy healing system. I bought books as they were written. (Unfortunately, at the time I learned Reiki there were very few books available. The few there were came all the way from the United States of America and were very expensive. Written for the American market they were full of hyperbole and often difficult to read because of the fonts chosen by the authors.)

Nonetheless I bought and devoured them. I gathered that there were other energy practices that could be combined with Reiki to obtain more 'power' or to have other affects. Then I discovered Frank Arjava Petter and his wife, Chetna. They had met and studied at Osho's ashram in Poona, India.

Immediately, I felt a strong connection with them. I knew that my Reiki Master, Ma Prem Pratiba, had spent a long time sitting at Osho's feet in the same ashram. Indeed, she had received the Reiki attunements there and my Reiki 1 certificate, a very beautiful document of hand calligraphy, states that I have received the first degree in *Osho Shamanic Reiki*.

Frank Petter had moved to the north of Japan to open an English Language School with his wife, and could not resist the opportunity to find out the truth behind the 'myth' of Doctor Usui. Because of the culture in Japan he found this difficult, but eventually he discovered a great deal — I will tell you more about this later — and when I found out about him he and Chetna were scheduled to teach a workshop in London to spread this knowledge. Of course, I had to attend.

As a result, I felt that there was great need for another workshop to plug the gap between Reiki 2 and Reiki Master.

So, to cut to the chase, I teach an Advanced Reiki Training (ART). This is the opportunity to revise all that has been learned in Reiki 1 and 2, as well as to share any experiences or learning that has occurred since taking those workshops.

In addition, I teach several ways of working with the Reiki energy, as well as particular ways to combine the power of the breath with the power of Reiki.

I love this workshop because it differs with each teaching depending on the experiences of the participants and what they need to learn. Many people experience energy differently after this workshop and feel that Reiki is more concrete and less 'airy-fairy'.

Of course, the participants are attuned to yet another level of Reiki and often have wonderful blissful experiences during those attunements.

I always suggest that if you are serious about making Reiki your own spiritual path you take this workshop before you continue to Reiki Mastership.

Reiki 3

Becoming a Reiki Master in the 1980s was both onerous and expensive. It was made that way by Hawayo Takata because she did not want people to 'dabble' in Reiki and to teach it only as a way to make money. She wanted to keep the way she thought Reiki 'pure' and, I believe, to honour the Japanese tradition of a kind of Reiki apprenticeship.

Reiki Mastership would take about a year all told and cost $10,000. During the year, the new Reiki Master, having received the attunements, would shadow Hawayo Takata for a few sessions. Then when s/he found students, their fees would be paid to Hawayo, who would conduct the first few classes, after that, she would sit in on classes given by the new Reiki Master. I understand that she was very strict.

I do not come from the same tradition as Hawayo Takata although she was the 'Reiki mother' of some of my own teachers. I have already told you that the first two degrees I took with Ma Prem Pratiba were 'Osho Shamanic Reiki' and incorporated a good deal of Osho's teaching about meditation, movement and the connection between mind, body and spirit. But my later Reiki Masters, who attuned me as a Reiki Master and a Karuna® Reiki Master were all part of Hawayo Takata's lineage.

A few of the 22 masters whom Hawayo attuned, decided that Reiki was so valuable to the global community, and so needed, that it should be made widely available and affordable. Unfortunately this caused a split in the Reiki community and I am one of those who became known as the 'Independent Reiki Masters'.

In my experience, there is a huge shift in energy between Reiki 2 and Reiki Master. Even between ART and Reiki Master, there is a great increase in the quantity and power of the Reiki energy one can channel.

Originally, Reiki Master Teacher was one degree. I prefer to teach it as two, for reasons that will soon become apparent.

So, I teach the Reiki Master Degree as Reiki 3 and The Reiki Master Teacher as Reiki 3a or Reiki 4.

When you become a Reiki Master, you take responsibility for your own healing and for making Reiki your own spiritual path. This is not something to be taken lightly. It is a matter for you alone, but if you choose to continue with Reiki for self-aggrandisement or merely to make money, you will never know its true power, nor the compassionate love which it is.

When you make Reiki your spiritual path, you find that you begin to feel different. By taking responsibility for your own beliefs, acknowledging your gifts and abilities and by making them available to the world, you begin to shine with your own light. You attract more light to yourself, and more of all that your heart desires. That is not to say that you will not suffer sadness and loss, but you will have a wonderful tool to help you to overcome those things.

At Reiki 3, Reiki Master, there are three more symbols to learn. These are used for connecting and healing at the soul level. They are very profound. You receive attunements to each of them in turn, and then to all of them.

These symbols are sacred, but they are also very practical and helpful.

Reiki Master Teacher

And so to:

Reiki Master Teacher.

This is where the magic happens. What an honour, privilege and joy it is to be able to pass the Reiki energy to another! Every time I see another person open to the Reiki energy, I am amazed and touched by the wonderful yet profound simplicity with which it occurs.

In this workshop, we revise all the symbols and make sure that each student knows them by heart. Then you learn the attunement process for each level. The attunements are all similar, but they are not the same, a fact which can make this workshop challenging as well as interesting.

You are also taught how to do a healing attunement.

24

Practical: Clearing the Aura

I THINK THAT'S enough listening for the moment. Let's move on to preparing for the third attunement.

This time we'll use sound to clear our energy fields and get our energy flowing.

First, as always, stand up. Close your eyes and take an inventory of how you are feeling at the moment. Are there any stuck areas? Any discomfort? Any pain? Any worries, anxieties etc.? No need to try and change anything. Just make a mental note.

We are going to take it in turn to feel through the other's aura. Now turn to the person next to you. That's right, give them a smile as you choose who will go first.

We are going to take it in turn to feel through the other's aura. Begin by gently floating your Reiki hands down their front. Start about a foot (25 centimetres) above the head and work slowly downwards about the same distance from the front of the body, all the way down to the floor. You can move your hands wherever they want to go, as long as it's down their front.

You are feeling for any change in the sensation in your hands. It may be warmth or cold, tingly, or empty — or all sorts of other sensations.

There is no right or wrong. Work together. See if the person whose aura you are sensing can tell you when s/he feels anything different.

Remember: this is just an experiment. If you sense nothing, that's fine. If you do, that's great — and fun, too.

When you have reached the floor, do the same down your friend's back and then down each side.

Have fun, enjoy.

Check with your friend to see if you have picked up areas that s/he knew about, or if you have found something new.

Now swap over so that the one who was doing the sensing is now being sensed. Again, work together and enjoy.

Are you all okay with this? Do you need any help? Or validation? I'll come and check if you would like me to, but it's best to trust your own perceptions.

Has everyone finished?

Good. Now choose what form of sound you would like to use. Any of these items will do … you see we have a tibetan bowl, some tuning forks, rattles, a drum, and a bell. You can use any of these, or if you prefer you can simply use clapping or sounding (singing).

But before we start, let me explain the purpose of the sound: it is to clear any disqualified energy from the person's aura so that it can return to its perfect blueprint. You need to have this in mind, because this is a form of healing.

Does anyone remember the Reiki Ethic? Let's say it together:

"This healing is for the highest good of all concerned."

So, the rest is easy, just take your desired instrument and use it all through the other person's aura. It doesn't matter who goes first: I'll leave that up to you, but when you have finished, give thanks. Wait a moment, with your eyes closed, and allow all that stuck energy to dissipate. Check again through the aura with your Reiki hands to see whether you can detect any changes. Share your experiences with each other.

Then, when you are ready, change places (and instruments, if you like) and repeat the process. Take your time. There is no hurry.

Relax. Enjoy. Share.

Good. How was that exercise? Did you enjoy it? Were you surprised by what you found? Did the sound make a difference?

Do you have any questions?

Well done. You all look shiny and new. But if you have anywhere that needs a stretch or a bend or a shake, just let it happen.

Now let's make ourselves comfortable for a meditation. After it, we will go straight into the third attunement, so make sure you've had a toilet break if you need one, or something to eat if you need that. And all of you have a good slug of water.

25

Meditation: Spiritual Mountain

We will go straight into the third attunement after this meditation. I expect you are getting used to this by now.

- Let's prepare by putting the chairs in a row.
- Now choose your place and put a cushion in your back and/or under your feet.
- Are you warm enough? If not, grab a cardigan, throw or blanket and have it nearby or put it around your shoulders or over your lap.
- Have your glass of water handy, and your notebook and pen in case you want to make notes about your experience.
- Make sure you are really comfortable as you will be sitting for quite a while. Wriggle around a little, if you need to, or have a stretch. Having said that, if you need to move, or cough or swallow or anything similar, allow yourself to do so, but try not to disturb the others.

Gently close your eyes. Become aware of where you are sitting. Feel the floor beneath your feet … feel your sitting bones on the chair. Let your shoulders be relaxed and in line with your hips. Feel a silver thread running from the top of your head up into the clouds and adjust your position until your nose is in line with your umbilicus. Take your awareness to your body …

Now, breathe out … all your breath. And take a long slow breath in … expanding your ribs and softening your tummy. Great. Let the breath escape though your mouth and feel yourself relaxing and letting go of all that you do not need right at this moment. Breathe in through your nose, softly, silently … and out through your mouth, softly, silently ….

...And now you find yourself walking through a summer meadow ... the temperature is just right, the surroundings are perfect ...

Become aware of the sun shining down on you from a clear blue sky ... the warmth is pleasant and comfortable. A light breeze ruffles your hair. You feel the wild flowers and grasses against your legs, the softness of the earth beneath your feet...

You are walking through a beautiful valley. On either side a gentle hill rises, topped with trees. Look at all the wild flowers which carpet the meadow, see their individual beauty and feel their transience. Beside you a small stream is gurgling along the valley ... you stop for a moment to gaze into the water and watch the fish ... the sound of the water fills your ears. As you listen, you hear the sweet sound of birdsong all around.

The air is so fresh and sweet that you can taste it on your lips and the scents of flowers, trees and water fill your nostrils ...

As you become aware of these things your intuition tells you that there is something in front that you can't quite see, but which feels as though it is important. Something is calling to you on the inner, subconscious plane. You hasten your steps and a mountain comes into view. This mountain is calling you and you know that it is a spiritual mountain and that you have to climb to the very top if you are to follow your own spiritual Reiki path.

Now you are walking even faster, up the gentle lower slopes as if you were wearing seven league boots. The way becomes steeper and your steps grow shorter. You are feeling the weight of all that you are carrying ... although you were unaware that you were carrying anything. You slow ... and slow some more as the foothills become steeper and the way narrows.

You wonder again ... why do you feel so heavy? It's as if you were walking through treacle. Most of the weight seems to be on your shoulders and back, so you feel around with your hands and discover that you are carrying a number of burdens, some are smaller than others, but all of them are heavy.

Well, you think, I don't need to carry all this up the mountain. It can't be important because I didn't know it was there, and anyway, I can pick it up when I retrace my steps.

So you reach up and take off the biggest and heaviest of the bags you are carrying. It's so heavy you almost drop it, but you manage to put it down carefully. You see that it is labelled 'physical burdens'. This puzzles you, so you take a peek inside to see what's there ... and you realise that you need none of the things that it contains, so you leave it there by the side of the path.

Ah. That's better. Now you feel so much lighter that you can walk faster and much more easily. You love the feel of the lightness in your step and the bounciness as you walk...

But soon the path becomes steeper and before you is a very narrow defile through which the path passes. You know you are still carrying too much, that it all makes you too wide to fit through the narrow passage, so you feel around behind you for the heaviest of the packages that you are still carrying and find a big squishy bundle. As you touch it, the handle gives way and the bag falls to the ground and ... out of it spills all sorts of emotional problems, some recent, some you remember and some that come from so long ago that you cannot remember why you were ever attached to them.

You examine the label but you aren't at all surprised to discover that this bundle was labelled 'emotional problems'. You are only too glad to leave them beside the track, but one or two emotions call to you. It is very hard to leave them there and continue on your way, but you know you can collect them on your way down.

Now it is as though you have taken off a fat suit. You feel so clear and slim, that it is easy to run through the defile without touching the rocks on either side. You feel a huge sense of freedom and release and continue to climb with renewed vigour.

Up and up you climb but gradually the going becomes more difficult. You are really climbing now, scrabbling for handholds and footholds ... They become more difficult to find and hauling yourself up the slope is becoming difficult again. If only you were lighter, slimmer, you could climb so much more easily.

You check your shoulders and back and are amazed to find that you still have another bundle. This one is more difficult to locate. It is as though it moves every time you put a hand on it.... Why, it's almost alive. Eventually you grab it and lift it off. Despite being much smaller than the other bundles, this one is even heavier than they were. What can be in there? You wonder and then you see the label 'mental constructs and beliefs'. No wonder it was so difficult to lay a hand on ... thoughts are always so ephemeral, so impossible to pin down. But now you realise that you have no need of these beliefs, thoughts and concepts. You are climbing a spiritual mountain and they have no place here. So you leave them by the side of the path knowing you can pick them up again on the way down, if there are any that still serve you after your journey.

Oh, but it was difficult to leave all your beliefs and thoughts behind ... and yet, now you are streaking up the mountain hand over hand. The summit is in sight ... there is just one bump ahead.

You round the bump ... and are faced with a sheer rock wall. There are no handholds, no crevices, no footholds ... just a sheer rock face. What can you do? How can you get to the summit?

Then you remember that you still have one small but very heavy parcel pressing down on you from somewhere … your head? … your neck? It doesn't matter .. . You don't need it. So you pull it off, little and heavy as it is … as heavy as lead, indeed. And it lands with a plop at your feet, like a small, laughing cartoon animal. You lean over to read the label and you see the words 'spiritual difficulties' before it scurries away.

As it does so, the smooth rock face in front of you suddenly moves, turns, and an amethyst staircase is revealed. You walk up it and find two beings waiting for you at the top. These are your Reiki guides and they may, or may not, be in human guise. They may have a form of some kind, or they may be simply a presence or a light.

They welcome you and praise you for finding the way to the top of your personal spiritual mountain. They take you to the very summit and show you your life spread out in the beautiful landscape below. You see the patches of light and shade, of sorrow and of gladness and you see that your future is hidden behind a mist. Your guides tell you that you are in charge of your own destiny, your own future. You have free will. But from this height you can look down and see that you can choose an easy path or one fraught with difficulties. You can see where you were heading and where you would like to go.

If you have any questions you can ask them of your Reiki guides now… or maybe they have a message for you … listen.

Now they tell you that it's time to go … but they have a gift for you. Take your gift and open it. If you need to ask anything about it, now is the time …

Holding in your heart all that you have experienced, all

that you have heard, and all that has been revealed to you, you thank your guides. And they give you a blessing … they remind you that, if at any time you feel unsure, uncertain, or uncomfortable they are there to support you and will always be available to you.

Then you say goodbye …

It is time to come down from the spiritual mountain. You can do this in any way you choose … maybe you float off the top and land like thistledown at the foot of the mountain, maybe you run down, maybe you find a big balloon waiting to carry you gently down.

Now you find yourself back in the lovely valley, walking through a summer meadow, back the way you have come … until you find yourself walking back into this room … you become aware of where you are, sitting in the chair. Again you take your attention back to your breath, feeling yourself softly breathing in and out.

Wiggle your fingers and toes … have a good stretch and when you are ready … and only when you are ready … gently open your eyes and come back into the room.

26

The Third Attunement

Now that you are back in the room, close your eyes again and we will go straight into the third attunement to Reiki 1.

Beginning

Check that you are sitting with your back straight. Your shoulders are in line with your hips. Take a breath and relax your shoulders. Make sure your nose is in line with your navel. If you find it relaxing, breathe in through your nose and out through your mouth, but that is not compulsory.

Now gently close your eyes and bring your hands to the prayer position (gassho, namaste) at your heart centre, in the middle of your chest. Remember that I will need to move them about.

Relax. Just allow this to be an experiment. Allow yourself to experience whatever happens.

I'm going to put on some music. Allow it to move through every one of your cells … Good.

Let's begin …

Take another deep breath and relax. This is for your unique self. Remind yourself that you are a magnificent being and capable of anything.

Take your attention to your breath. If you would like to invite our personal guides — or your angels or any other being who works for the highest good of all — to be with you, now is the time to do so.

This is the third of the four attunements to Reiki 1. Up until this moment, I have been holding the energy for the whole group, so the purpose of this attunement is to separate you from me so that you will each be a wonderful Reiki person in your own right. If your mind wanders, bring it gently back to this intention.

At the end of the attunement, keep your eyes closed until I ring the ting-sha three times.

Ending

Sound of ting-sha: three rings.

Silence for a few moments.

The third attunement to Reiki 1 is now complete.

Take as long as you need to open your eyes and come back in the room.

Now I would like you all, please, to spend a little while in your own energy, not speaking to anyone else — just until I come back into the room and ring the ting-sha again.

This is a special time for you to do exactly what seems right for you. There is no one who can tell you what that is ... Maybe you would like to stay exactly where you are ... maybe you would like to take a little walk outside in the garden ... or to snuggle up in a blanket on the settee. You may like to make a few notes of your experiences.

Do whatever feels right for you.

Do, also, drink some water.

I am going to leave the room now and will return in a few minutes.

Sharing

I return to the room and sound the ting-sha once.

Without speaking, I spend a little while putting the room back in order, being as quiet as possible as I tidy away chairs and cushions.

Okay, now it is time to come back into the circle. Make

yourself comfortable in the same place, or perhaps you would like to choose a different one.

Is everyone okay?

Would anyone like to share what they experienced?

There is no pressure. If you would prefer to keep your experience to yourself, that is absolutely fine.

If you have any questions, please ask them.

Is there anything in your experience about which you would like to ask me? If so, ask away.

If you feel you would like to keep things to yourself for the moment that is fine. But remember that I am here if you need me. Just text, telephone or email.

27

Preparation for Treating Others

Now we come to the exciting part: treating others. As I've said before it's important to allow the Reiki energy to run through your palm chakras as soon as possible after the attunement. So while I'm talking a little about preparing for a treatment, just put them anywhere on your body that feels comfortable with the intention of letting the Reiki energy flow.

Soon we'll go along to my Reiki treatment room to practice a Reiki treatment. But before we do, I would like to take a few moments to talk about preparing yourself and the room.

Before you give any treatment there are a few things it is imperative to check:

Self Check

Check that YOU are feeling well.

If you're not, or if you feel tired or washed out, it is best NOT to proceed. You will be using your own inner energy to connect to the Reiki energy and if you are depleted in any way, you will not be able to connect to it. The result will be that you will give away your own energy. The recipient may well feel better, but you will not. It is always best to make sure that you are feeling well and full of energy before you try to treat others. If you don't — you will end up feeling ill and unable to treat them in the future.

Check that you have plenty of time.

This should be a given. The thing most vital to a healing is that you are giving up your time to help someone else. It is important that you do not compromise this, either for yourself or for the clients. Sadly, some clients are very needy and the fact that you are listening to them — by which I mean *really* listening — means that they are loath to go. The only answer is to be determined. They do not deserve any more of your time than any other clients of yours. In addition, they often need to go home and reflect upon what they have experienced before they come for another session. So don't be rude, but do be determined. They will soon get the picture. If they don't get it, they don't deserve your time and attention.

Check that you will not be disturbed.

Sounds simple, doesn't it? But what I mean is don't make any arrangements for people to call (not one!) during your working hours. Even the postman. If you are expecting a parcel to be delivered, leave out a note asking for it to be left in a safe place. If you are anticipating a phone call, make sure that the answer phone is switched on and the volume at minimum. If you have one ear open for something else, you cannot give your client your full attention.

Of course, the unexpected happens to us all. But we owe it to our clients to minimise the impact of this. Just ignore the phone, or excuse yourself to turn it to silent. IF there is something to which you MUST attend, excuse yourself gently, deal with it quickly and take a deep breath in and out before you return to your client. That deep breath will re-centre you.

In the same way, ask your client to turn their mobile phone off, or to silent mode. I forget this far too often — and then I find that I have just managed to relax, and to calm and connect with my client — when their phone rings or the text alert pings and all is lost for another ten minutes.

Where to Give Reiki

The place where you give Reiki.

You can give anyone Reiki at any time and anywhere.

If you feel the need, or if your hands warm up, then just let the Reiki flow. This often used to happen to me, particularly when I was in a café having a coffee or a meal. A surreptitious eye-whizz round the room from under my eyelashes usually told me who it was, whether they were looking my way or chatting to friends. It doesn't matter whether you know who it is or not, though. Just let the Reiki flow for as long as it's needed. You'll soon get to know how long that is, because when the person has taken enough, your hands will cool down.

Obviously, it isn't ideal to give Reiki in the middle of something else, but sometimes it's necessary. I remember sitting in a circle in one of the many workshops I attended when I was recently qualified in Reiki. Suddenly I felt my feet warm up, and before I knew it Reiki was moving at lightning speed across the circle to my teacher. I still smile at the thought. It was only later that I discovered that she was fighting off a cold and needed all the energy she could get.

Generally, it's a more productive, more fun and a more comfortable experience to give Reiki in a quiet place where you will not be interrupted.

For this reason, I generally advise against going into someone's home to give them Reiki. They will find it more difficult to relax and so will you. The person in whose house you are working, will always be listening for small things, like the telephone or the doorbell, or they'll remember they forgot to put the dustbin out, or worry whether they turned the gas off. And you will probably find it difficult to make yourself comfortable while you are working.

Of course, sometimes there is no alternative. And many people will benefit from Reiki even in less than ideal circumstances. Older people whose movements are restricted or who are housebound, the very young, and those caring for others often find it difficult to leave the house. Later, I will return to this subject to show you how you can adapt to awkward circumstances, but for the moment, let's imagine that you have been invited to use a room in a health centre.

Make sure that the room is clean, tidy and comfortable. If you feel there is any left over 'stuff' from a previous client, or any feeling of anxiety, anger, sadness etcetera, you will need to clear it. The easiest way is to use your voice. Sing. Especially in the corners. If that makes you feel weird, or you think others will believe you've gone mad, then you can use the ting-cha, or a bell or a singing bowl. Ring them wherever there is 'heavy' energy, or just where you feel you need to.

If you prefer, you can use a crystal or two, or spray the room with essential oils, or simply open your hands and let Reiki flow into every part of the room, paying particular attention to the corners and to the couch on which your client will lie.

Imagine the violet flame of St Germain — which, you will remember, has been given to us as a swift method of purification and transformation — to cover the floor and the couch or chair in which your Reiki client will sit.

You could smudge the room with sage, but this can make some people feel a little peculiar, or set them coughing, so I suggest you try the other ways first.

If you do not feel comfortable in the room, even after doing all this cleansing, then do not use it. Find somewhere else.

All these suggestions apply wherever you are going to undertake a treatment. If you are lucky enough to have your own therapy room, or are using another room in your own house, do the same there.

And on that note, we'll go into my treatment room ...

28

Treating Others: Front

This is my treatment room. I cleared it earlier and filled it with Reiki. I also asked that the floor and the couch are covered with the violet flame of St Germain so that anything inappropriate is transformed in the flame.

Before You Begin

'Who would like to be a demonstration model? Thank you.

Have you had a drink of water recently? If not, please have one now. It is very important that the body is hydrated, since energy flows through water.'

'Let me make you comfortable on the couch. Here's a pillow for your head, and one for under the knees to take any pressure off the back. I'm going to cover you with a blanket … is that all right? Or will it be too hot?'

There are three reasons we cover the body with a blanket.

- ✓ First, it makes the client feel nurtured and comfortable, especially because someone is taking care of them.
- ✓ Second, when one is lying still for a while, blood pressure tends to drop, so you will feel cold.
- ✓ And third, it helps the person on the couch to feel less exposed and vulnerable.

'Before we begin, please remember that this is *your* time. I suggest that you allow yourself to let go of anything you do not need at this moment. Please tell me if anything is uncomfortable, or if you have any pain, or if you wish me to move my hands to some other place. Honour your own needs.

I also encourage you to allow your body to do anything that it needs. You can move, or jerk, or shudder, or stay still. You can talk if you need to. If you feel any emotion, there is no need to try and work out why. You can just allow it to be there. Give it space and it will fade. If you have to cough, cry, shout, sneeze, sigh, laugh, yawn … anything and everything is okay.'

'You may also find that I am sneezing or coughing or sighing or yawning. I'm not getting a cold, nor am I bored. It's just that sometimes you may not be able to reach and let go of some old emotion that no longer serves you. In that case it may come through me in one of these guises.

- ✓ A sneeze is something quite recent, easily dispatched.
- ✓ A cough is something that is ready to go, but which needs a little more energy.
- ✓ A sigh is something older, deeper: perhaps something from many years ago.
- ✓ And a yawn is something ancient, possibly even from a previous life.
- ✓ There is no need to investigate further. Just allow whatever it is to pass out of your life.'

'Are you quite comfortable? Good. I'm going to place my hand gently here, on your belly. Take a deep breath in, right down to my hand. That's good. Sigh the breath out slowly through your mouth, letting go of anything — any thoughts or worries or emotional stuff, any pain or discomfort — that you don't need right at this minute.

Let's do that once more. Breathe in deeply …. And sigh the breath out.

And again: but this time breathe in peace … and breathe out calm. Now, if you would like, take yourself off to a special place in Nature that you love. Really be there. Feel the earth beneath you and the sun on your cheek … hear the sounds …

see all the beautiful surroundings … smell the fragrance of the place … and taste it … feel its special significance to you …'

Beginning

Now that your client is settled, you need to link in to the Reiki energy by repeating the ***Reiki Ethic: 'This healing is for the Highest Good of all concerned'*** Remember that you can add in any other form of prayer that you like , or that seems appropriate. I use part of St Francis' Prayer.

Then slowly sweep your hands through your client's aura. Hold your hands about two hands' breadths above the body with the fingers spread apart and the thumbs almost touching. Starting slightly above the level of the forehead, move backwards slowly, keeping one hand on each side of the client's body. When you reach the feet, take your hands over the feet and right down to touch the floor.

This grounds anything that is ready to be removed from the client's aura. You will remember that we learned that every disease comes in through all the layers of the aura and leaves the same way. This is a way of dealing with things before they become an issue for the client.

The other reason for taking your hands through the aura in this way, is to give you the opportunity to sense any areas that need Reiki. I like to keep my eyes closed the better to sense what is happening in the aura. Remain open to any sensations in your hands. You may feel heat, cold, tingling, or some other sensation. You can check in with your client as to whether they have any pain or problem in the areas you sense. Usually, they will be pleasantly surprised by what you have picked up.

If you have no sensations, there is no problem. You may be able to later when you have sensitised your hands, or you may have another way of knowing: an inner knowing, perhaps, or words in your head, or you may see a disturbance in the energy surrounding the client.

On that subject, I must mention that some practitioners do pick up the client's pain. It can feel appropriate and easy to feel another person's pain in our own body. It validates the experience. That is fine. We all have our own methods of understanding and validating. But make sure that you register that the pain is the client's. Feel it, if you must, then let it go. You will feel ill yourself if you hang onto it. Just let it flow away.

Actually, it is best to find some other means of assessing the nature of the disturbance or imbalance in the client's energy. Find your own individual way.

I used to take on pain, but it can wear you down. Now I have learned my own system for feeling it. It's hard to explain, but it's the nature of the vibration I sense that tells me whether the pain is deep, shallow, recent or chronic, sharp or dull. I suggest you play with the energy and ask your hands to communicate with you. It will suddenly come, I promise.

Hand Positions

In the appendix to this book there are photographs of the hand positions that we use for others.

We keep our hands soft, thumbs close to fingers, in just the same way as when we are using them to give ourselves Reiki.

Seat yourself comfortably at the head of the couch. Take a breath, and feel the Reiki energy coming in through the crown of your head, passing down through your body and out into the earth. With the next breath feel the flow of energy from the earth through to your crown. With the third breath feel the energy coming through your crown and your base chakra, meeting in your heart centre and flowing down your hands. If you feel nothing, use your imagination. It will happen, I promise.

If you feel yourself drawn in towards the client, consciously withdraw by keeping your posture upright. If you still find yourself moving forwards, it may help to throw out an imaginary metaphysical anchor about nine yards behind you.

When we treated ourselves yesterday, I mentioned about headaches. This is a good time to check whether the client is aware of any ache or pressure or pain in the head. If so, it is important that they have another drink of water first. Then use the '*dustpan and brush*'.

Just to remind you, this is how you do it:

- With one hand (the brush) sweep the excess energy lightly towards the other hand (the dustpan). Keep the action light.
- Your hand can come close to their head or not — it's your choice. Go with where you feel the headache to be: you will be correct. And do whatever seems best.
- You can repeat this action as often as needed.
- Remember: when the 'dustpan' is full it needs to be emptied. Either go out into the garden and allow the 'dust' to fall into the earth, or imagine a violet flame — the violet flame of St Germain has been given to us as a swift method of purification and transformation. Empty the contents of the dustpan into the violet flame and watch as they are consumed by it.
- N.B. You can do this at any time or in any place (and for any part of the body).

Eyes

Gland: pineal

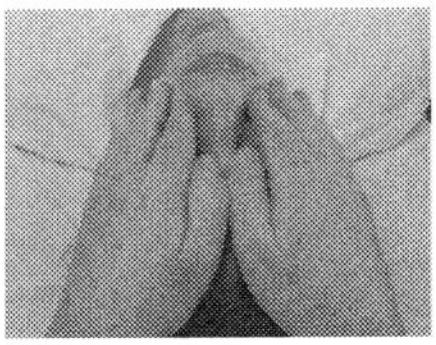

Again, we start by treating the eyes. Bring your hands in slowly and gently. The client will sense it if you move abruptly and will find it unsettling. Keep your hands particularly light here.

Place your thumbs just above the bridge of the nose, between the eyebrows. If this is a narrow space you can put them one on top of another. Then softly curl your fingers and allow them to fall one by one beside the nostrils and along the cheekbone. Make sure you do not pinch the nose or cover the mouth. Soothe your client's eyes. They work hard all the time, constantly stimulated, particularly if the client works on computers a lot.

Stay here for at least a minute, and up to 5 minutes. Longer is seldom necessary.

As you sensitise your hands you will know when to move to the next position. Sometimes it simply happens without your knowing why, but if you are wondering, you can wait until the energy in your hands subsides a little, or the client takes a sigh. Both are indications that the Reiki energy has done its work.

Temples

I often miss out this hand position, but if it seems to be required, move your hands to the temples. Letting the Reiki flow here can be very calming, helping consciousness move towards the centre of the client's being, but some people find it restrictive. Be aware.

Ears

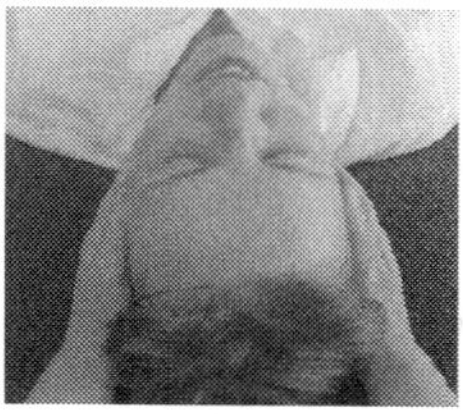

Next, move your hands gently so that they cup the ears. Remain aware that you are treating all that the ears do — hearing, listening, balancing. They are a holograph of the body, so you can also work on the body as a whole from here.

Back of Head
Gland: pituitary

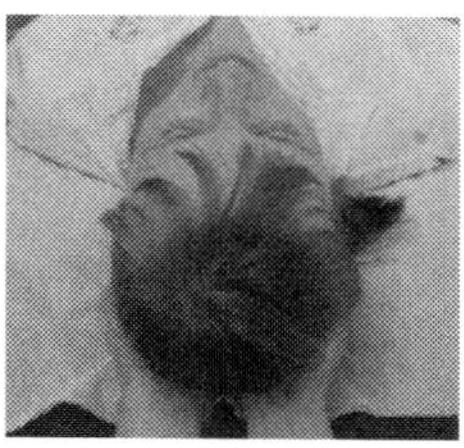

To move to this position, it is best to manoeuvre the head from the 'ear' position.

- Using your right hand, turn the client's head sideways, onto your left hand.
- Mould your free right hand carefully around the client's head, with your little finger running the length of the centre of the head, from the base to the top.
- Now, using the thumb of your left hand roll the clients's head right over onto your right hand.
- Mould your left hand over the left side of your client's

head, so that your little fingers touch.
- Using your right thumb gently roll the head back to a central position, so that it is resting on your two hands.

Relax your hands into the pillow. Your middle fingers will be in contact with the client's occiput, the brain stem, and thus with the fluid that bathes the brain and the spinal cord. This has a very slow pulse — usually much slower than the breath. See whether you can feel it.

In any case, this contact means that you are able to send a message of healing down the whole spine. You might feel the Reiki energy gently adjusting the nerves of the spine. Be aware and simply allow. The Reiki energy has its own intelligence and will go to any place that is in need of healing. Again, if you can't feel anything, just be aware that Reiki is flowing and imagine it as clearly as possible.

Throat

Gland: thyroid

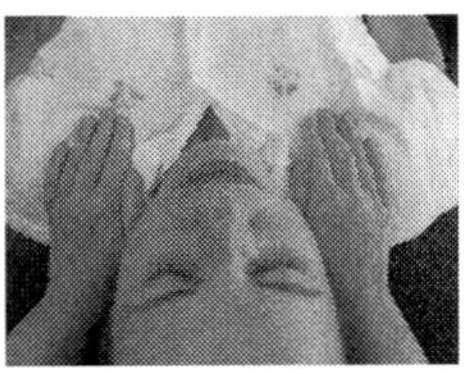

While treating your own throat can be reassuring and comforting, to a client it can feel threatening to have the hands wrapped around the throat. Instead, place them either side of the neck, with the heels of the hands on the client's 'shoulder seams'. The fingers point straight down the body, but your intention is to treat the throat chakra and any issues that arise from there.

This position is good for the voice, helpful for sore throats, and stimulates the throat chakra. You will remember that this is the centre of our creativity, and also the place from where we communicate with all levels of existence, both speaking (even on the inner plane) and listening/hearing.

It is particularly useful for freeing emotion which has been repressed, so if your client (or you) feels tearful, encourage them to let the tears flow, without judgement.

The Heart Centre

Gland: thymus

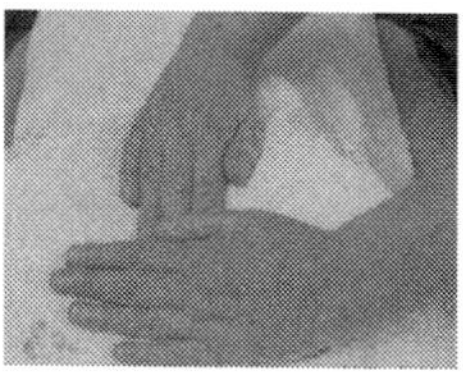

Next we move on to the heart centre. This is in the centre of the chest, *not* exactly over the heart. Place one hand over the thymus gland horizontally, that is, in line with the shoulders. Tuck the ends of the fingers of your other hand under the palm of your hand so that you have a T-shape, with one hand touching lightly between the breasts. If this feels too invasive, place the second hand on the chest below the breasts and imagine the Reiki energy entering the heart space.

This is the place of compassion for all things, of empathy and unconditional love. Giving Reiki here really stimulates the immune system.

I often find that there is very little energy in the heart centre itself, while the energy can be felt strongly a foot or so above the body. In such a case the client is so busy loving others that s/he has kept very little for themselves. This leaves the immune system vulnerable so concentrate on using Reiki to bring some of this energy back to the client.

The Solar Plexus
Gland: pancreas

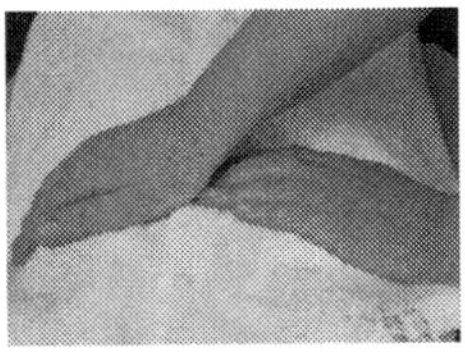

Place whichever of your hands is nearest the client's head across the ribs so that the tips of your fingers touch the hollow beneath the client's breastbone. Place the other hand across the ribs on the further side, so that the heel of that hand covers the fingertips of the first hand, and both palms rest along the lower ribs.

The Solar Plexus is the place of the client's inner fire: his/her will. Energy is often lacking here. On the physical level, this hand position is helpful to the digestion. On the emotional level it is how the client deals with problems and life events. Here is the place of sweetness in life — or sourness. The pancreas is often overworked and depleted.

Hara, abdomen
Glands: ovaries and gonads

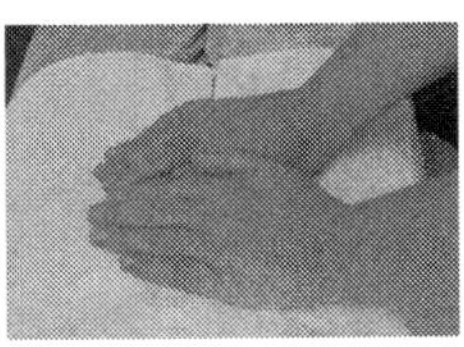

When you are ready, move your hands down so that they rest in the centre of the abdomen, one above the other. The lower hand's thumb rests gently over the umbilicus, or tummy button.

Like the heart, the intestines also have a brain. How often do we talk about a 'gut feeling'? How often do we pay attention to it?

As you may have guessed, or already know, the abdominal chakra (often referred to as the sacral chakra or the hara) has to do with our relationships with others. This is where we connect with the emotions others are feeling. This is where our own emotions sit, and where we nurture ourselves. It is also the place of the womb and the ovaries, where new life grows within and is nourished by its mother's body. For this reason, in men it relates also to the gonads.

Base, pubic bone

Gland: adrenals.

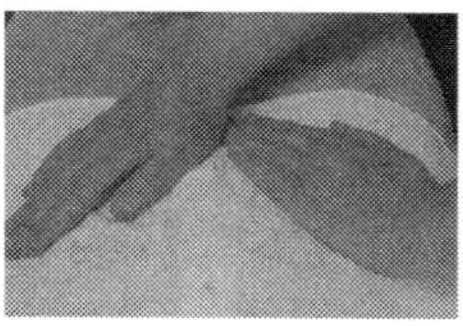

From the *hara* position above, move your lower hand across the body until you contact the client's hip. Move the other hand towards you and down until you contact the other hip.

Turn the first hand so it slants along the hip-bone with the fingers pointing up.

Turn the second hand in the opposite direction so the fingers point downwards and towards the pubic bone.

If you are treating a man, leave your hands there, although your attention is to heal the base chakra.

If you are treating a woman, gently slide your hands towards the pubic bone, until their fingers meet. Rest here. Most people find this feels very supportive and comforting, but if you are at all uncomfortable leave the hands on the hips as for a man, and concentrate on sending Reiki to the base chakra.

The base chakra relates to all our basic needs, and

whether or not they are met. It is a place, often, of fear; and in particular, the fear of lack.

The adrenals are the glands which regulate the fight, flight or freeze response. Each of those is our reaction to a current event. The adrenals will become easily overworked if we spend a lot of time stressed and anxious. Reiki here helps us to realise that we are able to supply all our own needs. We do not have to rely on anyone else. Events which have scarred us are simply that — past events.

Encourage your client to look to the future with hope and courage, while endeavouring to remain fully present in the here and now.

Legs

Many Reiki Masters don't teach any hand positions for the legs, but I have found that it is really important to make sure that Reiki energy runs down the legs because a large number of people, through extreme or constant emotion, often grief, seem to 'cut off' their legs. This means that their energy no longer runs all the way down to the earth for grounding and transformation, and thus the find it difficult to access the Earth's wonderful healing energy. This can be exacerbated if they wear shoes with manmade soles, or walk on artificial fibres, or journey in cars, rather than walking.

I have already mentioned the wonderful flow of natural energy through us: from the universe down through the body and into the earth: from the earth it flows the other way. It is like the breath. We are the breath and the universe is breathing us.

You can either work across the body; or down one side and then, walking to the other side of the couch, working down the other leg.

If you are working across the body, make sure that it is the hand that is closest to the feet that goes across to the other side. The Reiki energy will run more smoothly because there is nothing blocking the flow of energy down from the head towards the feet.

Thighs

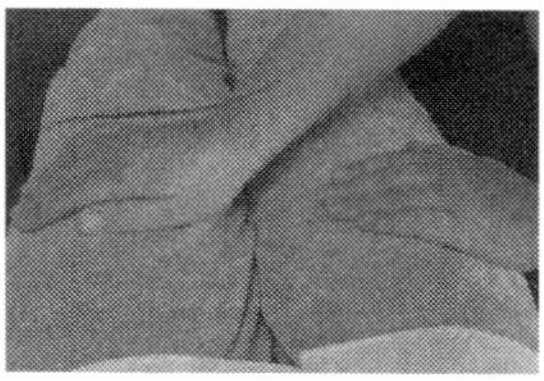

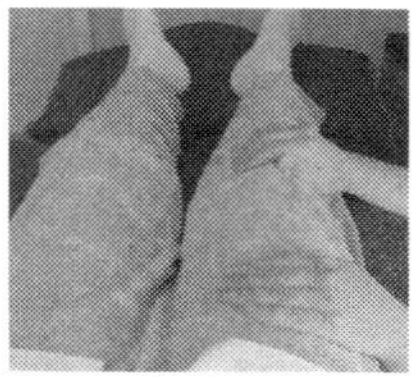

The simplest position is to place each hand on a thigh, as in the first photograph. If you prefer to work down one side of the body, on a hip and thigh, and then a thigh and knee. Repeat on the other leg.

The thigh muscles are the strongest in the body. They have to do with bearing us through life, and, when necessary, with running. In Ayurveda, it is believed they link to the digestion.

Knees

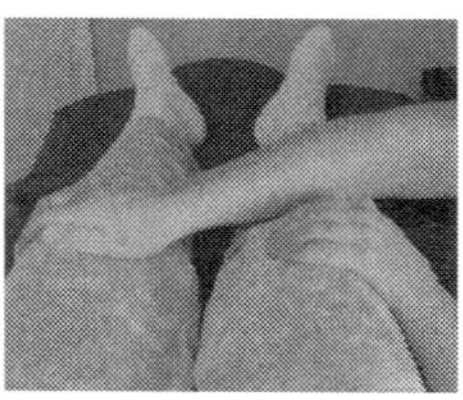

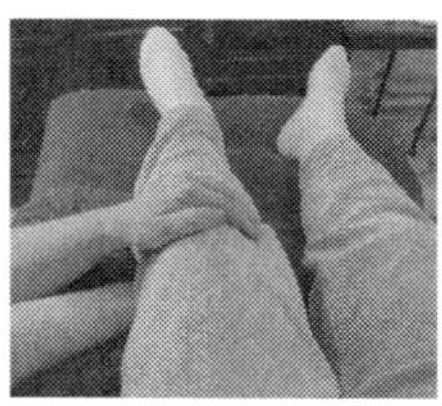

Cover the client's knees very gently. You can put one hand on each knee, or bend the knee slightly and make it the filling in a sandwich between your two hands. Imagine this area, perfect, beautifully oiled and easily moved.

The knees hold our fear. We know this because they tremble when we are frightened. We even talk about knees knocking. No wonder they often crumple and let us down, or hurt or creak. Often the fear of death — our own or another's — is held here.

We expect a lot of our knees, but we seldom give them any thought other than an occasional rub. Concentrate on imagining the joint moving easily and smoothly.

Shins

The shins are not often considered in Reiki or other healing modalities, but I have found them to be very responsive to Reiki, and, consequently, I have learned how often they need some tender, loving care.

Again, you can Reiki them both simultaneously, or connect a knee and a shin one side, and then connect the others in similar fashion. Remember to move to the other side of the couch if you do this.

If it feels right you can use your Reiki hands to give the shins a massage, or just to smooth and stroke them, using as much or as little pressure as feels appropriate, remembering to err on the light side if you aren't sure.

Ankles

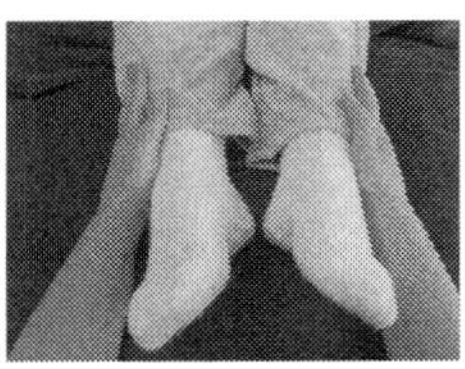

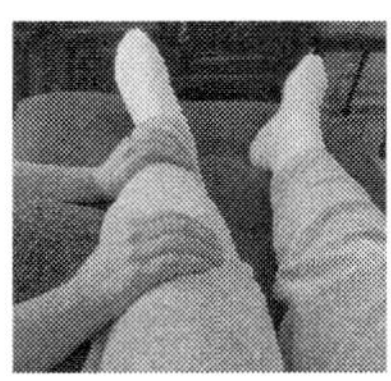

Stand at the end of the couch and place one hand round the outside of each ankle, cupping the bone and making sure that your thumbs are close and parallel to your fingers.The ankles are about flexibility. If the ankles lock, walking becomes almost impossible and certainly very painful.

We need flexibility in our lives because the only constant

in life is change: we need to be able to move with that change both mentally and physically, so keep Reiki-ing your client's ankles until you feel the energy move through them.

Feet

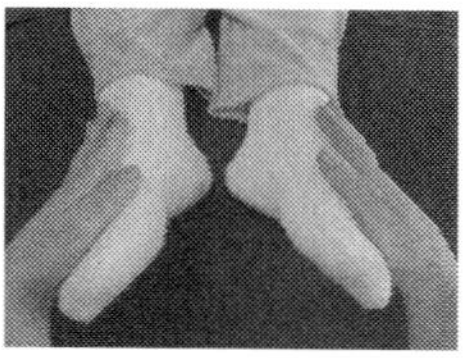

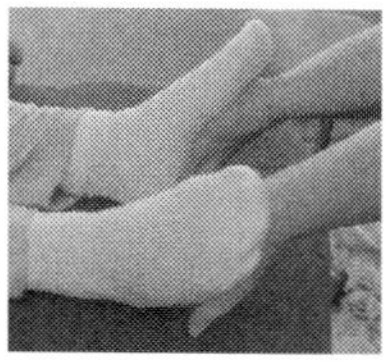

Feet are such important parts of our anatomy and yet are so often neglected.

One word of warning. Although it's not shown in the photograph above, it is best to stand to one side of the client while working on the feet. Otherwise they are discharging disharmonious energy straight into your belly.

If you stand to one side, facing the end of the couch, your hands will cover the feet easily, the heels of your hands covering the heels and your fingers falling near the toes.

You can choose which way is easiest for you to give Reiki to your client's feet. You can put a hand on the top of each foot for a minute or two, and then move on to put a hand on the sole of each foot.

Or you can make a 'foot sandwich' with one hand on top of the foot and the other on the sole.

Feet not only support us, they are the means by which we move from place to place. They are also our connection to the earth. Through them we are able to discharge 'disqualified' energy into the earth, but, even more important, we are also able to draw up the earth energy which gives us our *oomph*, or vital force.

Finish here. If you feel the need, touch the floor to make sure that all that unwanted energy is grounded.

Ending

Auric Sweep

This is similar to the way we began the treatment. It has the effect of decluttering the aura of any negative energy which has been released, but has not completely cleared during the Reiki treatment.

Hold your hands about two hands' breadths above the body with the fingers spread apart and the thumbs almost touching. Starting slightly above the level of the forehead, sweep your hands gently through the aura, right down and over the feet. Touch the floor to clear and ground the energy.

- Finish with your hands folded in the prayer position at your heart centre.
- Give thanks to the Reiki energy, to your client, and to yourself.
- Visualise your client safely wrapped in golden light.
- Make a big circular sweep with your hands to bring this into manifestation.

Kenyoku Ho

Next, to clear your own energy, and to disconnect you from your client, we will practise:

Kenyoku - *Dry bathing*

✓ Put your right hand on your left shoulder.
✓ Stroke across your body from left shoulder to right hip.
✓ Repeat with the left hand — right shoulder to left hip.
✓ Repeat once more with the right hand — left shoulder to right hip.

- ✓ Put your right hand on the top of your left arm and stroke along the inside of your left arm, across your palm and off the fingertips.
- ✓ Repeat with your left hand along right arm and palm.
- ✓ Complete by bringing your hands to the prayer position at your brow centre.

This technique may be used at the beginning and end of a Reiki session or at any time that you feel you need to cleanse your personal environment. This may be from people, things, situations, thoughts, emotions or any other attachments,

Finishing

So now you've finished your Reiki session, you've made sure that your client is safe and protected in a gorgeous Reiki bubble and you've cleared yourself with Kenyoku Ho.

What's next ?

Yes, it's time to take care of your client. I usually gently stroke his/her hair and say something along the lines of:

"Hello again, Sam. The Reiki treatment is finished. Is there anywhere else you feel needs any healing?"

If the answer is yes, honour your client's needs. However, usually the answer is no.

"Good. Come back into the room very slowly. Take your time. I'm just going to wash my hands. There's absolutely no hurry. I'll help you off the couch when I come back."

It is good spiritual hygiene to go and wash your hands, up to the elbows in cold water. You may also need to use the toilet. Reiki helps to rid both you, and your client, of toxins — and water is the medium.

When you come back, gently announce your presence — something like:

"I'm back. Are you ready to get up now?"

If they seem to need a little longer to come back to full consciousness, let them have a *little* more time. However, don't allow them to take too much. You can move them on by saying: "I'll help you sit up."

Ease them into a sitting position on the edge of the couch. Suggest they have their feet on the floor, and lean back against the couch so that they are connected to the ground but have support from the couch.

If you have anything you want to share with your client, this is the time, but before you launch into all the things that you have experienced, give them time to tell you anything they want.

Then give them any advice that feels apposite. Write down your suggestions for their self-care at home until they come to see you again, and give the paper to them.

When you have both said all you need to, go round to the other side of the couch, so that you are facing the client's back.

The following exercise will help to ground them, but if they feel a bit 'out of it' wait a moment or two before starting.

Grounding

Changing the Blood: *a technique for grounding a client's energy after a treatment.*

- Stand at the client's back. As I have explained, I suggest that the client stands close to the couch and half-sits on it for support.
- Gently place your non-dominant hand on the client's shoulder. This is a soft balancing touch.
- Curl your dominant hand over the back of the client's head, with your fingers pointing up towards the crown of their head.
- With medium pressure, since you are doing this to

ground your client, sweep your dominant hand down the spine to the pelvic girdle and then along the pelvic girdle towards one hip. Stop at the hip.
- Repeat this sweep, but sweep the dominant hand along the pelvic girdle towards the other hip.
- Repeat each movement alternately so that you have done a total of at least ten sweeps — five towards the client's left hip and five towards the right hip.If you feel more sweeps are required carry on until you feel satisfied that you have done enough.
- For the final stroke, make a V by parting the index and middle fingers of your dominant hand. Curl the remaining two fingers and the thumb underneath.
- With slightly more pressure sweep down the back from the occiput, with the opened fingers either side of the spine.
- When you reach the point below the pelvic girdle where the two dimples are to be found — there's no need to check exactly where they are. Just guess — you press in.
- Release. That's it.

Check that your client is back with you. If they are still light-headed, try the following:
- Go round to the front of the client.
- With medium pressure, run your two hands, from the shoulders along the arms, on to the legs, down the legs, to the feet. Hold the feet for about five seconds.
- Repeat twice, holding the feet a little longer on the last sweep.

Give the client a glass of water. When s/he has finished it check that she/he is grounded enough to be able to drive home.

If more grounding is needed give them a biscuit or something sweet to eat and/or put a few drops of rosemary essential oil on a tissue and ask the client to sniff it.

Finally

Finally, make sure you're paid. When you have given the client such a marvellous treatment, it's easy for such mundane things to slip their mind. This has happened to me so often that nowadays I usually ask nicely for my payment before I begin the session. I find the client usually approves of this, if only because they do not have to remember to pay, when all they want to do is to float away happily.

Do remember, too, to tell them to contact you if they experience any difficulties, emotional imbalances, or pain so that you can give them advice.

Finally, this is the time to make another appointment. I usually suggest the best way to receive the full healing from Reiki is to have six appointments over six consecutive weeks, followed by four fortnightly sessions, and then two monthly sessions, but I often vary this depending on my availability and the client's finances.

Well done. Now I reckon you must be famished, so let's go and get some lunch.

DAY TWO, AFTERNOON

29

Permission and Payment

This morning you all did very well to give and receive a whole treatment on the front. Did you enjoy it? You probably don't realise how much of your energy you've been using — in a good way, of course. But do take care of yourself. I'm always famished after I've given and/or received Reiki. Make sure you are well hydrated, too.

As I've said, the Reiki energy works through the water in our bodies, so it's very important to drink, not only so that Reiki can work better, but also so that any toxicity which has been released by the Reiki energy can be dissolved in water and pass out of the body in the usual way.

Asking

Before we move on, I'd like to clarify a few things.

First, if you would like to treat someone, even a member of your own family, you must obtain their permission before you give them Reiki. Everyone has free will. Even though we know Reiki would really help them, some people are quite anxious about what Reiki is. That anxiety will mean that they are less likely to benefit from Reiki.

Please do **not** try and explain Reiki until you are sure you can talk about it confidently and happily. Any apologetic inclination will make another person nervous. In any case, there is no need to go into detail. Tell people it is experiential: it's not the sort of thing that's easy to explain, but they will understand when they feel it. Remind them there is no need to undress because Reiki works through clothes.

Sometimes you can just ask: "May I put my hands on your

back? I think I may be able to help with the pain?"

If the person says yes, or nods, that is sufficient consent.

Occasionally, you will find that Reiki will flow when you simply touch someone, even though you had no intention of giving them Reiki. That's fine. Their subconscious has given consent.

Money

Now we must talk about money and payment.

I know that a lot of people feel strangely anxious when it comes to charging money for healing — and that includes Reiki. I say 'strangely', but that is exactly how I used to feel about healing in the 'old days'. I know better now.

The point is that you are giving something to them. Your time, your knowledge, your attention and your energy. You need some acknowledgement, some validation. Not only do you need this, but the person you have been treating also needs to give you something, however small.

Over the years I have given lots of free treatments. I have also given lots of concessions. Of course, that's why we've come to learn Reiki — so that we can help others. Especially others in need.

Imagine you have attended a trade fair and been given a free pen. Do you value that pen? Do you keep it safe and appreciate it every time you use it? Speaking only for myself, the short answer is 'no'. It has come to me free as part of an advertising campaign. I put it with all the others and before long I've forgotten about it.

Now consider that beautiful fountain pen that you have always wanted. It's beautiful, its easy to write with and somehow your writing improves every time you use it. Do you remember saving up for that pen, looking at it in the shop, drooling over it? And the delight when you finally managed to save up enough to buy it?

See how much more you value the thing you have paid for? How much more attention you give it. How much more you enjoy writing now you can use it?

I have learned the hard way that those who pay for Reiki heal more quickly and permanently than those who just turn up for a free treatment now and again.

In fact, I now believe that I am doing those 'free' people a disservice. They do not truly value Reiki, so they do not truly benefit from it. In fact, sometimes it is just enough to free them from pain for a little while, but they then embrace the pain when it returns. That pain gives them a reason for being. It also gives them an excuse (reason) to stay stuck where they are.

There are also those to whom you give a free treatment and they won't come back when they need to because they think they will be taking advantage. They, too, would have done better to have paid something for their treatment.

Those who pay *expect* results. They want to see themselves getting better. They want to help themselves. Generally speaking, they will improve.

Now I know that thirty pounds is nothing to some people: to others it is a huge amount of their disposable income. The lovely thing is that you have the freedom to charge whatever you want. You can have a sliding scale, or you can have a fixed one. You can ask for donations to the costs you have incurred, or donations towards your training. You can barter one treatment for another. You can agree any recompense you like.

I remember that when I was first in practice as a solicitor, I survived on barter. A friend who came from Australia and helped me in my first tiny office said: "Marion, you don't make much money, do you? But we eat very well."

It was true. I didn't charge as much as I should, but a lovely old lady (probably younger than I am now, come to think of it!) gave me pots of jam in exchange for a Will, and the greengrocer gave me weekly vegetables when I helped him with the lease on his shop. The butcher gave me a whole jointed lamb in return for a Power of Attorney .... I won't go on because I know you've caught my gist.

Don't forget that you have already incurred the cost of your training. There will be other things too, not only your time. So start now by asking for some sort of recompense.

Of course, when you are practising your Reiki on friends and family, you feel a little constrained about asking for payment. After all, you've only just started and you're using them for practice. And naturally, with your family there is a constant movement of energy, give and take, so there is no problem with treating them for free. However, there should be some exchange of energy. Perhaps they could make you a cup of tea, or do a small household chore for you? Or take you out to tea or dinner?

At this time, I suggest you have some sort of container labelled 'Donations: £5 suggested'. To most people, £5 is not a lot, but it is sufficient to make them appreciate what you have given them. And it will help you to save up for your Reiki 2 workshop, as well as to learn to charge for Reiki.

PRACTICAL: OILING YOUR JOINTS

BEFORE WE TACKLE giving Reiki on the back, I'd like to retrace my steps a little way. We didn't have much time this morning; and we'd already done some exercise before we started working on the front of someone else.

However, before you give any Reiki treatment, it's important to make sure that your energy is running smoothly and to do this we need to 'oil' the joints. I suggest you do this each morning, or at least before you do any healing.

We are moving *with* the body's energy, not against it. ONLY do what you can without discomfort. NEVER force your body.

We'll start with the head and work down.

HEAD

Shrug your shoulders a couple of times to release any tension in them.

Then slowly turn your head from side to side, as far as you comfortably can. Don't force it. Repeat a couple of times

Now gently move your head up and down. Lift your shoulders slightly to protect your neck as you slowly circle your head one way and then the other.

Lower your shoulders.

Let your jaw hang loose with your mouth open.

Move your lower jaw from side to side, up and down, or wherever it wants to go.

SHOULDERS

Shrug your shoulders.

Take them right up to your ears.

Then release and let them drop.

Now lift them up and circle them backwards.

Try to make your shoulder blades touch.

Change direction and circle them the other way.

ELBOWS
Circle the forearms at the elbow joints.
First one way, and then the other.

WRISTS
Circle the hands at the wrist joints.
First one way, and then the other.
Shake your hands up and down like a mad piano player.

HANDS
Open and close the fists.
Wriggle the fingers.

TORSO
Bend forward a little at the waist.
Circle one way, then the other.
Start with small circles and let them get larger.

HIPS
Put your hands on your hips.
Circle your pelvis first one way, and then the other.
Again start with small circles.

KNEES
I like to do this lying on my back, so I can circle both knees at the same time, but you can do it standing on one leg if you prefer.
Circle your knees first one way and then the other.
Repeat with the other knee if you are doing this standing.

ANKLES
Just the same as for the knees and wrists.

Let them circle one way, then the other.
Move them up and down.

FEET
Scrunch up your feet, curling your toes under.
Then extend the foot, turning the toes right up.
Repeat.
Massage foot against the floor: heel, ball, toes.
And back.
Repeat on the other foot.

Good. Now close your eyes, take a deep breath in … and as you let it out see how relaxed your body feels. If there are any areas of tension, you can repeat any of these exercises as necessary.

30

Meditation: Angel Journey

As before, we will go straight into the final attunement after this meditation. I expect you are getting used to this by now.

- Let's prepare by putting the chairs in a row.
- Now choose your place and put a cushion in your back and/or under your feet.
- Are you warm enough? If not, grab a cardigan, throw or blanket and have it nearby or put it around your shoulders or over your lap.
- Have your glass of water handy, and your notebook and pen in case you want to make notes about your experience.
- Make sure you are really comfortable as you will be sitting for quite a while. Wriggle around a little, if you need to, or have a stretch. Having said that, if you need to move, or cough or swallow or anything similar, allow yourself to do so, but try not to disturb the others.

Gently close your eyes. Become aware of where you are sitting. Feel the floor beneath your feet … feel your sitting bones on the chair. Let your shoulders be relaxed and in line with your hips. Feel a silver thread running from the top of your head up into the clouds and adjust your position until your nose is in line with your umbilicus. Take your awareness to your body …

Now, breathe out … all your breath. And take a long slow breath in … expanding your ribs and softening your tummy. Great. Let the breath escape though your mouth and feel yourself relaxing and letting go of all that you do not need right at this moment. Breathe in through your nose, softly, silently … and out through your mouth, softly, silently.

Take your awareness now to where your body touches the chair. Feel yourself becoming lighter … and lighter … until you are as light as an angel's feather, as light as thistledown.

A white fluffy cloud drifts down towards you from a blue, blue heaven. You are so light that it simply floats beneath you and raises you up, slowly and gently. Feel the comfort of being so light, so weightless. Enjoy the sensation as the cloud rises slowly up into the sky … you feel as soft and comfortable as if you were wrapped in a silken shawl. As you wonder at the purity and beauty of your surroundings, you feel yourself embraced, ever so gently, ever so kindly. As if you were being carried on the wings of an angel.

As you look upwards you see a beautiful countenance of light. You note that it wears a beautiful smile and you hear words that aren't words. The knowledge comes to you in your heart. Your guardian angel is enveloping you.

You ask where you are going … and your angel gently hushes you. You do not need to know. This is a time for experiencing, not for knowing. As she speaks, you feel yourself smiling, you have not a care in the world, your brain is too peaceful to think. The whole sensation is so wonderful, so warm, so kind, so exquisite that you only want to bask in it.

For a while you drift there in the warm light of heavenly blue sky, held in your angel's bosom.

Your angel communicates that whenever you want a rest from the busy-ness of the world, you only have to ask. She will be there to raise you up as soon as you have that desire. You may rest in her for as long as you wish.

But right now she is taking you to meet some powerful beings. This will open your eyes to the magnificence of All-That-Is, and to the magnificent being that you also are.

Now you feel the cloud that is your angel's wings slowly descending. Below you a range of mountains lift their peaks towards the heavens. You hear a thunderous sound as lightning flashes from the mountaintop. But you are still held, warm and safe in your angel's arms.

Don't be afraid, she says, *it is just the voice of the Mountain. Feel the power of his spirit.*

Mountain says: *I am your strength.* And you feel its strength within you.

Next you fly over the ocean. You watch as huge black waves rise and fall. A tempest rises and churns up the water even more. The sound of the waves crashing and the howling of the wind make you tremble a little.

Don't be afraid, your angel says, *it is just the voice of the Ocean. See how changeable she is.*

Now you drift over the peace of a calm sea, small wavelets caressing the shore.

Ocean says: *I am your flexibility*. And you rejoice within to feel the elasticity of your body, your mind and your spirit. All, all are flexible and changeable.

You drift on ... the cloud slowly descends until you see you are high, high above a vast and beautiful jungle forest. Even here, you can feel the change in the air, its vivacity and cleanliness. You would like to go down and touch the branches, but some innate vulnerability makes you hesitate. And then you suddenly hear it, the sound of tropical rain pounding on the trees beneath and the sound of the forest leaves laughing

Don't be afraid, your angel says, *it is just the voice of the Forest. Feel the vibrant aliveness of his spirit.*

Forest says: *I am your Aliveness.* And you feel at once the tingling joy of being alive, as you breathe in the wonderful, cool, clean air of the forest and it fills every cell of your body.

You would like to stay here, just to rejoice in these

feelings, but your angel is carrying you on, on. You rest back in her arms and allow yourself to be transported.

Now you are borne over a huge desert. Below you trace the lines of rocky dry mountains and endless wastes of beige desert sand. Now you see a wind has arisen. It swirls and howls, drawing the sand up from the desert floor as if to consume it. Sand is flying, swirling around you. Then the wind lets it drop... because the wind is moving ...ever onwards ... churning sand before it. You hear the dry sound of the desert wind.

Don't be afraid, your angel says, *it is just the voice of the Desert. Feel the freedom of her spirit.*

Desert says: *I am your freedom.* And you feel within the sudden exhilaration of spontaneity. You are free. You are the author of the whole of your life. You can write the story any way you wish.

Exactly, says your angel. Now tell me, what have you learned?

But you cannot answer for what you have experienced is too deep to be expressed in words. So you open your heart and show:

That from the mountain you have discovered your power;

That from the ocean you have discovered your flexibility;

That from the forest you have discovered your aliveness;

And that from the desert you have discovered your freedom;

Ah, that is good, says your angel. But there is one more thing to learn and that is the greatest of all.

Now she slowly drifts down, down, down, until you find yourself lying not on a cloud, but on soft green grass. Beneath you, you feel the solid Earth. You put your ear to the ground and hear the drum, drum, drum of the Mother's heartbeat.

All around you, down here, where you are lying on the

Earth, you see life ... insects ... animals ... plants ... and hovering all around them you are aware of their little live spirits. Small and joyful, the spirits smile at you. They beckon, and in come the Nature Spirits ...fairies and elves, brownies and pixies, ...and the Elementals ... the salamanders of fire, the undines of water, the sylphs of air, and the gnomes of the earth.

Are you listening, asks your angel, *Can you hear the language of love?*

And the Earth, and the Spirits of all living things, the Nature Spirits and the Elementals all start to sing a beautiful song. You feel it warm in your heart, the essence of all Life ... LOVE.

Yes, says your angel. *LOVE is all. In it is power, flexibility, aliveness and freedom. But none of these can exist without LOVE.*

You take these words to your heart.

Seeing this, your angel smiles. She strokes your hair and moves away.

Remember, I am here whenever you need me, she says. *But now it is time for you to return to your life.*

As she says this she floats upwards. You watch as she dissolves into the ether.

And then you begin to come back from your journey ... to slip back into this room.

Now you become aware of where you are, sitting in the chair. Again you take your attention back to your breath, feeling yourself softly breathing in and out.

Wiggle your fingers and toes ... have a good stretch and when you are ready ... and only when you are ready ... gently open your eyes and come back into the room.

31

The Fourth Attunement

Now that you are back in the room, close your eyes again and we will go straight into the fourth and final attunement to Reiki 1.

Check that you are sitting with your back straight. Your shoulders are in line with your hips. Take a breath and relax your shoulders. Make sure your nose is in line with your navel. If you find it relaxing, breathe in through your nose and out through your mouth, but that is not compulsory.

Now gently close your eyes and bring your hands to the prayer position (gassho, namaste) at your heart centre, in the middle of your chest. Remember that I will need to move them about.

Relax. Just allow this to be an experiment. Allow yourself to experience whatever happens.

I'm going to put on some music. Allow it to move through every one of your cells ... Good.

Let's begin ...

Take another deep breath and relax. This is for your unique self. Remind yourself that you are a magnificent being and capable of anything.

Take your attention to your breath. If you would like to invite your personal guides — or your angels or any other being who works for the highest good of all — to be with you, now is the time to do so.

This is the last of the four attunements to Reiki 1. It is a blessing that you will always use Reiki for the highest good of all concerned. If your mind wanders, bring it gently back to this intention.

At the end of the attunement, keep your eyes closed until I ring the ting-sha three times.

Sound of ting-sha: three rings.

Silence for a few moments.

The fourth and last attunement to Reiki 1 is now complete.

Take as long as you need to open your eyes and come back in the room.

Now I would like you all, please, to spend a little while in your own energy, not speaking to anyone else — just until I come back into the room and ring the ting-sha again.

This is a special time for you to do exactly what seems right for you. There is no one who can tell you what that is ... Maybe you would like to stay exactly where you are ... maybe you would like to take a little walk outside in the garden ... or to snuggle up in a blanket on the settee. You may like to make a few notes of your experiences.

Do whatever feels right for you.

Do, also, drink some water.

I am going to leave the room now and will return in a few minutes.

I return to the room and sound the ting-sha once.

Without speaking, I spend a little while putting the room back in order, being as quiet as possible as I tidy away chairs and cushions.

Okay, now it is time to come back into the circle. Make yourself comfortable in the same place, or perhaps you would like to choose a different one.

Is everyone okay?

Would anyone like to share what they experienced?

There is no pressure. If you would prefer to keep your experience to yourself, that is absolutely fine.

If you have any questions, please ask them.

Is there anything in your experience about which you would like to ask me? If so, ask away.

If you feel you would like to keep things to yourself for the moment that is fine.

32

DO AND DON'T

REIKI IS NOT just a quick fix. It requires ongoing commitment and willingness to take complete responsibility for yourself.

DO

DO : *Supporting the Healing Process*

As you go about your everyday life, allow time for several of the following activities to help sustain your healing progress:

- ✓ Drink lots of clean spring water
- ✓ Rest
- ✓ Eat healthy food
- ✓ Spend more time in Nature
- ✓ Exercise - yoga and tai chi are excellent
- ✓ Laugh - be happy and carefree
- ✓ Feel your feelings without judging them
- ✓ Meditate
- ✓ Repeat affirmations to create and maintain a positive attitude
- ✓ Keep a diary to record changes for the better
- ✓ Practise telling the truth
- ✓ Take risks
- ✓ Use Bach Flower essences to support your feelings of harmony
- ✓ Be gentle with yourself
- ✓ Listen to your inner guidance
- ✓ Listen to soft music

- ✓ Buy yourself a small present — flowers are good
- ✓ Concentrate on your goals and on what your heart desires
- ✓ Be creative

These things relate to those you treat as well, so do mention them to your client before he/she leaves your presence.

Don't

DON'T : *Allowing the Healing Process*

As I have mentioned very often, your cleared energy field needs a little time to stabilise and balance. So I suggest you avoid doing anything like these things — at least for **48 hours** after a Reiki Workshop or Reiki Session.

- ✓ Explaining what you have experienced to people who may not understand it. This often includes a spouse or partner
- ✓ Intellectualising what you have experienced
- ✓ Venting your anger on anyone
- ✓ Beating yourself up about trifles
- ✓ Blaming anyone else for your experiences/pain
- ✓ Processing your experience with friends and family. Allow yourself to integrate it fully first
- ✓ Even thinking that change can't be so
- ✓ Denying the beauty and divinity within you
- ✓ Making major decisions in your life (e.g. change jobs, marry, divorce, separate)
- ✓ Not accepting the lessons that are being made available to you
- ✓ Believing that the Reiki Practitioner/Teacher is responsible for the healing, rather than you yourself.

33

Fears, Doubts and After-effects

There are some ***common after-effects*** from Reiki treatments (and attunements) so I'm going to run through a list of them. You don't need to remember them all. Just look at the list if and when you need to. Of course, you can always telephone me if you have a problem after this workshop.

Similarly, I will run through a list of ***fears and doubts*** that are common. You may not notice any of them, but if you do, they will soon pass.

Common After-effects

I know this list seems very long. But do stay calm: Few people experience any of them, but it's good to be aware that you might experience any of these after this workshop, or you might find yourself feeling like this after a Reiki treatment.

In some cases you may find one of your Reiki case-studies or clients experiences one of these things. If this happens, either to yourself or to a client, re-assure yourself and/or your client that such feelings and experiences are quite normal. The reason for them is simply that Reiki helps to release blocked energy and this will often lead to the experience of a wide range of emotions.

You may also feel an increase or decrease in vitality. Or you may feel nothing at all.

The following results are usual:

✓ **Positive feelings** — increased vitality, happiness, self-confidence, joy, serenity, peacefulness, freedom.

✓ **Headaches** — often caused by resistance to change or by release of toxins from the brain. Breathe deeply into the pain, drink lots of water, have a hot bath with a handful of sea salt in it (remembering to dip your head beneath the water at the end), then rest.

- ✓ **Flu-like symptoms** — fever is an indication that the body is burning old memory patterns. Body aches and pains are the result of release of tension. At first sign, acknowledge your feelings and express them in any way possible.
- ✓ **Exhaustion** — Often precipitated by tension, resistance to change or the depletion of energy used for healing. If you feel tired or depleted, allow yourself to slow down and rest.
- ✓ **Anger** — Often old suppressed anger that could not be expressed to parents or authority figures. Sometimes it is rage directed at oneself for a failure to meet your own or others' expectations.

  Remember that the feelings are coming up for release and that, ***provided the anger is not judged,*** healing will follow. If rage erupts, shout, scream or hit a soft object. A pillow is ideal — you can scream into it as well. Strenuous physical exercise is also good.

  Ask yourself:
  "Who am I really angry with?"
  "What happened to me?"
  "When did it happen?"

  Tell yourself that you are ready to know the truth and then invite memories to come up for healing.

  But remember: do not direct your anger at another person, animal or solid object.
- ✓ **Fear** — If you become engulfed by fear, breathe into it, filling yourself with white light and unconditional love. If you face fear in this manner it will lose its hold on you.
- ✓ **Grief** — releasing outgrown patterns can cause

sadness, grief and loneliness. Allow yourself to grieve, filling yourself with white light and unconditional love.

- ✓ **Shaking —** usually induced by reluctance to move on or by stuck energy. Find out whether the shaking is as a result of energy (not) moving or of your holding on. If the latter, allow yourself to find out why you are so afraid of letting go. In either case, drink plenty of water, love yourself unconditionally, give yourself lots of Reiki, have a hot bath and surrender to the shaking. If it still persists book a Reiki session.
- ✓ **Healing Crisis** — a major breakthrough is often marked by a combination of the symptoms described above and may also include confusion, disorientation and frustration. This situation often takes 24 to 48 hours to resolve itself gradually as old patterns are discarded and new ones come into being. Pamper yourself with lots of Reiki, drink plenty of water, have hot baths. If you need support, call your Reiki practitioner.

ANOTHER REIKI SESSION?

More Reiki treatments are indicated if any of the following happen:

⇒ Feeling stuck and unable to move on

⇒ Feeling frightened

⇒ Feeling disoriented for more than a few hours

⇒ Depression that lasts more than 24 hours

⇒ Anger that lasts more than 24 hours

⇒ Additional issues come up with which you need assistance

Fears and doubts

Fears and doubts often surface before a Reiki session because your subconscious recognises that change is imminent, and consequently feels anxious and unsafe. These ripples of fear, doubt and uncertainty will definitely interfere with your healing if they are not addressed.

If you experience any of the feelings listed below recognise them as limiting beliefs. Realise that this reaction is normal. Breathe through it and don't give up or make excuses.

- ✓ Fear of change
- ✓ Fear of losing control
- ✓ Fear of the unknown
- ✓ Fear of making decisions which may upset others
- ✓ Fear of making a wrong decision
- ✓ Fear of losing your mind, of going crazy
- ✓ Fear of love, joy, happiness
- ✓ Fear of being told that your feelings are not acceptable
- ✓ Fear of what others might say/think
- ✓ Denial that a problem exists
- ✓ Belief that Reiki may not be acceptable to your family culture or religion
- ✓ Belief in the need for struggle, pain and suffering
- ✓ Belief that you are limited by your parents' teaching, behaviour and commitments

- ✓ Lack of faith in yourself
- ✓ Lack of faith in Reiki
- ✓ Fear of the cost in terms of money, time, relationships
- ✓ Fear that you have to "do it alone"
- ✓ Fear of forgiveness
- ✓ Doubt as to whether you can forgive others, or yourself.

Many of these doubts and fears also masquerade as "reasons" or excuses not to commit to your own healing.

Recognise them and let them go — or even better, chuck them out. If you really need them, you can always pick them up again later.

34

Treating others: back of the body

Now we are going to learn the hand positions for treating the back of the body.

Beginning

Normally, these days I only treat the front of the body, with variations that I will teach you if you come to learn more Reiki with me. But a 'usual' Reiki treatment is to spend about thirty-five minutes on the front of the body, as we learned yesterday, and then to ask the client to turn over so that you can work on their back.

The reasons I seldom ask a client to change positions are these:

1. They are usually nice and relaxed by the time you've covered the whole of the front and it seems a great pity to disturb them so that you can work on their back.
2. It can become quite complicated as you try to alter the placement of cushions while at the same time trying to ensure they don't fall off the couch.
3. Some people find it very difficult to lie on their front.
4. Reiki will go to the places it is needed even if we can't put our hands on those places.

Having said that, however, it is sometimes beneficial to work on the back rather than the front:

- ✓ Some clients feel very vulnerable if they are lying on their backs.
- ✓ This position can be more naturally appropriate for sleep and relaxation.
- ✓ You can reach parts of the anatomy through the spinal

cords and the ganglions of nerves which come out from either side of each vertebra.

- ✓ You find that you are more relaxed because no-one is watching what you are doing.

I will not go through all of the things I said about preparation yesterday — because it was only yesterday and you can check your notes if you need to — but I suggest that you watch carefully how I place the pillows on this couch. This arrangement is very relaxing. It supports the back, gives a soft pillowing for the breasts, means that the neck is held straight and not twisted, and that the client has room to breathe.

You will need four normal-sized pillows and a small cushion or a rolled up hand towel for the head.

- ✓ Place the small pillow, or small, rolled towel, at the head of the couch for the client's forehead.
- ✓ Leave a space to allow the client to breathe.
- ✓ Then pile two pillows together — one on top of the other — to go under the breasts/chest.
- ✓ The edge of the third pillow is placed between the others. This extends the padding and helps support the body, so that the back is soft and relaxed. I usually fiddle with these pillows until I have just the right height and length for the client.
- ✓ Cover them all with a towel or sheet, tucking it under at either end to keep the pillows together.
- ✓ A last pillow, usually a soft one, is placed at the end of the couch to cosset the client's feet.

Once you are happy with the arrangement, show your client how to lie on the pillows by demonstrating. When s/he gets onto the couch, make sure that s/he is comfortable. You can adjust the pillows again if necessary. Everyone's body shape is slightly different.

Cover your client lightly with a blanket. It is best to use

natural materials, particularly cotton or silk, on your Reiki couch. The reasons for this are that your client will be more comfortable, and that Reiki energy flows more smoothly through natural fibres.

Ensure that you have washed your hands recently, so that they smell of soap rather than what you had for lunch!

Next, prepare the client as we did yesterday, like this:

'Are you quite comfortable? Good. I'm going to place my hand gently here, on your lower back. Take a deep breath in, right down to my hand. That's good. Sigh the breath out slowly through your mouth, letting go of anything — any thoughts or worries or emotional stuff, any pain or discomfort — that you don't need right at this minute.

Let's do that once more. Breathe in deeply .... And sigh the breath out.

And again: but this time breathe in peace ... and breathe out calm. Now, if you would like, take yourself off to a special place in Nature that you love. Really be there. Feel the earth beneath you and the sun on your cheek ... hear the sounds ... see all the beautiful surroundings ... smell the fragrance of the place ... and taste it ... feel its special significance to you ...'

If you have already worked on the client's front there is no need to re-link into the Reiki energy unless you feel you want to.

But for practice and because we are only working on the back today, we will link in to the Reiki energy again. It's just the same way as when we were working on the front:

1. Fold your hands together in the prayer position at your heart centre.
2. Say a short, potent, heart-felt prayer in the words of the Reiki ethic: *this healing is for the highest good of all concerned*. You can add in any words of your own that you like. Personally I add a couple of lines from

St. Francis' prayer:

Make me a channel of your peace
Where there is hatred let me bring your love
Where there is despair let me bring hope
Where there is darkness let me bring light
And where there's sadness let me bring joy.

3. Then step to one side. Now you have left your personality to one side and have become a vessel for Reiki ... a Reiki channel without all the hopes, fears and wishes or your ego.

Now, just as you did yesterday, you are going to sweep through the client's aura with your Reiki hands. Do you remember why?

Yes, that's right — first, to ground and remove any disturbance in the aura that has not yet become manifest in the physical body. And, second, to find areas that need our attention.

Again you put your hands either side of the client, about six inches above the body, and starting slightly above the head, but leaving the crown chakra undisturbed. Step slowly backwards, bringing your hands along the client's body in a smooth motion.

Touch the floor to ground any energy that is not in harmony with the client.

Repeat this action, but this time see if you can sense any areas where there is coldness, or lack of energy. Or there might be a vibration of some sort: pins and needles, perhaps? Or you might find heat, or even feel pain.

You may want to experiment by taking your hands lower or higher in the aura as you sweep. Play with the energy. Keep it light. There is no right or wrong. There is only what you can sense. You will only find what is appropriate for you, or that require the client's attention in order for them to be healed.

If you sense something, make a mental note of it. Sometimes you may 'receive a message' or 'just know' what the problem is. Because you are working on the back and your client is probably already relaxed and drifting off to their beautiful place in Nature, there is no need to disturb him/her by asking questions out loud. However, if they ask, or of you feel the need to ask, go ahead. Listen to your intuition. It is your greatest gift, your greatest asset, in healing. Trust it. Sometimes you may hear words. At other times you may find your hands or your eyes are drawn towards a certain area. That's great. You can rationalise it later. At this moment simply follow where your hands and intuition lead.

If you don't feel anything, or know anything, that is fine. Reiki has its own intelligence. It will always find and release what is appropriate, even if you sense nothing.

Hand positions for treating the back

If you have already worked on the front there is no need to cover those areas that have already been treated. You can leave out the, ears, temples, back of the head and throat.

But today we are doing a whole treatment on the back, so we will cover those areas that are available to us ... but we will ignore the eye position, and the temples.

If you feel that your client has a headache or too much energy in the head that might develop into a headache or migraine, I suggest that you start with our good old 'dustpan and brush' technique to take away any excess energy.

- Make yourself comfortable, sitting on a chair at the head of the couch.
- Take a breath, and feel the Reiki energy coming in through the crown of your head, passing down through your body and out into the earth.
- With the next breath feel the flow of energy from the earth through to your crown.

- With the third breath feel the energy coming through both your crown and your base chakra, meeting in your heart centre, and flowing down your hands.

If you feel nothing, use your imagination. If you feel yourself drawn in towards the client, consciously withdraw by keeping your posture upright. If you still find yourself moving forwards, it may help to throw out an imaginary, metaphysical anchor about nine yards behind you.

Ears

Gland: pineal

When you are ready bring your hands slowly through the client's energy field and gently cup the ears. Remain aware that you are treating all that the ears do — hearing, listening, balance etc.— but that they are a holograph of the body, so you can also work on the body as a whole from here.

Back of head

Gland: pituitary

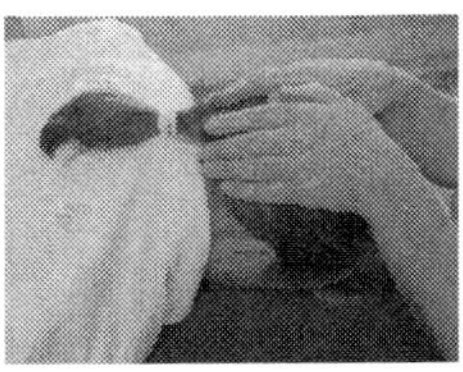

Move your hands carefully into the position for the back of the head, your fingers rest softly over the occiput, and the heels of your hands lie on top of the client's head. Overlap your thumbs slightly to make sure that the whole of the middle of the back of the head is covered.

A reminder: your middle fingers are in contact with the client's occiput, the brain stem, and thus with the fluid that bathes the brain and the spinal cord. Feel its slow pulse as its tide moves up and down the spine. It's much slower than the breath. Some people can sense it easily, others find it more difficult. It doesn't matter which sort you are. Trust and imagine space between each of the vertebrae. Sometimes you can feel the head move towards you as the spine lengthens in response to your intention.

Remember that, as with the similar position described when you were working on the front of the body, this contact means that you can send a message of healing down the whole spine, and you may feel the Reiki energy gently adjusting the nerves of the spine. Be aware; and simply allow.

Throat

Gland: thyroid

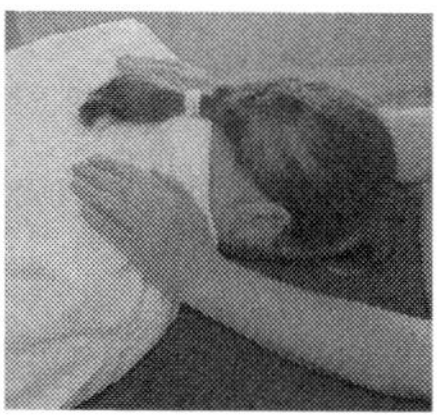

The throat tends to need a lot of Reiki. It is the centre of our creativity as well as the place from which we communicate with all levels of existence.

Place your hands either side of the neck, as we did on the front, with the heels of the hands on the client's 'shoulder seams'. The fingers point straight down the body, but your intention is to treat the throat chakra and any issues that arise from there.

This position is good for the voice, helpful for sore throats, and stimulates the throat chakra. Often Reiki here will have the effect of freeing emotion which has been repressed, so if you or your client feel tearful, just let the tears flow, without judgement.

Remainder of the back

Now we will move to one side of the couch so that we can move easily down the client's body. There are two ways that you can give Reiki down the back.

The first way is to follow the chakras. For this, you will recall that the hand nearest the feet ('feet hand') is the one that you place across the far side of the body, while the hand nearest the client's head ('head hand') stays on the near side of the client's body.

I know this sounds complicated, but it's really quite simple. Remember the reason: because the Reiki energy is sweeping down from the client's crown chakra. If you place the 'head' hand across the body, you will be blocking the energy and it will not run so smoothly. It *will* run, of course, so this is not going to ruin a treatment.

Actually, this would be a good time to experiment with this, especially as your client cannot see what you are doing and so can't cheat. Play with the energy and the different positions. Ask your client if he/she can feel the difference, and if so, which feels better and why. Remember it may be difficult to tell you exactly why it feels better but I'm sure they will have an opinion.

Heart Centre

Gland: thymus

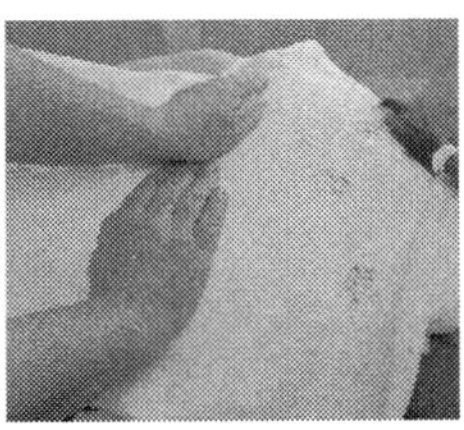

Use your non-dominant hand to sense where the heart chakra is. It's usually in the centre of the chest, *not* exactly over the heart. Place the 'feet' hand over the ribs furthest from you with the heel of the hand resting on the heart chakra. Nestle the tips of the fingers of the 'head' hand under the heel of the other hand, and allow the rest of the hand to mould itself over the ribs of the side nearest you. The two hands are in a straight line, roughly parallel to the shoulders.

This is the place of compassion for all things, of empathy and unconditional love. Giving Reiki here stimulates the immune system.

Solar Plexus

Gland: pancreas

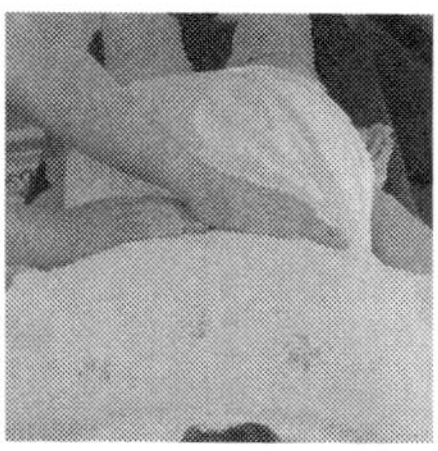

When you are ready to move on, use your non-dominant hand to sense where the solar plexus chakra is. Then place the 'head' hand across the ribs, so that the tips of your fingers touch the chakra. Place the 'feet' hand across the ribs on the further side, so that the heel of that hand covers the fingertips of the 'head' hand, and both palms rest along the lower ribs.

The Solar Plexus is the place of the client's inner fire: his/her will. Energy is often lacking here. Remember that, on the physical level, this position eases the digestion. On the emotional level it is how the client deals with problems and life events.

Hara, Abdomen
Glands: ovaries and gonads

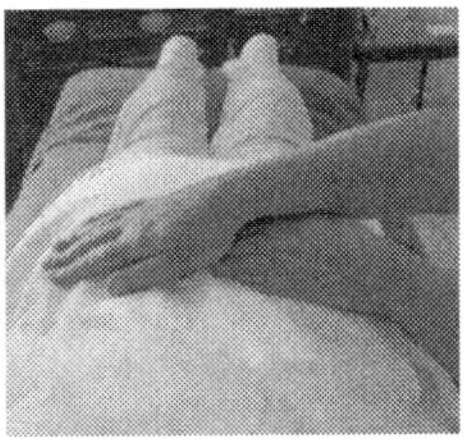

When you are ready, move your hands down so that they rest along the sacrum. Of course, you can use your non-dominant hand to sense exactly where to place your hands. This part of the back is often tender and overworked, so be gentle.

Base, pubic bone
Gland: adrenals

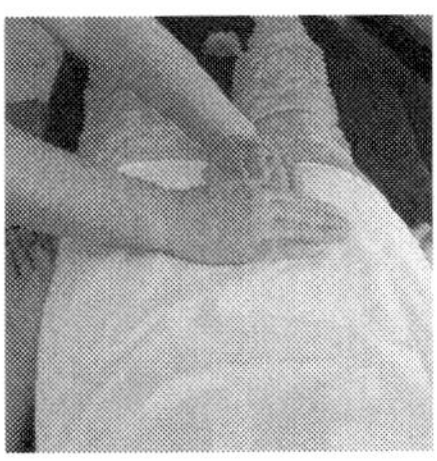

Like the hand position on the front of the body, this hand position is sometimes considered a little personal. Nonetheless I invite you to try it as most people find it very comforting and reassuring, and some even find it supporting. You place your 'head' hand across the base of the spine — just before the parting of the buttock ways, so to speak!The 'feet' hand gently moulds itself over the crack of the buttocks with the tips of the fingers nestling under the upper hand. If you find this feels uncomfortable, invasive, or you are not happy doing it, then just raise your hands about an inch above the client's body.

The base chakra relates to all our basic needs, and whether or not they are met. The emotions that relate to this chakra are fear and courage. Reiki here helps us to realise that we are able to supply all our own needs, so we don't need to rely on anyone else.

This chakra relates to the adrenal glands which regulate the fight, flight or freeze response. They are often overworked because we spend a lot of time stressed and anxious.

Legs

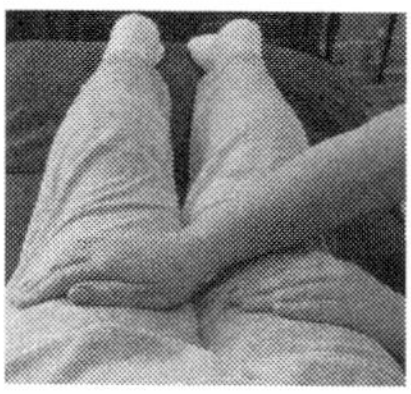

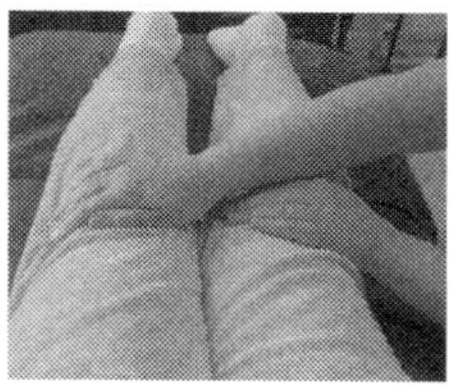

As I'm sure I've mentioned before, many Reiki Masters don't teach any hand positions for the legs, but I believe treating the legs is particularly therapeutic, especially when you have a client who is not grounded and who spends too much time in his/her head to be balanced.

You will also remember that many people, through extreme or constant emotion, often grief, seem to 'cut off' their legs. Reiki helps to restore the connection between the legs and the rest of the body.

As we continue to work down our client's body, we carry on along the legs in much the same way as we have worked down the back. Putting our hands in turn on:

Both *thighs*

Both *knees*

Both *calves*

As before, the 'feet' hand is placed on the far side of the body, and the 'head' hand on the side close to you.

Ankles

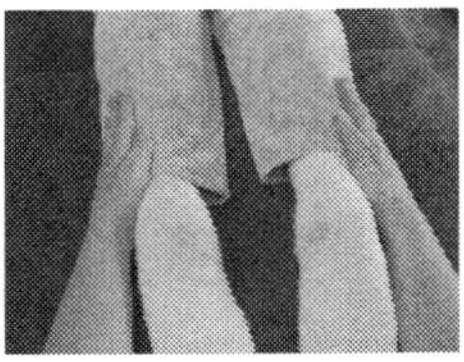

Move to the foot of the couch. Place your hands, fingers pointing up towards the head, along the outside of each leg so that the protruding ankle bones nestle in the palm of each hand. Make sure that your thumbs are parallel to your fingers.

The ankles are about flexibility and the ability to cope with change.

Feet

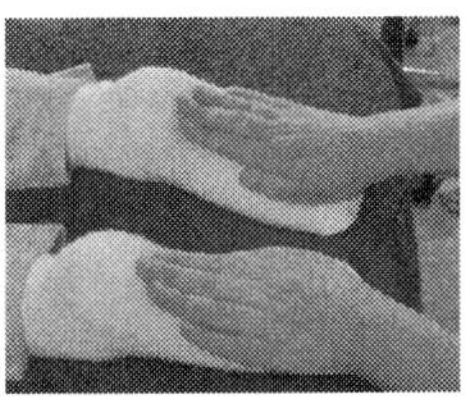

A reminder: do not stand for long directly in front of the feet while working on them (although this is shown in the photograph above) because they may discharge disharmonious energy into your belly. Instead, stand to one side.

Allow your hands to cover the whole of the sole of each foot. If you stand to one side, facing the end of the couch, your hands will cover the feet easily, the heels of your hands covering the heels and your fingers falling near the toes. Imagine the energy flowing smoothly down the body towards the earth and then, receiving some extra Reiki energy, flowing smoothly back up towards the crown. Wait until you feel this flow.

Finish here: touch the floor to make sure that all that unwanted energy is grounded.

Nota Bene

You can work across the body: or, if you prefer, down one side and then (after walking to the other side of the couch) down the other.

35

Alternative Hand Positions for the Back

This is an alternative system of hand positions for the back. I emphasise that it is an alternative, not that it is better than the previous system. However, I have had very good results from these hand positions. I believe this may be because I have more experience and a deeper knowledge of physiology than when I began to give Reiki. Now I know where the ganglions of nerves for the various physical systems exit the vertebra.

You can be more precise, it is true: but that is not always a 'good thing' as it brings the ego into play. We begin to use our thinking brain rather than our intuitive brain.

If you are interested in physiology, I suggest you obtain a good diagram of the spinal column and the associated nervous system. You will find it fascinating. However, having said that, I suggest you try first to see what you can sense with your hands. Float your Reiki hands down the body and see where they come to rest.

You may find a desire to place them in some position that is not mentioned in this book. Good. Go with the feeling. Intuitive understanding is very powerful — more powerful and effective than any system of academic study. At least, that is my experience when Reiki is involved.

This is an exercise, which you may find useful, since it helps us to access our intuition without worrying about whether we are over-thinking, or whether we are putting our own hopes and wishes before the healing needs of our client.

First, make sure that you do all the preliminaries that I described earlier.

Reiji-Ho - Listening to the intuition

A short, potent, heart-felt prayer before a Reiki treatment. This prayer increases your awareness that you, the practitioner, are merely a channel for the Reiki energy. It also teaches you to listen to your intuition.

There are three parts to **Reiji-Ho:**

1. **Fold** your hands in the prayer position at your heart centre
2. **Pray** for the well-being and healing of your client on all levels — physical, mental, emotional and spiritual.
3. **Move** your folded hands so that your thumbs touch your forehead between the eyebrows. Ask the Reiki energy to guide your hands to where they are needed.

Proceed with the healing, allowing your hands to rest on those parts of the body to which they are drawn.

Be aware:

- ✓ of any changes in the body as you touch it
- ✓ of your own thoughts and emotions
- ✓ of your intuition and/or guidance

Remember to use Reiji-Ho for self-treatments too.

Alternative Hand Positions for the Spine

I haven't included photographs of these positions in the appendix to this book because they are not precise: rather they are as fluid as your intuition is when you use the Reiji-Ho technique.

However, I offer the following guidance.

As I have said so many times before, the spinal cord contains all the nerves to the body. Reiki energy is carried along the nerves.

If I may digress for a moment, I would like to marvel at the magnificence of the body and its cells. Bear in mind that we have about three trillion cells in our bodies. Each one has a cell wall and its own tiny organs. In fact, it is a constellation in its own galaxy. Why it might even *be* a galaxy! We know that each cell contains infinite space within it, so why not? It also contains infinite possibilities. Each cell has an unbounded ability for change. It is our consciousness working on that infinite space that makes the difference.

Now, let's take one nerve cell or neuron. A microscopic neuron is long and thin. Invisible to the naked eye. Thirty-thousand neurons would fit on the head of a pin. *Thirty-thousand.* And yet, one nerve cell runs all the way down from the brain to the very end of your longest toe. Isn't that amazing?

Whenever we put our Reiki hands on anyone, we are contacting neurons. As the Reiki energy reminds them of their energetic blueprint, it gives them the opportunity as well as energy to heal or 'whole' themselves. But only if that is for the highest good of the person who is receiving the Reiki energy.

Now the place where it is easiest to contact the nerve cells that serve the respective parts and organs of the body is ... the spine. Or rather, to be exact, the bunched neurons (ganglions) that come out from either side of the spine. If you have some knowledge of anatomy, it's easy to see the relation between these ganglions and the organs they serve, because they are in roughly the same region of the body. The exception to this are the nerves which serve the legs because they come from the sacrum and travel all the way down.

So to return to the back of the body ... look at the one in front of you. You may be able to see subtle or not-so-subtle twists in the spine. It may seem to be contracted one side. Maybe it's looser one side than the other. Use Reiji-Ho and see whether your hands follow your eyes. In front of you, you have a blank canvas. You can put your hands anywhere they are drawn to.

If you find this difficult, there is a simple way to cover the whole of the spine. Stand to one side and put your 'head hand' over the occiput, making sure you cover the place where the skull meets the spine. This hand will be covering the atlas and the axis vertebrae. Place your other hand next to it, with one thumb covering the other.

When you feel you need to move on, take your 'head hand' gently away. Cross it over the other hand and snuggle the little finger next to the little finger of the 'foot hand'. Then move the 'foot hand' next to it, linking the thumbs.

In this way you work gradually down the spine, all the way down to the coccyx. Make sure you do not skimp at the 'buttock end'. This is a place where a lot of tension is held. The coccyx itself is often damaged in accidents, or sometimes in childbirth. Because it is near the root chakra, such accidents can badly affect a person's sense of security.

Yet Another Alternative for the Spine

Another way of working with the spine is to work with the polarity in the body. The 'polarity' is the electro-magnetic energy of the body. Again, this is a whole workshop or more in itself, but briefly, the body has an electrical charge. It has negative and positive poles at the feet and head respectively. At the centre of the body is the neutral area. Thus the feet are negative, the head is positive and the hands are neutral. This is one of the reasons we use the hands for Reiki healing.

If you connect the positive and negative poles you begin to allow the energy to run freely, thus allowing healing and reducing pain.

To take this a little further, the base of the spine relates to the top of the spine. So if you put one hand (preferably your non-dominant hand) on the base of the skull and the other (dominant hand) over the base of the spine you can adjust the energy to run smoothly through the whole spinal column. This position is very good for bringing the whole body, including the mental and emotional bodies, into balance.

You can make it even more effective by gradually moving the hands closer together, a hand-width at each end. Rest here to give Reiki before again moving the hands a hand-width closer from each end. Continue until your hands meet in the centre of the spine.

Then move on to the legs.

Alternative Hand Positions for the Legs

When you have covered the whole of the spine in one of the ways mentioned above, continue on down the legs in a similar manner.

Upper legs

I suggest the you do one leg at a time. Stand to one side, and start on the buttocks on the same side.

Move on, as described above, a hand-width at a time until you have covered the whole of the thighs and upper legs. Then move round the couch and work down the other buttock, thigh and upper leg.

Knees

Be gentle with the knees. The backs of the knees are very tender and vulnerable. I suggest that you do a 'knee sandwich' by slipping the 'head hand' under the knee and placing the 'feet hand' gently over the back of it.

Do one knee and then the other.

Calves and Ankles

Continue on down the calf a hand-width at a time until you come to the ankle.

Go round to the other side and work down from knee to ankle in the same way.

Feet

A reminder: stand to one side of the client while working

on the feet.

Simply allow your hands to cover the whole of the sole of each foot. Imagine the energy flowing smoothly down the body towards the earth and then, receiving some extra Reiki energy, flowing smoothly back up towards the crown. Wait until you feel this flow.

Finish here: touch the floor to make sure that all that unwanted energy is grounded.

36

Uses for Reiki

Just to recap: over these last two days you've learned:

- ✓ to use Reiki for treating yourself
- ✓ how to give yourself a chakra balance.
- ✓ how to treat others with Reiki, working down the front of the body
- ✓ how to treat others with Reiki, working down the back of the body.

The big question is… what else can you use Reiki for?
Do you have any ideas?
That's right. You can use it for practically anything.

Do *play* with the Reiki energy. Have fun with it! Keep it light and try anything that comes to mind. You can only use it for good. That is built into the attunements.

Now I'm just going to run through a few of the more common uses.

Pets and animals

Pets and animals.

If you are going to work with animals professionally or for money, you have to have the consent, and preferably the presence, of a veterinary surgeon. However, your own pets are a different matter, as are those that come and sit near or on you. You will be giving them Reiki just by stroking them.

Pets can feel the Reiki energy. If you have a dog, you may find that s/he is a little unsure of you after this workshop. That's because they feel the alteration in your vibrational energy. But don't worry. Leave them to adjust and they will soon be back to normal.

Horses, too, are very aware of our energy and may be a little more skittish or stand-offish for a few days. Again, just give them time. Act normally.

If you are a cat owner, you will probably find that your cat is more affectionate than usual. Cats tend to love Reiki energy from the very beginning. However, animals are as individual as we are, and may react differently from these basic rules.

In my experience they will all come to love Reiki.

Two other things about animals: they always know where they want you to put your hands; and they always know when they have received enough. In the first case, they will come up to you and manoeuvre themselves into the right position under your hands. When they want your hands somewhere else, they will move.

When they've had enough, they simply walk away. Easy. Never try to give them Reiki after that, and never *insist* on giving them Reiki. Animals have not lost their inner knowing or intuitive powers.

I have a lovely story to illustrate this. A friend of mine had a special cat. One of those wonderful animals who just seem to know everything about you and are loving and affectionate as well. Sadly, the cat — I'll call him Ziggy — was less than a year old when he was run over by a car. The driver drove off. Probably he hadn't realised. Anyway, my friend found Ziggy almost dead.

She rushed him to the vet. The cat had a broken pelvis and a broken skull. The vet had no idea how many internal injuries he had also sustained. He said it would be merciful to put Ziggy to sleep, but my friend couldn't bear to do that without at least trying. So the vet patched him up and sent him home. My friend gave him constant Reiki. He loved it.

When she took Ziggy back to the vet, he couldn't believe

that the cat hadn't died. His pelvis required a long and serious operation, but there was nothing the vet could do for the skull. He said Ziggy *might* live, but he doubted it. Well, you've guessed I'm sure. The cat came for Reiki every night for a couple of months; and every time my friend took him back for a check-up, the vet was amazed at the way he was healing. It took about four months for the healing to be completed but Ziggy lived to a ripe old age — and the vet said he hd never seen a cat recover so amazingly well after such serious injuries.

My friend said that she knew Ziggy's head hurt him from time to time because he would always come to her for Reiki healing, and manoeuvre himself so that he was almost upside down with his head in the palm of her hand. He had done that each day after his accident, several times each day.

I've heard several similar stories, but this is my favourite.

Plants and Nature Spirits

Plants

Plants love Reiki. And as you can imagine there are many ways that you can give it to them. I like to wander round the house, holding the indoor plants' pots in my hand as I let the Reiki flow to their roots.

When I do the dusting — with Reiki in the dusters, of course. — I wave my hand and a duster over their leaves. My orchids get the occasional Reiki duster. I Reiki the water in the watering cans, too.

When I buy a new plant, I may have an idea of where I would like it to go, but I walk round the garden with it and ask it. Usually it's quite insistent on the place it wants to be. Seldom does it end up where I intended.

I bless with Reiki the place I'm to dig, and fill the hole with 'Reiki'ed water. Then I ask its Nature Spirit if it wishes to have more Reiki to help it settle. If I get no answer — nature spirits can be shy — I give it some Reiki with the intention that if it's not wanted by the new plant it should go to another one: one that would like the energy.

Sometimes, I just stand in my doorway and open my Reiki hands to send it out into the garden.

It's useful to Reiki seeds before you plant them, too. You can Reiki the compost, the water, the pots or trays.

Use Reiki with plants in any way that you imagine.

Nature Spirits

I mentioned Nature Spirits. You probably know that every living thing has a spirit, and plants have very definite ones. I always try to remember to ask before I pick flowers, and to give a plant Reiki whenever it needs it.

When you wish to prune a shrub or tree, talk to its spirit and ask it to withdraw its energy from the branches you are planning to cut. It helps to touch the branches briefly. Sometimes, you may feel that you have chosen to prune the wrong one. If so, correct what you have asked. Wait a day or two before cutting. It's helpful to give Reiki to the plant after pruning.

All weak and fragile plants benefit from Reiki, but if their time has come to die, Reiki will not help them to recover.

One word of warning. If the plant has a pest, or is diseased, make sure that you are clear in your intention. I once gave Reiki to a plant that was covered in spider mites. I obviously had some muddled thinking because the spider mites increased exponentially and killed the plant!

Lesson: make sure your intention is clear.

Maybe the spider mites needed to grow and the plant was the means.

We do not know the big picture. We trust.

First Aid

Emergency

Reiki is wonderful in an emergency. It is always with you, whatever happens to you or someone close to you.

Reiki helps with shock and pain. It also helps to keep the person present and conscious.

One day I had a stall at a 'green' event in the local park. I was offering Reiki treatments and advertising my Reiki training workshops. As I was talking to a lady about learning Reiki, a couple came up to me, introduced themselves — I'll call them Mr and Mrs Green — and said they had overheard me. They just wanted to say how wonderful Reiki was. In fact, they knew that Reiki had saved both their lives. It transpired that they had been involved in a serious road accident on a motorway. Another motorist stopped. He and his passenger came over to see if they could help. The couple were trapped in their vehicle, barely conscious. The motorist and his companion, sat by the car and held the Greens' hands. Immediately they both felt warmth envelop them and much less pain. The Reiki people stayed, giving Reiki, until the Greens were cut from the car and stretchered away. The Reiki-givers left. The Greens recovered after a long stay in hospital. The medics said they could not believe that they had survived and still less that they recovered so quickly. The Greens said that they never learned the names of their helpers, so were unable to thank them. Instead, they lauded Reiki whenever they had the opportunity.

Lesson: You can give Reiki simply by holding someone's hand.

Shock

If you are close enough and the injured person is in the right position, the best Reiki remedy for shock is to put one hand on the person's solar plexus in the front, and the other in a matching position on her back. Hold it for as long as seems right, or at least until the person's heart rate settles.

Quick Healing

Just remember that Reiki really does assist healing and it works very fast.

A friend of mine's mother fractured her leg. My friend rushed to help. She gave her mother's leg Reiki while the ambulance took her to hospital. The emergency staff at the hospital were amazed that it was such a recent break as it had already started to heal.

Moral: With fractures and breaks it is best to wait until the break has been set before giving Reiki direct to the site of the break. Instead, give Reiki elsewhere to reduce the pain.

Another 'quick healing' story is about a little girl of three, called Maya. Maya's mother had taken Reiki 1 and 2 with me and Maya loved receiving Reiki. She loved it so much that she sometimes 'gave' it to her mother, too. One day, Maya was playing at school with a little boy called James when he fell over and cut his forehead badly. Immediately, Maya pushed the two edges of the cut together and placed her hand over it. While the school staff rushed around to take James to hospital, Maya refused to remove her hand. "I'm giving him Reiki," she said. She went with him to the hospital, hand still firmly over the wound.

By the time they arrived at the Accident and Emergency department, the cut had ceased to bleed and was already almost healed. When Maya's mother told me this story, she said Maya had wished that there should be no scar — and within a few days there wasn't!

Homes, Houses and Workplaces

I'm sure that you have all walked into a room at some time and felt uncomfortable with the energy in that room? I remember looking over a property in Sawbridgeworth many years ago, long before I even thought about anything like Reiki. Although the day was bright and sunny, a shadow seemed to loom over the house. Every hair on my arms stood up as I entered the front door. The whole place felt dark and the air inside was heavy and smelled dirty. Although the rooms were empty and clean, they seemed full of some dark, heavy 'something'. I could hardly bring myself to climb the stairs.

When the Estate Agent flung open a door into the main bedroom, I fled. The feeling that came out of that room was black despair. I couldn't run out into the sunshine fast enough — and in those days I was much fleeter of foot than I am now. Later, I found out that the man who had lived there had suffered from severe depression and had hanged himself in that very room.

If I'd known then what I know now, I would have had the tools to help to change the energy in that house, but all I could do then was flee.

Most houses do not build up anything as heavy and dark as I have described, but nonetheless, energy does cling to walls and ceilings and soft furnishings. It builds up particularly in corners. This is why some rooms feel joyous and others feel sad or depressed or full of anger.

It is good to clear them sometimes, and don't forget the soft furnishings and places that you sit. One of the easiest ways is to Reiki some sea salt with the intention of transforming energy from negative to beneficial. Then throw the salt all over the room. Leave it for no longer than half-an-hour to soak up any negativity and then vacuum it up. Make sure you empty it from the vacuum cleaner and place it outside or in the bin. If you leave it indoors it will become saturated with negativity and then it will leak out again. In the garden, or compost bin, Mother Nature will transmute it.

Or you can just let Reiki flow from your hands as you move them over the walls, about two feet out to begin with — you can always move closer as the energy clears.

You will be surprised how much people notice the difference. I did this once in my office, and my secretary thought I'd moved an old, dark piece of (non-existent!) furniture out of the room.

To keep the energy sweet, Reiki a small crystal with that intention. Leave it in the room and give it Reiki when you pass by it.

Computers and Electrical Equipment.

COMPUTERS, WIFI AND electrical equipment are ubiquitous nowadays.

Unfortunately, very little research has been done on the effect on the human energy system of living in the middle of electrical ring mains. Still less has been done on the effects of wifi and the artificial microwaves that pervade the whole of the space in which we live. There is a great deal of evidence that these waves exacerbate the effects of 'ordinary' electromagnetic energy. Some sensitive people suffer a great deal: from headaches, depression, general malaise, exhaustion, skin and eye problems ... you name it, someone suffers from it as a result of being exposed to this sort of energy.

This has been the case for some time. Paints have been developed to counter the effect of it. Some houses have to be swathed in special materials to protect the sensitive occupiers — occupiers who cannot venture outside their houses and are virtually imprisoned.

Have you read the instructions for nearly all mobile phones? The bit that says they should never be held closer than two inches away from the head? Have you heard about the young girl who developed breast cancer from keeping her mobile phone in her bra? I'm sure you've heard of the viruses that infect computers and phones?

Well, after all that bad news: here's the good news. Reiki can help with all these things.

Reiki is a strong beneficial energy. It is even stronger when combined with crystals, orgone or other shielding methods.

Here are some ways you can use Reiki. There is no need to use them all, though. Just choose.

1. You can put yourself and your family in Reiki bubbles. Know that they are safe and protected. You can do

this in the same way that we did at the end of Reiki Session, or just with your imagination. Your intention is that it is for the highest good and should last forever. You can renew it whenever you feel it's appropriate or necessary, but if you had a strong intention in the first place that will be sufficient.

2. Imagine that Reiki is spreading across the whole of your home and garden. Your home and its over-lighting spirit will rejoice and so will the Nature spirits in your garden. Do the same for your workplace, your car — in fact anywhere and everywhere you go. Everyone will benefit.
3. Program a clear quartz crystal by giving it Reiki and asking that the Reiki either transforms any negative energy or directs it to a place where it will be useful to other life forms. Place the crystal on the electrical fuse box/meter, with the point directed away from the house. Renew the Reiki from time to time, asking it to clear the crystal of any negative energy it has absorbed.
4. Program an amethyst or black tourmaline crystal that you place near your computer, or tape to your mobile phone or tablet. In this case ask that the crystal transforms the negative energy into positive beneficial energy. You can also ask that the Reiki energy transforms any virus attacks or hacks into beneficial energy that is then returned to the sender. This is much more powerful than returning negative energy. It does *good*, and good is always more powerful that evil.
5. A small black tourmaline crystal worn next to the skin, or kept in a pocket, will absorb negative energy. Clear it after every outing.

Food and Drink

AH. TWO OF my favourite things.

Food

In this amazing symbiotic world, we are what we eat. It's as simple as that. So what we eat is vital to our well-being. Of course, I suggest that we try to eat a wholly organic wholefood diet, with an emphasis on vegetables and fruit, but we cannot always achieve that aim.

If you are eating out, unless you go to an organic wholefood restaurant, you have no idea whether you are eating organically or not. I believe that generally restaurants do not use organic produce. Added to this, all the cook's emotions go into the food he prepares, so although the food may look great and taste wonderful, it will have no nurturing, nourishing quality.

Generally, everyone loves homemade cooking, especially if your parent is a good cook. Even if the cooking is not good, we can often dine on the joy and nurturing that has gone into the preparation of our food.

When I was in my very early twenties, an impecunious articled clerk — as trainee solicitors used to be called — by a strange series of coincidences I managed to find myself a weekend job of cooking for the boys in an approved hostel for young offenders. It's true that I have always loved food and I have always enjoyed nourishing others with food. But it was surprising how different my Sunday-roast-with-all-the-trimmings tasted depending on who had helped me peel the vegetables.

Sometimes it was a dark, violent, brooding boy of few words called Tiger. His crimes had been vicious. Unsurprisingly, I was a little scared of him, although he never really gave me cause. Those weekends nothing tasted as delicious as when I had been assisted by Callum, a tall, beautiful youth of about seventeen with an amazing sense of rhythm and dance. We would put on the radio and dance and sing our way round the kitchen. How different the food tasted.

Now we have Reiki to help us when we feel the food we are given to eat is less nutritious, and less nourishing than it could be.

Wave your Reiki palms over the food to enliven it. Anything that is not of the highest good is wafted away. Bless the food itself. Whatever its journey has been, and whether it is vegetable, fruit, meat or fish, some other sentient being has given its own life force to nourish yours. Bring gratitude to the table, so that the food's sacrifice is not in vain.

Even the most organic, fresh, food will be enhanced with a good dollop of gratitude.

Drink

One day, my friend and I were about to co-teach a Reiki workshop. We poured out water for ourselves from the bottled water that we'd purchased only that morning. It tasted terrible. We looked at each other and wondered what we could do. The only alternative was unfiltered tap water that smelled and tasted of neat chlorine. The bottled water was marginally better.

"Let's practice what we preach," my friend suggested, taking a large bottle and cradling it in her arms.

"Great idea," I said, albeit a trifle doubtfully. I grabbed a bottle and did the same as we sat together and worked out the framework for the Reiki lesson.

I'm sure you've guessed, but to me a true miracle occurred. When we next tasted the water, it was fine — tasting clear, clean and ever-so-slightly sweet. I was immediately reminded of Jesus' first miracle when he turned the water into wine. Reiki healing energy really does work on the nano level of vibration to heal and transform.

I am certain that the bottled water we drank that day was healing as well as comforting.

This is not surprising, for it has been proved again and again that water has a memory. Water has always been worshipped for its cleansing, healing powers — consider the sacred springs that abound around this country. Combine that with Reiki energy and you have water that is wholing, nourishing mind, body and spirit.

So whatever you are about to drink, give it Reiki. You don't need to cradle it as we did. A hand over the top with a heart full of intention, is fine. Or you could wrap your Reiki hands around the mug or glass. Do this for others, too: particularly those who have come for healing.

Crystals and Other 'Inanimate' Objects.

Are crystals, rocks, stones, wood and other objects really inanimate? We know they are compacted energy, just like everything on this planet, don't we?

This was brought home to me very clearly when I was attending a dowsing conference. One of the speakers told how he had made a photographic lens that 'saw' through rocks. He showed us various photographs that he had taken with the lens. The one I remember best was a picture of a standing stone. *Through* it, you could see the line of the landscape behind. The stone itself looked solid, but in a way that I can only describe as shadowy. We all thought he must have cheated somehow— perhaps by amalgamating two photographs — but he promised he had not. As you can imagine, there was a rush to buy the lenses. I tried mine out the following day at East Kennet Barrow. A stone had been placed to seal the entrance. I couldn't resist taking a photograph of the solid stone. When I looked at the picture, the stone seemed almost transparent: behind it the entrance to the barrow was clearly (though mistily) visible.

Unfortunately, the phone 'died' on my way home and I could not recover the photograph. I felt that I had received a message: the lens was not for me. I put it away and some time later I gave the lens to my great-nephew in Australia who loves photography. I'm not sure whether he has used it yet.

Since then I have looked at such objects very differently. Sometimes I hear them whispering to me. Okay, I know they're not really whispering, just vibrating!

I love crystals: I have no doubt that they have a consciousness. For more about this, and their healing properties, take a look at the work of Dr Marcel Vogel. There are several YouTube videos of him, even though he died in 1991.

Let's go back to Reiki. Reiki has a particular affinity with crystals, but before you use them for healing you need to learn more about crystals than I can teach you in this workshop.

Use Reiki to clear crystals. Using your intention, hold Reiki in your mouth with the intention that your breath will clear the crystal. Then just breathe on it, turning it so that your breath has reached every part of it.

Use the same technique to programme a crystal for healing. And you can use it to charge the crystal with Reiki energy too.

Every man-made object has its own spirit or deva. Sometimes it is good to acknowledge the spirit of the object by giving it Reiki, or simply by thanking it. This includes every item in your house, workplace and car.

Because computers have a chip that is quartz crystal, they, too will delight in a Reiki blessing.

Before I move on from talking about crystals, I can't resist telling you a little story from my childhood. When I was two-and-a-half I lived with my parents in the Lebanon. My mother and I spent many hours on the beach there, mostly because I was so insistent. I couldn't bear to see the rocks dry in the sun when the tide went out. Somehow I just knew they wanted to be wet. My mother bought me a watering can and I would spend hours happily watering the rocks.

Laundry

I'M SURE YOU will think of many more uses for Reiki, but I think the best one I have heard is from a student of mine who decided to see if it would work on loosening stains in her laundry.

She told me it worked. Unfortunately, I haven't had much success myself. But that may be because my mind is too rigid. I can't see any other reason why it wouldn't work for me.

37

Closing

We are coming towards the end of this second day so while I nip out to the kitchen and make some tea, please think whether you have any questions, or whether there is anything that is not clear. Have a chat to each other. Take a comfort break. I'll be back shortly.

Tea and Cake

This is where I go and make a pot of tea, set out my best china cups and saucers and put an organic cake on a plate. Then I carry the whole lot into the room where I've been teaching and start serving it out.

"Okay, did you think of anything?"

I'll answer any questions and try to sort out any difficulties. I find that people are more relaxed while they're cradling a cup of tea, so the questions pop out easily.

The cake also serves another purpose. Sugar and sweet things ground people fast, so sharing a cake provides a quick and easy way to bring people back to normality after they have been 'high' on energy.

We have been working at a very high vibrational rate, which can make some people feel 'spacey'. But now it's almost time to go home. For those who are about to drive cars it is particularly important that they are grounded before they get behind the wheel, but this applies equally to those who are simply going home and back into their everyday lives.

Certificates, Manuals and Comments.

I hope I've answered all your questions … or at least, all those that you can think of at the moment.

Do remember that you can contact me if you have any queries or problems, can't recall something you feel you need to know, or just want a chat or some reassurance. I take my responsibilities as your Reiki Master very seriously.

It's time to celebrate your achievements. You have all done very well indeed and here I have the Certificates to prove it. I shall sit here and ask you to come up, one at a time, so that I can present you with yours ... and a manual, of course.

A word about the manuals: I suggest you read them through when you are at home tonight. They aren't very long, but they are packed with information. Read your manual again tomorrow, from start to finish. If you can read it once more within the first three days, you will remember all the information easily. After that, do leave your manual handy so that you can use it for reference.

While we're doing this, I'm going to hand round this *Happy Book*. It serves two purposes: the first is to keep the energy of this lovely group together. The other is to provide a record I can turn to if I ever need to redo your Certificate, or need to confirm the date on which I taught you Reiki. You may ask me to do one of these things if you do another Reiki course with a different teacher, or for the purposes of a professional organisation.

As well as putting down your name, address, email address and mobile phone number, I'd be very grateful if you could write a comment or two about this weekend. Thank you, it all helps me improve my teaching.

If you'd like to exchange details with anyone else here, now is a good time.

Closing circle

It's time to draw this lovely workshop to a close, so let's have our last Reiki circle for a while.

As we come together, turn your left hand palm upwards, and your right hand palm downwards, then place your right palm gently on the upturned left hand of your neighbour. In this way, all hands should be meeting palm to palm.

Gently close your eyes.

Make sure your shoulders are relaxed … your elbows are relaxed … your hands are soft and resting gently against those of your neighbour on each side. Your hips are relaxed … and your knees. Become very aware of your feet and your connection with the floor and through the floor, with the Earth below. Spread your toes and wriggle your feet against the floor.

Breathe in deeply and gently out, feeling centred in your body and connected with the earth.

Now, for the last time in this workshop, begin to allow energy to pass round the circle. Receive it with your left hand … imagine it passing up your left arm … through your heart centre in the middle of your chest … down your right arm … and out through your right palm. Watch the energy as it passes round the circle joining each of you at the heart centre. Thank each other, feeling your connection, and knowing that in some form this circle of souls will always exist.

Now we thank that all those who work for our highest good, on all levels of existence — including the Reiki Masters who have gone before, the ascended Masters, the angels, archangels, beings of light and Reiki guides — and who have been with us to help us on our Reiki journey.

We thank, too, the column of light that fills this room, coming up from the centre of the earth, through our circle and out into the universe.

We allow it now to rise up, up ... out into the universe ... and we ask that it showers down upon us so that we can each shine a little more brightly as we go about our everyday lives.

It is a great honour to be chosen to be your Reiki Master, so I thank you all for coming and lending your special energy to this workshop. I do hope that you have enjoyed it as much as I have and that you will always find Reiki to be a huge blessing in your life. Thank you.

Breathe in slowly... breathe out slowly. And again, breathe in slowly and breathe out ... gently, calmly, bring your consciousness back into the room.

And let us have another Reiki hug. As you place your arms around your neighbours let yourself relax into silence. And feel the connection, warmth and togetherness...

It's so hard to move away ... but there's one last thing we have to do:

Okey-Cokey

It's the okey-cokey..

Do you know it? It's easy. The words tell you what to do.
We stay in our circle and ...

You put your right arm in,
You take your right arm out,
In. Out. In. Out
And shake it all about.
You do the okey-cokey
and you turn around
and *(clapping)* that's what it's all about.
(Join hands and move into the middle raising hands)
Ooooh ... okey cokey, cokey
(Step back and swing hands down)

Ooooh … okey cokey, cokey
(move into the middle raising hands)
Ooooh … okey cokey, cokey
Knees bend
Arms raise
Clap, clap, clap.

You put your left arm in,
You take your left arm out,
In. Out. In. Out
And shake it all about.
You do the okey-cokey
and you turn around
and (*clapping*) that's what it's all about.
(Join hands and move into the middle raising hands)
Ooooh … okey cokey, cokey
(Step back and swing hands down)
Ooooh … okey cokey, cokey
(move into the middle raising hands)
Ooooh … okey cokey, cokey
Knees bend
Arms raise
Clap, clap, clap.

You put your right leg in,
you take your right leg out,
In. Out. In. Out
And shake it all about.
You do the okey-cokey
and you turn around
and (*clapping*) that's what it's all about.
(Join hands and move into the middle raising hands)
Ooooh … okey cokey, cokey
(Step back and swing hands down)

Ooooh … okey cokey, cokey
(move into the middle raising hands)
Ooooh … okey cokey, cokey
Knees bend
Arms raise
Clap, clap, clap.

You put your left leg in,
you take your left leg out,
In. Out. In. Out
And shake it all about.
You do the okey-cokey
and you turn around
and (*clapping*) that's what it's all about.
(*Join hands and move into the middle raising hands)*
Ooooh … okey cokey, cokey
(Step back and swing hands down)
Ooooh … okey cokey, cokey
(move into the middle raising hands)
Ooooh … okey cokey, cokey
Knees bend
Arms raise
Clap, clap, clap.

You put your whole self in,
you take your whole self out,
In. Out. In. Out
And shake it all about.
You do the okey-cokey
and you turn around
and (*clapping*) that's what it's all about.
(*Join hands and move into the middle raising hands)*
Ooooh … okey cokey, cokey
(Step back and swing hands down)

Ooooh … okey cokey, cokey
(move into the middle raising hands)
Ooooh … okey cokey, cokey
Knees bend
Arms raise
Clap, clap, clap.

Well that certainly raised the energy again. Look at yourselves, laughing. It's good to leave on a high note....

Thank you very much indeed for making this time together so memorable and enjoyable. I've loved every moment.

Drive carefully tonight. Drink lots of water over the next couple of days. Take great care of yourselves, and sleep well.

Thank you.

APPENDIX OF MEDITATIONS

The Spiritual Mountain

Gently close your eyes. Make sure you are comfortable. Wriggle around a little, if you need to, or have a stretch. Become aware of where you are sitting. Feel the floor beneath your feet ... feel your sitting bones on the chair. Let your shoulders be relaxed and in line with your hips. Feel a silver thread running from the top of your head up into the clouds and adjust your position until your nose is in line with your umbilicus. Take your awareness to your body ...

Now, breathe out ... all your breath. And take a long slow breath in ... expanding your ribs and softening your tummy. Great. Let the breath escape though your mouth and feel yourself relaxing and letting go of all that you do not need right at this moment. Breathe in through your nose, softly, silently ... and out through your mouth, softly, silently ....

...And now you find yourself walking through a summer meadow ... the temperature is just right, the surroundings are perfect ...

Become aware of the sun shining down on you from a clear blue sky ... the warmth is pleasant and comfortable. A light breeze ruffles your hair. You feel the wild flowers and grasses against your legs, the softness of the earth beneath your feet...

You are walking through a beautiful valley. On either side a gentle hill rises, topped with trees. Look at all the wild flowers which carpet the meadow, see their individual beauty and feel their transience. Beside you a small stream is gurgling along the valley ... you stop for a moment to gaze into the water and watch the fish ... the sound of the water fills your ears. As you listen, you hear the sweet sound of birdsong all around.

The air is so fresh and sweet that you can taste it on your

lips and the scents of flowers, trees and water fill your nostrils …

As you become aware of these things your intuition tells you that there is something in front that you can't quite see, but which feels as though it is important. Something is calling to you on the inner, subconscious plane. You hasten your steps and a mountain comes into view. This mountain is calling you and you know that it is a spiritual mountain and that you have to climb to the very top if you are to follow your own spiritual Reiki path.

Now you are walking even faster, up the gentle lower slopes as if you were wearing seven league boots. The way becomes steeper and your steps grow shorter. You are feeling the weight of all that you are carrying … although you were unaware that you were carrying anything. You slow … and slow some more as the foothills become steeper and the way narrows.

You wonder again … why do you feel so heavy? It's as if you were walking through treacle. Most of the weight seems to be on your shoulders and back, so you feel around with your hands and discover that you are carrying a number of burdens, some are smaller than others, but all of them are heavy.

Well, you think, I don't need to carry all this up the mountain. It can't be important because I didn't know it was there, and anyway, I can pick it up when I retrace my steps.

So you reach up and take off the biggest and heaviest of the bags you are carrying. It's so heavy you almost drop it, but you manage to put it down carefully. You see that it is labelled 'physical burdens'. This puzzles you, so you take a peek inside to see what's there … and you realise that you need none of the things that it contains, so you leave it there by the side of the path.

Ah. That's better. Now you feel so much lighter that you

can walk faster and much more easily. You love the feel of the lightness in your step and the bounciness as you walk...

But soon the path becomes steeper and before you is a very narrow defile through which the path passes. You know you are still carrying too much, that it all makes you too wide to fit through the narrow passage, so you feel around behind you for the heaviest of the packages that you are still carrying and find a big squishy bundle. As you touch it, the handle gives way and the bag falls to the ground and ... out of it spills all sorts of emotional problems, some recent, some you remember and some that come from so long ago that you cannot remember why you were ever attached to them.

You examine the label but you aren't at all surprised to discover that this bundle was labelled 'emotional problems'. You are only too glad to leave them beside the track, but one or two emotions call to you. It is very hard to leave them there and continue on your way, but you know you can collect them on your way down.

Now it is as though you have taken off a fat suit. You feel so clear and slim, that it is easy to run through the defile without touching the rocks on either side. You feel a huge sense of freedom and release and continue to climb with renewed vigour.

Up and up you climb but gradually the going becomes more difficult. You are really climbing now, scrabbling for handholds and footholds ... They become more difficult to find and hauling yourself up the slope is becoming difficult again. If only you were lighter, slimmer, you could climb so much more easily.

You check your shoulders and back and are amazed to find that you still have another bundle. This one is more difficult to locate. It is as though it moves every time you put a hand on it.... Why, it's almost alive. Eventually you grab it and lift it off. Despite being much smaller than the other bundles, this one is even heavier than they were. What can be in there? You wonder and then you see the label 'mental constructs and beliefs'. No wonder it was so difficult to lay a hand on … thoughts are always so ephemeral, so impossible to pin down. But now you realise that you have no need of these beliefs, thoughts and concepts. You are climbing a spiritual mountain and they have no place here. So you leave them by the side of the path knowing you can pick them up again on the way down, if there are any that still serve you after your journey.

Oh, but it was difficult to leave all your beliefs and thoughts behind … and yet, now you are streaking up the mountain hand over hand. The summit is in sight … there is just one bump ahead.

You round the bump … and are faced with a sheer rock wall. There are no handholds, no crevices, no footholds … just a sheer rock face. What can you do? How can you get to the summit?

Then you remember that you still have one small but very heavy parcel pressing down on you from somewhere … your head? … your neck? It doesn't matter .. . You don't need it. So you pull it off, little and heavy as it is … as heavy as lead, indeed. And it lands with a plop at your feet, like a small, laughing cartoon animal. You lean over to read the label and you see the words 'spiritual difficulties' before it scurries away.

As it does so, the smooth rock face in front of you suddenly moves, turns, and an amethyst staircase is revealed. You walk up it and find two beings waiting for you at the top. These are your Reiki guides and they may, or may not, be in human guise. They may have a form of some kind, or they may be simply a presence or a light.

They welcome you and praise you for finding the way to the top of your personal spiritual mountain. They take you to the very summit and show you your life spread out in the beautiful landscape below. You see the patches of light and shade, of sorrow and of gladness and you see that your future is hidden behind a mist. Your guides tell you that you are in charge of your own destiny, your own future. You have free will. But from this height you can look down and see that you can choose an easy path or one fraught with difficulties. You can see where you were heading and where you would like to go.

If you have any questions you can ask them of your Reiki guides now… or maybe they have a message for you … listen.

Now they tell you that it's time to go … but they have a gift for you. Take your gift and open it. If you need to ask anything about it, now is the time …

Holding in your heart all that you have experienced, all that you have heard, and all that has been revealed to you, you thank your guides. And they give you a blessing … they remind you that, if at any time you feel unsure, uncertain, or uncomfortable they are there to support you and will always be available to you.

Then you say goodbye …

It is time to come down from the spiritual mountain. You can do this in any way you choose … maybe you float off the top and land like thistledown at the foot of the mountain, maybe you run down, maybe you find a big balloon waiting to carry you gently down.

Now you find yourself back in the lovely valley, walking through a summer meadow, back the way you have come … until you find yourself walking back into this room … you become aware of where you are, sitting in the chair. Again you take your attention back to your breath, feeling yourself softly breathing in and out.

Wiggle your fingers and toes … have a good stretch and when you are ready … and only when you are ready … gently open your eyes and come back into the room.

By the Ocean

Gently close your eyes. Become aware of where you are sitting. Feel the floor beneath your feet … feel your sitting bones on the chair. Let your shoulders be relaxed and in line with your hips. Feel a silver thread running from the top of your head up into the clouds and adjust your position until your nose is in line with your umbilicus. Take your awareness to your body.

Now, breathe out … all your breath. And take a long slow breath in … expanding your ribs and softening your tummy. Great. Let the breath escape though your mouth and feel yourself relaxing and letting go of all that you do not need right at this moment. Breathe in through your nose, softly, silently … and out through your mouth, softly, silently.

And now you find yourself walking along a beautiful, deserted beach … the temperature is perfect, neither too warm nor too cold … the sand beneath your feet is firm but soft … the sky is the blue of high summer … and beneath the green trees that come down to the edge of the sand … wild flowers bloom … their fragrance is borne to you on a fragrant breeze.

The breeze ruffles your hair … you feel the sun on your face, your arms, your legs … the clothes on your body.

Gentle waves wash against the shore … you walk at the edge of the sea … feel the water caressing your feet.

You become aware of the salt smell of the sea combined with the fragrance of wild flowers and the green scent of the trees at the edge of the beach.

Taste the freshness of the air and the slightly dry salt on your lips.

A seagull swoops away over the sea, giving a sense of freedom and you hear its inimitable cry … let the swish of the waves against the shore fill your ears and lull you … feel the smile on your lips.

As you look around, you take in the perfect harmony of the scene, the blue sky reflected in the smooth water … the golden-white sand of the beach … the contrasting darkness of the trees behind.

The peacefulness of this beach … the comfortable aloneness … allows you to reflect, without effort, on the interconnectedness of all things … you and the beach are one … you and nature are one.

Now you turn to face the water and are seized with a great desire to feel its freshness all over your body. You strip off any clothes you may be wearing, and leave them above the water line … Now you walk, skip or run into the sea … you can bask in the shallows … go a little deeper … or dive in for a long swim.

Take some time to play in the water. Maybe fishes nibble at your toes … or a dolphin comes to take you for a ride … or a seagull lands on the water, bobbing up and down just out of reach, as though to tease you …

Then take a little time to luxuriate in the feeling of the water … its freshness … its coolness … its saltiness … its exhilarating quality … its cleanliness. Allow your body to float, feeling the gentle waves uplifting you, feeling the water's support.

Be aware that the water is cleansing you of anything you no longer need, on all levels … spiritual, mental, emotional … particularly emotional … and physical. Feel how there is no gap between you and the water, it embraces you completely.

Accept its support, and allow all troubles or pain to disperse into the sea. Let the water take all negativity from you … Feel how all the sea creatures rejoice in all that you give them … let the sea cleanse and transform you.

As you feel your troubles and pain float away, you give grateful thanks to the water … you call down a blessing on the water that brings life to the Earth … to the sea that encompasses such a great proportion of the life force on this planet … for giving us the food that we eat … that nourishes our body … We give thanks to the sea and all it contains …

Now it's time to leave the water … You allow yourself to float towards the shore and as you find your feet, you notice how refreshed, invigorated … clear and clean you feel … you are washed clean of all the mental constructs and belief systems that limit your amazing creativity…

Smiling, you walk up the beach to where you left your clothes … and … they are gone. In their place lies a huge fluffy white towel. Pick it up and dry yourself … perhaps you give yourself a brisk rub, perhaps you dab gently at the places where water still lurks, or maybe you spread it out on the sand and lie on it so that the sun can dry and energise you.

When you are dry, you see that your old clothes have been replaced by shining new white garments perfectly designed for you. You put them on …if you wish … or you may prefer to stay naked…

Whichever you choose, you give thanks again for the feeling of purity which encompasses you and start to walk back along the beach the way that you came…

As you go, you notice again the smells, the tastes, the sounds, the sights and the feelings all around you … You acknowledge that you are part of Nature …and you realise that all that you do or think or feel emotionally has an effect on All-That-Is.

You are unique, you are special … you are you.

Bring this knowledge with you as you walk back the way you have come … until you find yourself walking back into this room … you become aware of where you are, sitting in the chair. Again you take your attention back to your breath, feeling yourself softly breathing in and out.

Wiggle your fingers and toes … have a good stretch and

when you are ready ... and only when you are ready ... gently open your eyes and come back into the room.

Native American

Gently close your eyes. Make sure you are comfortable. Wriggle around a little, if you need to, or have a stretch. Become aware of where you are sitting. Feel the floor beneath your feet … feel your sitting bones on the chair. Let your shoulders be relaxed and in line with your hips. Feel a silver thread running from the top of your head up into the clouds and adjust your position until your nose is in line with your umbilicus. Take your awareness to your body …

Now, breathe out … all your breath. And take a long slow breath in … expanding your ribs and softening your tummy. Great. Let the breath escape though your mouth and feel yourself relaxing and letting go of all that you do not need right at this moment. Breathe in through your nose, softly, silently … and out through your mouth, softly, silently ….

Let the music thrum into your bones … you are lying on the floor, covered by skins … feel yourself awake … as you stretch out your limbs, you pull yourself back from your dreams. And remember who you are … a Native American brave.

Open your eyes and take in your surroundings … your teepee, anyone else asleep near you, see the things you see everyday when you wake and look around … your clothes, your bow … the domestic clutter for hunting, skinning, cooking.

Everyone else is asleep. Silently, you rise and take your clothes with you as you softly open the tent flap and venture outside into the early morning.

You stretch your arms and legs, feeling the strength in the muscles and sinews, feeling the muscles flexing along your back as you stretch backwards and then forwards. You joy in your strength, your flexibility and the beautiful harmony of your body. You say a small prayer of thanks to the Great Spirit, as you look around you, surveying the beautiful scenery.

Your teepee is on the edge of the small temporary settlement, on one grassy slope of a small valley, overlooking virgin forest which rises on the other slope, straight ahead of you. As you watch, the sun blinks at you from between the branches.

You smile with pleasure and anticipation, feeling the joy of being alive bubbling in your chest as you set off down the slope, towards the forest, feeling the soft dampness of the grass beneath your bare feet.

As you come to the tree line, you bow your head, asking for permission to enter the forest. You hear a sign of assent from the trees ... you smile and leave a few threads of tobacco as an offering.

Then you enter the forest. All around you is dark and warm, you see the sun glistening through the leaves high above your head, and note the differing colours of green and brown around you. The forest is your friend. You walk softly upon the earth so that you leave no mark of your passing, but you feel the coolness around you, the differing nature of the trees and their individual energy. You see the undergrowth, green and shining where a gap in the canopy lets in a shaft of sunlight.

You listen to the sounds of the forest, the scurry of an animal, the call of birds, the movement of the treetops in a gentle breeze.

Your nose picks up fragrance of the forest, the green smell of leaves and the musky smell of decay, overlaid with the scent of the other occupants of the forest, small and large. You taste the freshness on your lips, feel the air, cool and fresh, as you breathe it deeply into your lungs.

Your intuition, your inner knowing, acknowledges the forest being into which you are treading. You feel the life-force all around you, nourishing and nurturing your own.

As you walk, you hear the sound of water, and see a place where the trees are thinning and the sun is shining into the darkness. The sound grows louder as the trees thin, and soon you walk out into a clearing.

A stream runs through the clearing … its clear water chuckling and gurgling over its rocky bed. You notice the sound of rushing water and looking upstream you see a waterfall gushing into a wide shallow pool.

You walk towards the pool, taking off your garments as you go, and dive straight in. As you surface, you shake the water from your long hair and watch the sun glinting on the drops. Your body tingles from the cold, clear water and you laugh again with pure delight, the joy of being alive.

Now you move to stand under the waterfall and feel it washing all the sleep and all the toxicity from your body. You feel alive, clear of mind and clean of body.

Stay and play in the water for a while. Do whatever comes naturally. This is your moment to strip yourself naked and feel the coldness of the water as it cleanses you of all you no longer need.

When you are ready, you step out of the pool, and lie on the rocks to dry in the heat of the sun. Feel how clear, how young, refreshed and comfortable you are. Rejoice in your strength, and youth.

… Now you see from the sun that it is time to go back to the village. The cooking fires are lit and breakfast will be cooking. Suddenly you feel ravenous.

You take a few more strands of tobacco from your pouch and leave an offering to the spirit of the waterfall before you collect your clothes and leap up from the rock.

You enter the forest again, walking back the way you came, taking care that there is no sign of your passage through the forest. All your senses are alive as you acknowledge all that you can see, hear, touch, smell and taste

... all those other animals and living beings that share your awareness of all that the forest means and supplies.

Now the trees begin to thin, and soon you can see the open clearing and the circle of your tribe's teepees. You call down a blessing on the whole of Nature as you step out of the forest ... and walk back up the slope towards the village.

Slowly retrace your steps ....until you find yourself walking back into this room.

Now you become aware of where you are, sitting in the chair. Again you take your attention back to your breath, feeling yourself softly breathing in and out.

Wiggle your fingers and toes ... have a good stretch and when you are ready ... and only when you are ready ... gently open your eyes and come back into the room.

Angel Journey

Gently close your eyes. Become aware of where you are sitting. Feel the floor beneath your feet … feel your sitting bones on the chair. Let your shoulders be relaxed and in line with your hips. Feel a silver thread running from the top of your head up into the clouds and adjust your position until your nose is in line with your umbilicus. Take your awareness to your body …

Now, breathe out … all your breath. And take a long slow breath in … expanding your ribs and softening your tummy. Great. Let the breath escape though your mouth and feel yourself relaxing and letting go of all that you do not need right at this moment. Breathe in through your nose, softly, silently … and out through your mouth, softly, silently.

Take your awareness now to where your body touches the chair. Feel yourself becoming lighter … and lighter … until you are as light as an angel's feather, as light as thistledown.

A white fluffy cloud drifts down towards you from a blue, blue heaven. You are so light that it simply floats beneath you and raises you up, slowly and gently. Feel the comfort of being so light, so weightless. Enjoy the sensation as the cloud rises slowly up into the sky … you feel as soft and comfortable as if you were wrapped in a silken shawl. As you wonder at the purity and beauty of your surroundings, you feel yourself embraced, ever so gently, ever so kindly. As if you were being carried on the wings of an angel.

As you look upwards you see a beautiful countenance of light. You note that it wears a beautiful smile and you hear words that aren't words. The knowledge comes to you in your heart. Your guardian angel is enveloping you.

You ask where you are going … and your angel gently hushes you. You do not need to know. This is a time for experiencing, not for knowing. As she speaks, you feel yourself smiling, you have not a care in the world, your brain is too peaceful to think. The whole sensation is so wonderful, so warm, so kind, so exquisite that you only want to bask in it.

For a while you drift there in the warm light of heavenly blue sky, held in your angel's bosom.

Your angel communicates that whenever you want a rest from the busy-ness of the world, you only have to ask. She will be there to raise you up as soon as you have that desire. You may rest in her for as long as you wish.

But right now she is taking you to meet some powerful beings. This will open your eyes to the magnificence of All-That-Is, and to the magnificent being that you also are.

Now you feel the cloud that is your angel's wings slowly descending. Below you a range of mountains lift their peaks towards the heavens. You hear a thunderous sound as lightning flashes from the mountaintop. But you are still held, warm and safe in your angel's arms.

Don't be afraid, she says, *it is just the voice of the Mountain. Feel the power of his spirit.*

Mountain says: *I am your strength.* And you feel its strength within you.

Next you fly over the ocean. You watch as huge black waves rise and fall. A tempest rises and churns up the water even more. The sound of the waves crashing and the howling of the wind make you tremble a little.

Don't be afraid, your angel says, *it is just the voice of the Ocean. See how changeable she is.*

Now you drift over the peace of a calm sea, small wavelets caressing the shore.

Ocean says: *I am your flexibility.* And you rejoice within to feel the elasticity of your body, your mind and your spirit. All, all are flexible and changeable.

You drift on … the cloud slowly descends until you see you are high, high above a vast and beautiful jungle forest.

Even here, you can feel the change in the air, its vivacity and cleanliness. You would like to go down and touch the branches, but some innate vulnerability makes you hesitate. And then you suddenly hear it, the sound of tropical rain pounding on the trees beneath and the sound of the forest leaves laughing

Don't be afraid, your angel says, *it is just the voice of the Forest. Feel the vibrant aliveness of his spirit.*

Forest says: *I am your Aliveness.* And you feel at once the tingling joy of being alive, as you breathe in the wonderful, cool, clean air of the forest and it fills every cell of your body.

You would like to stay here, just to rejoice in these feelings, but your angel is carrying you on, on. You rest back in her arms and allow yourself to be transported.

Now you are borne over a huge desert. Below you trace the lines of rocky dry mountains and endless wastes of beige desert sand. Now you see a wind has arisen. It swirls and howls, drawing the sand up from the desert floor as if to consume it. Sand is flying, swirling around you. Then the wind lets it drop… because the wind is moving …ever onwards … churning sand before it. You hear the dry sound of the desert wind.

Don't be afraid, your angel says, *it is just the voice of the Desert. Feel the freedom of her spirit.*

Desert says: *I am your freedom.* And you feel within the sudden exhilaration of spontaneity. You are free. You are the author of the whole of your life. You can write the story any way you wish.

Exactly, says your angel. Now tell me, what have you learned?

But you cannot answer for what you have experienced is too deep to be expressed in words. So you open your heart and show:

That from the mountain you have discovered your power;

That from the ocean you have discovered your flexibility;

That from the forest you have discovered your aliveness;

And that from the desert you have discovered your freedom;

Ah, that is good, says your angel. But there is one more thing to learn and that is the greatest of all.

Now she slowly drifts down, down, down, until you find yourself lying not on a cloud, but on soft green grass. Beneath you, you feel the solid Earth. You put your ear to the ground and hear the drum, drum, drum of the Mother's heartbeat.

All around you, down here, where you are lying on the Earth, you see life ... insects ... animals ... plants ... and hovering all around them you are aware of their little live spirits. Small and joyful, the spirits smile at you. They beckon, and in come the Nature Spirits ...fairies and elves, brownies and pixies, ...and the Elementals ... the salamanders of fire, the undines of water, the sylphs of air, and the gnomes of the earth.

Are you listening, asks your angel, *Can you hear the language of love?*

And the Earth, and the Spirits of all living things, the Nature Spirits and the Elementals all start to sing a beautiful song. You feel it warm in your heart, the essence of all Life ... LOVE.

Yes, says your angel. *LOVE is all. In it is power, flexibility, aliveness and freedom. But none of these can exist without LOVE.*

You take these words to your heart.

Seeing this, your angel smiles. She strokes your hair and moves away.

Remember, I am here whenever you need me, she says. *But now it is time for you to return to your life.*

As she says this she floats upwards. You watch as she dissolves into the ether.

And then you begin to come back from your journey ... to slip back into this room.

Now you become aware of where you are, sitting in the chair. Again you take your attention back to your breath, feeling yourself softly breathing in and out.

Wiggle your fingers and toes ... have a good stretch and when you are ready ... and only when you are ready ... gently open your eyes and come back into the room.

ILLUSTRATIONS

SELF HEALING

The following Hand positions are a guide.

If you use these you will cover all the main chakras and give yourself a wonderful Reiki treatment.

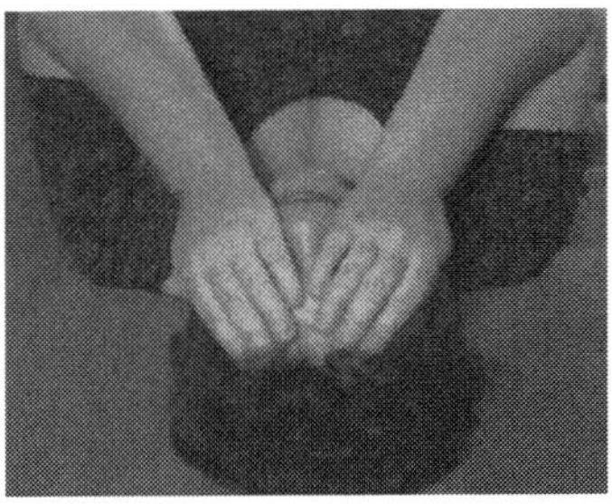

1. Brow

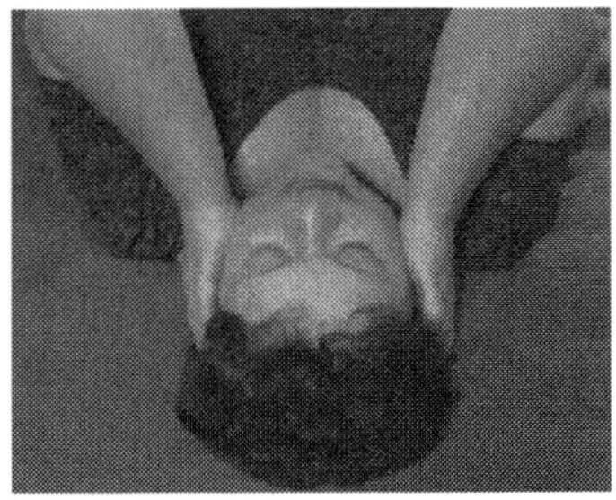

2. Ears

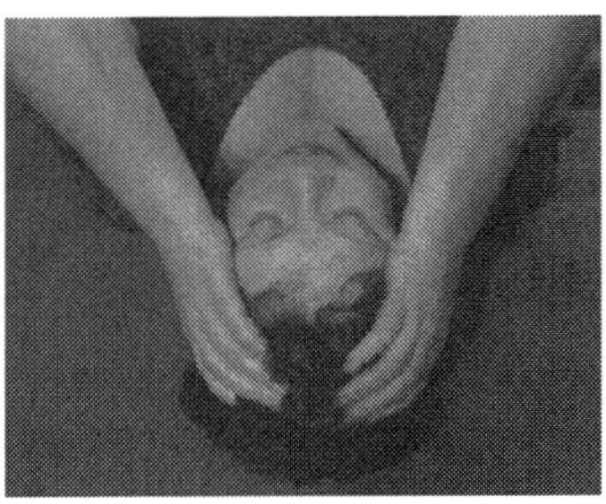

3. Temples

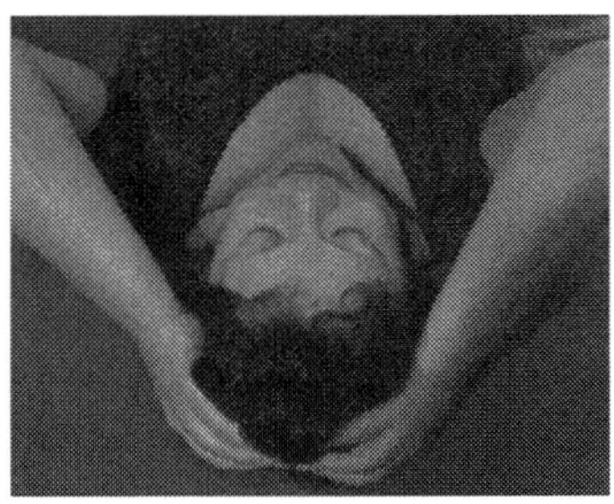

4. Crown

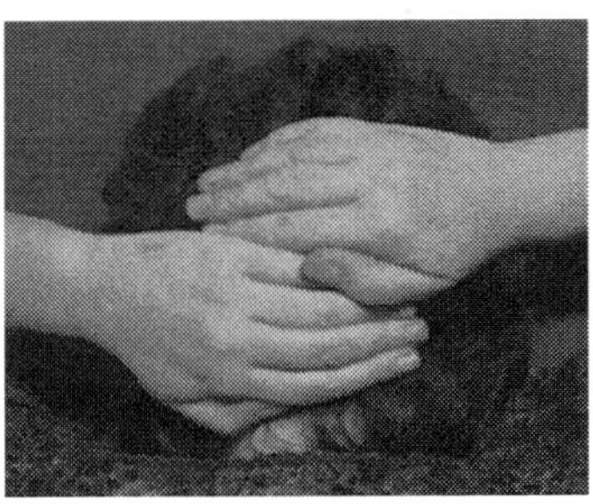

5. Base of Skull

6. Throat

SELF HEALING: 2

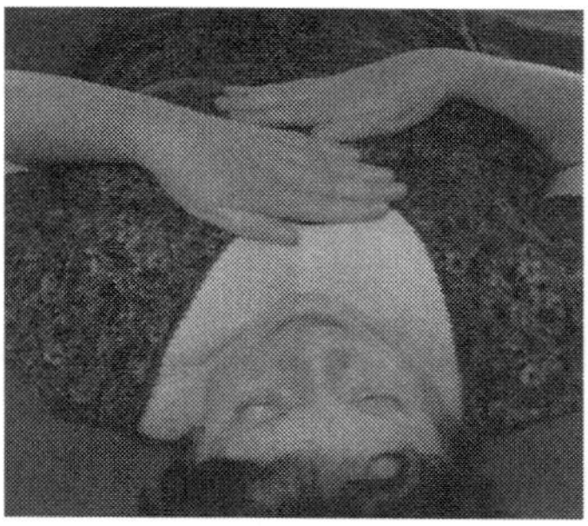

6. Heart

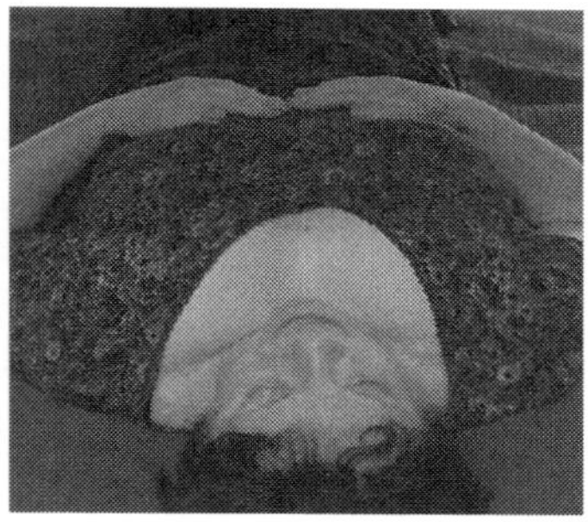

8. Solar Plexus

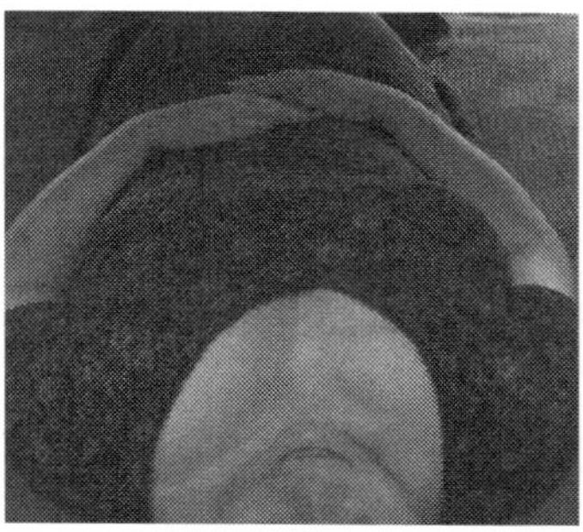

9. Hara Chakra

10. Base Chakra

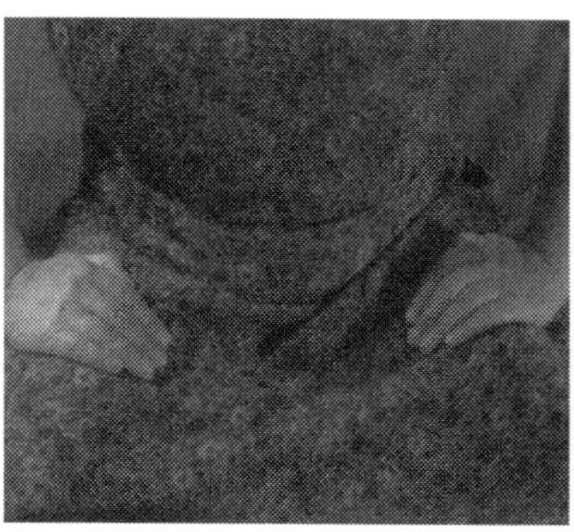

11. Thighs

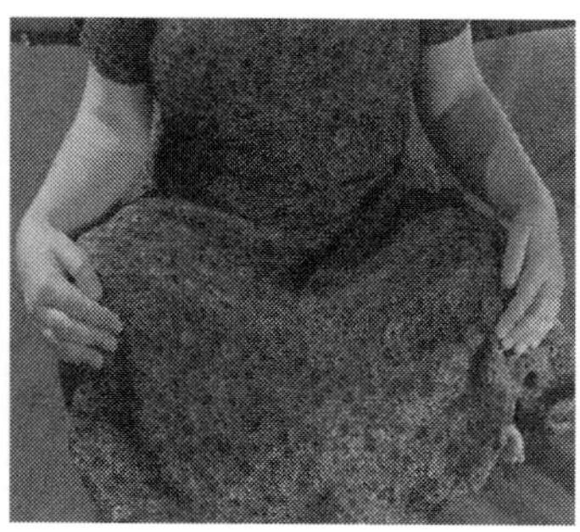

12. Knees

SELF HEALING: 3

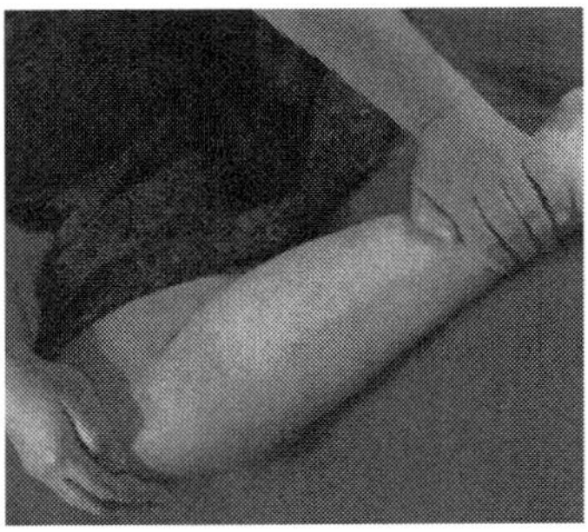

13. Knee/ankle

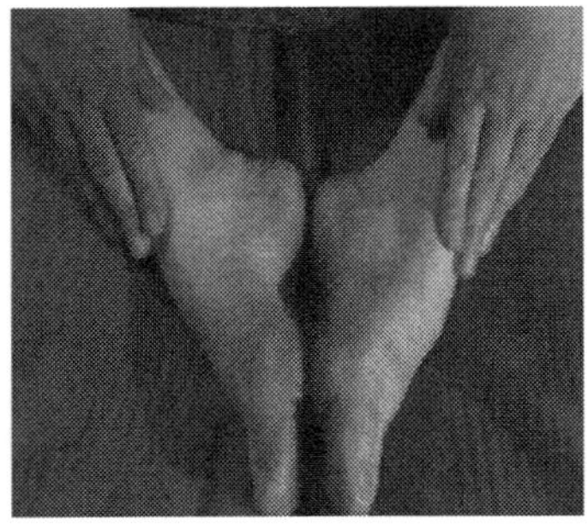

14. Both ankles

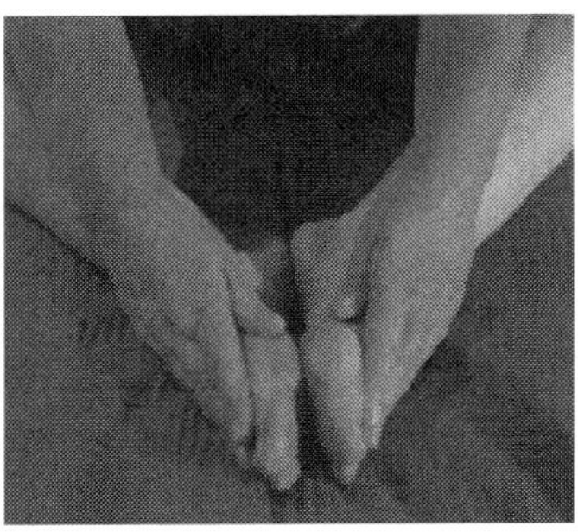

15. Tops of feet

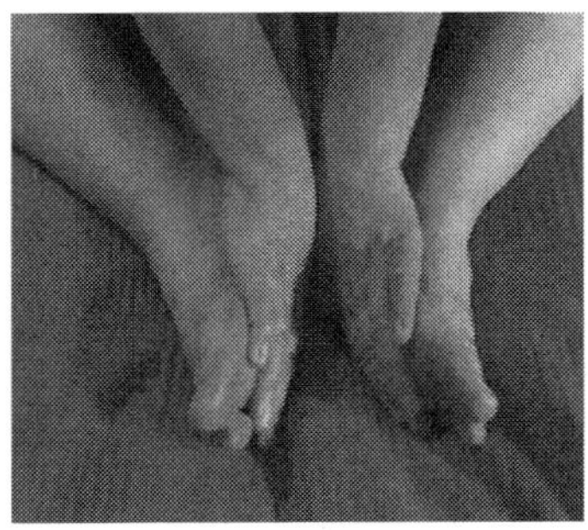

16. Soles of feet

HOW TO USE THE HAND POSITIONS FOR **HEALING OTHERS**

Once again, the following hand positions are a guide only. If you use these positions you will cover all the main chakras and give another person a wonderful Reiki treatment.

Remember to ensure that **you** are comfortable and adapt the positions to suit you. Because the recipient will pick up any discomfort that you feel.

With this in mind, I have included positions 12, 13 and 14 which enable you to work from one side of the couch. If you use these positions, it is unnecessary to use the other thigh and knee positions, although I do recommend that you also treat both ankles as shown in photo 15.

You can adapt these positions to work on the back of the legs as indicated in back position 9.

Notes:

- ✓ Keep your hands soft and light, as if you were cradling a baby bird. Do not press or lean on your client.
- ✓ Ensure your fingers and thumbs are together, as if you were wearing socks on your hands.
- ✓ If you are uncomfortable, gently remove your hands and have a shake, stretch, dance (or all three) before you gently replace them. Your client will probably not even notice.
- ✓ Try not to move, stretch or shake unless you remove your hands or your client will notice and will not feel so relaxed.
- ✓ Make sure that the hand nearest the feet is the one that crosses the body. The Reiki energy will flow more easily.
- ✓ Allow yourself to be guided by your intuition as to how long you stay in each position.
- ✓ Above all relax and enjoy: even if you forget all of the above your client will be happy and relaxed.

HEALING OTHERS — FRONT: 1

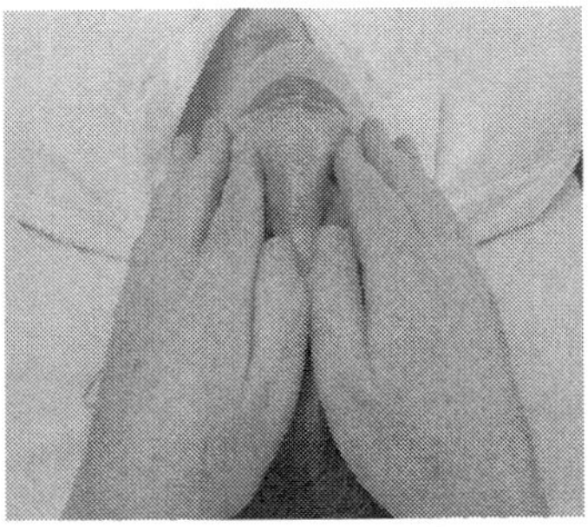

1. Eyes

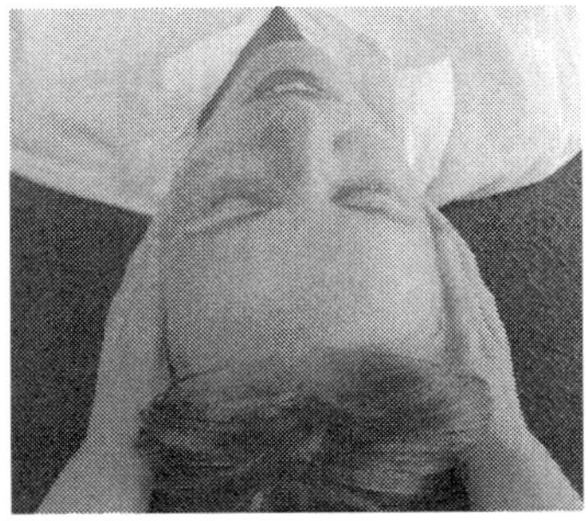

2. Ears

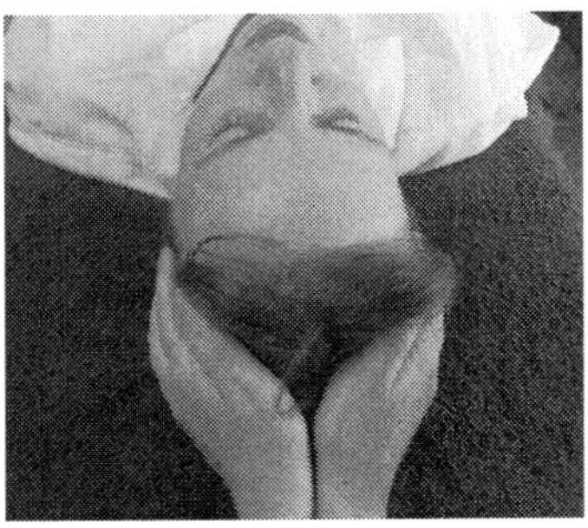

3. Crown

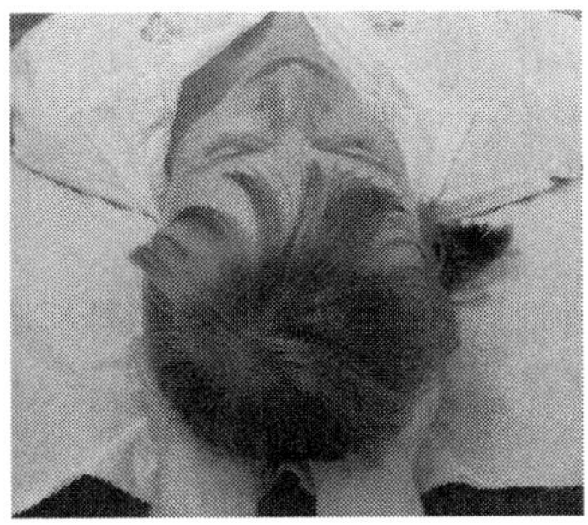

4. Occiput

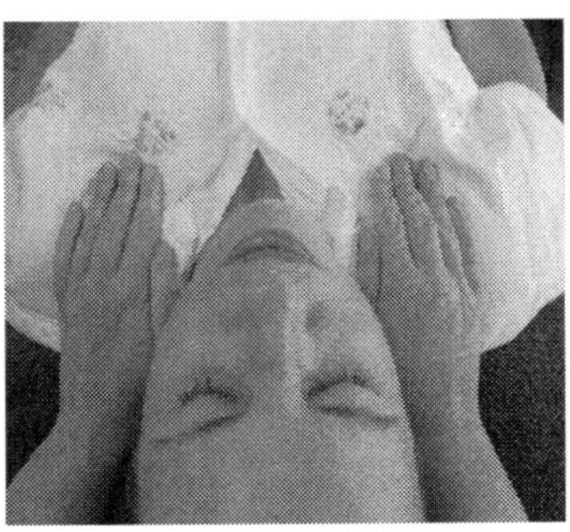

5. Throat

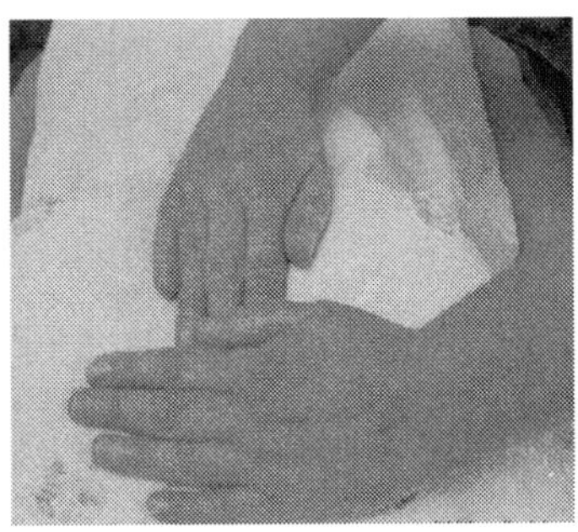

6. Heart

HEALING OTHERS — FRONT: 2

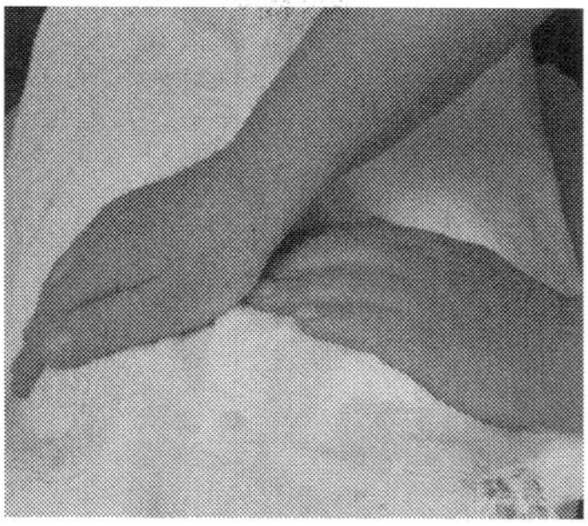

7. Solar Plexus

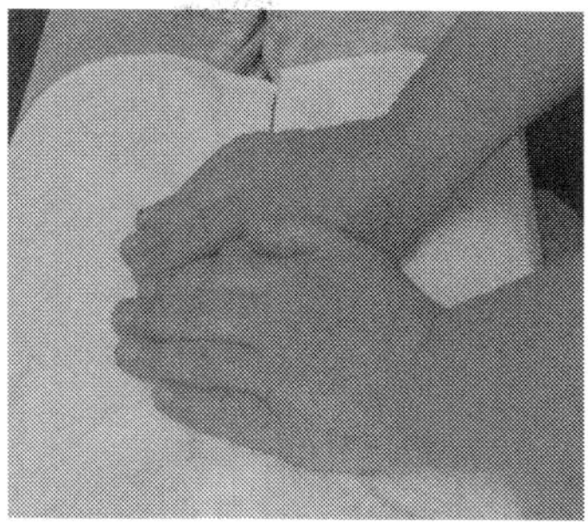

8. Hara

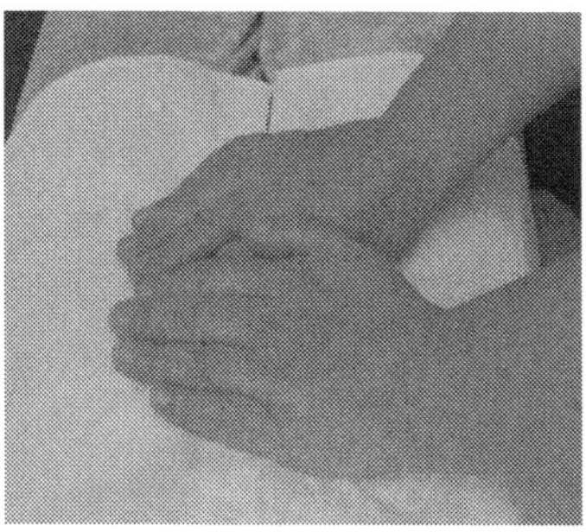

9. Base

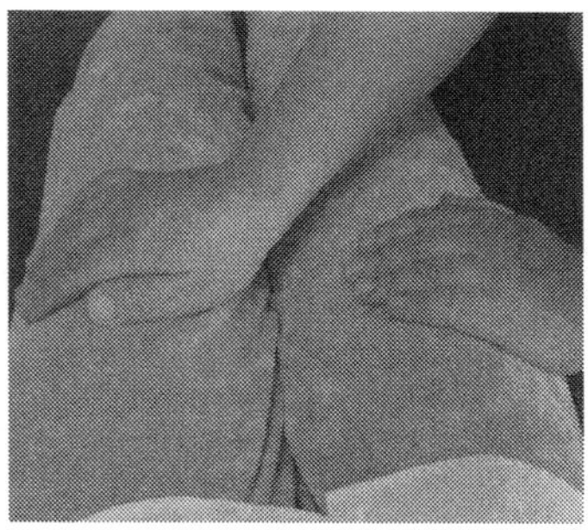

10. Thighs

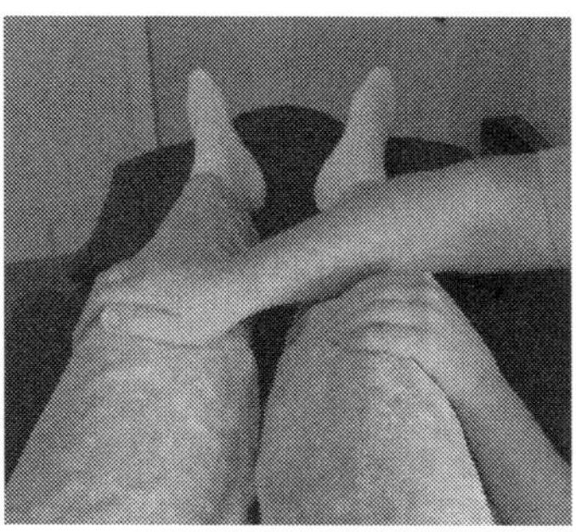

11. Knees

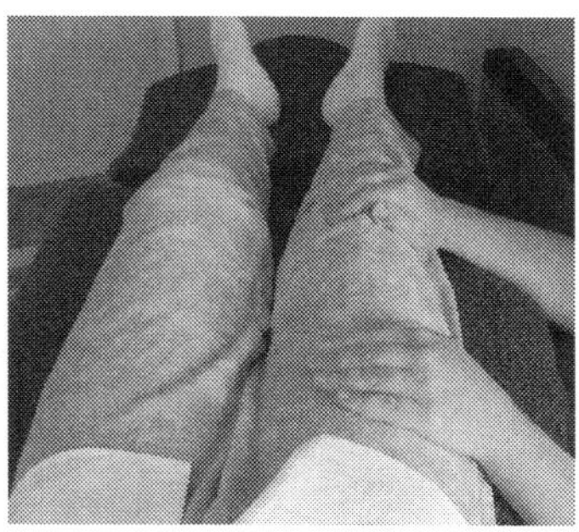

12. Thigh and Knee
(repeat other side)

HEALING OTHERS — FRONT: 3

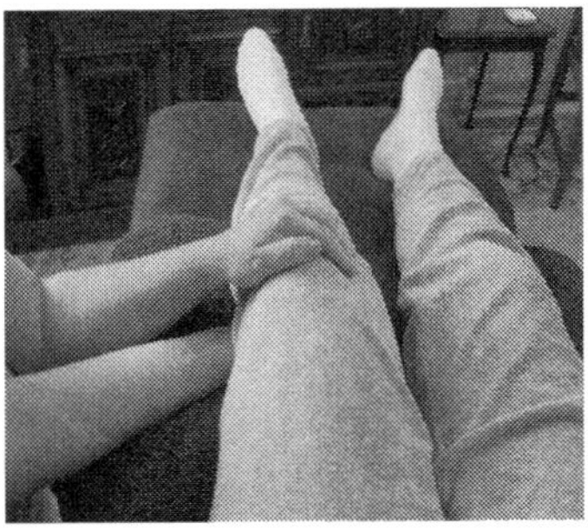

13. Knee Sandwich

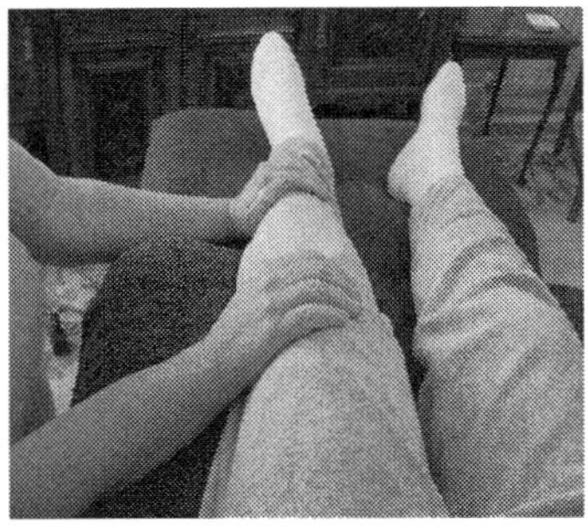

14. Knee and Ankle
(repeat other side)

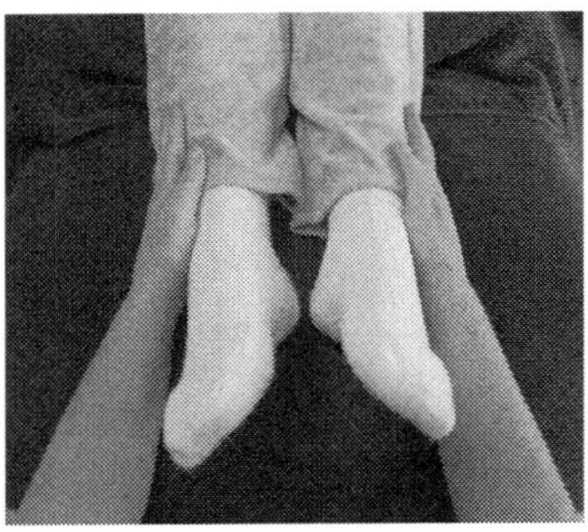

15. Ankles

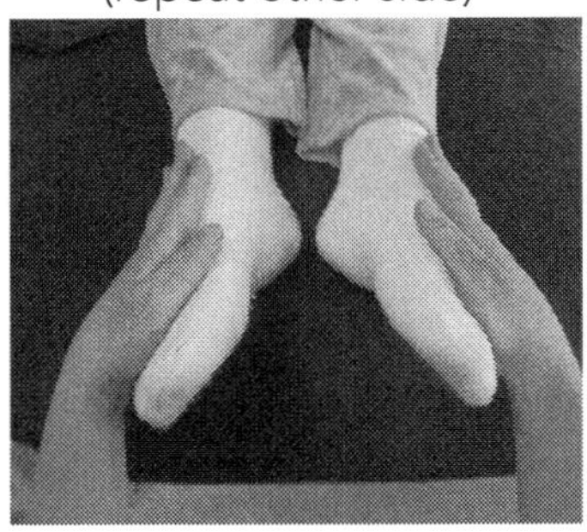

16. Tops of feet

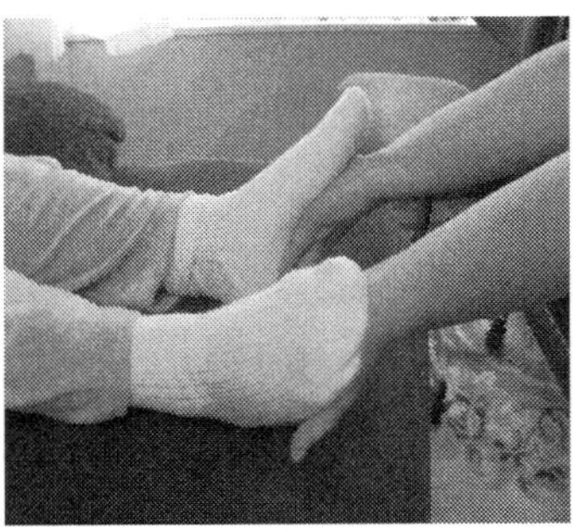

17. Soles of feet

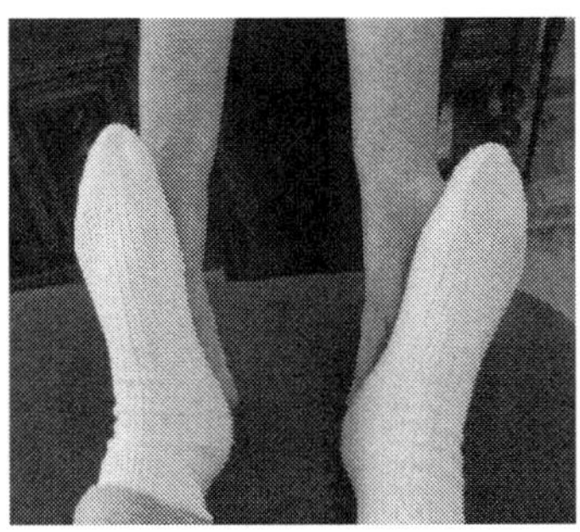

18. Soles of feet
(same position, another view)

HEALING OTHERS — BACK: 1

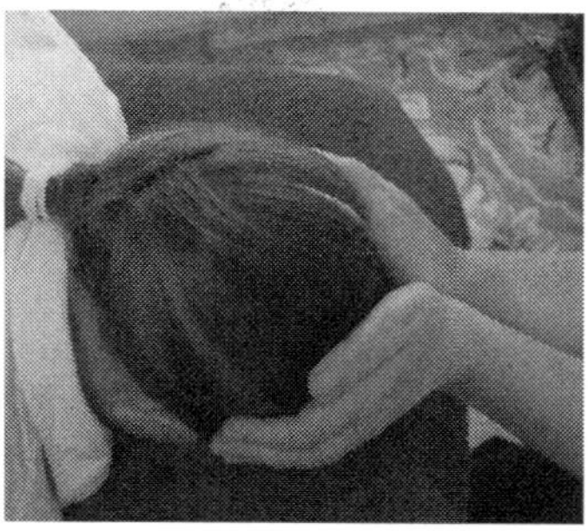

1. Crown

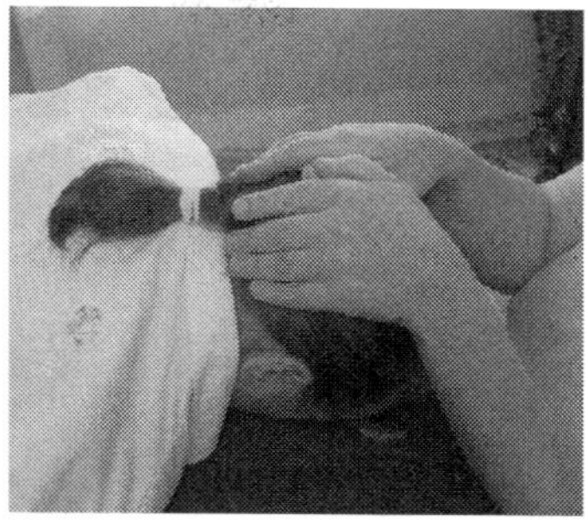

2. Occiput

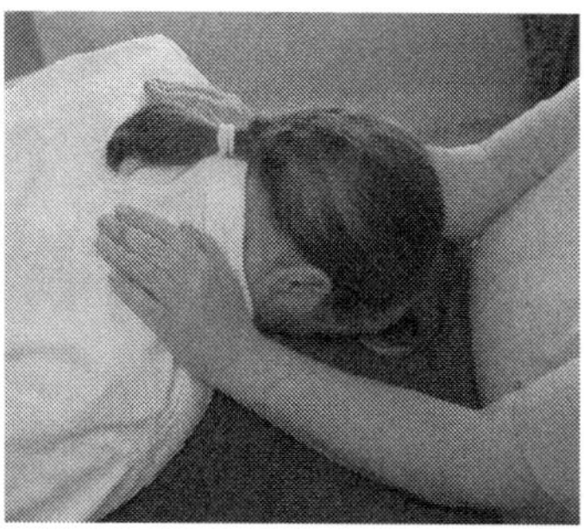

3. Throat

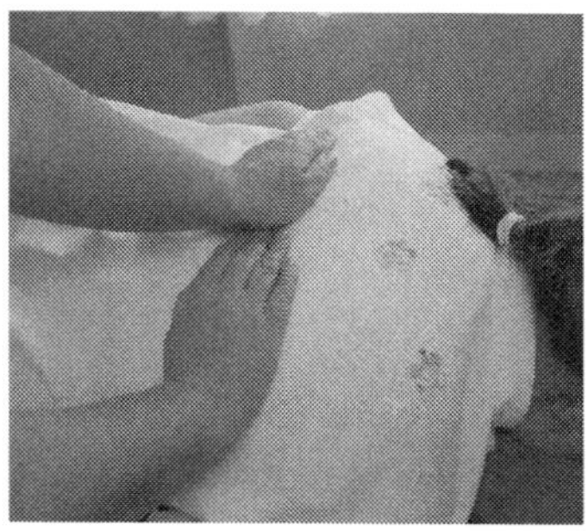

4. Heart

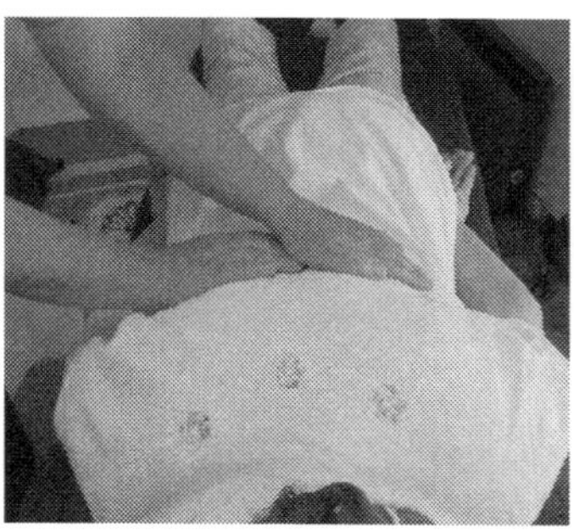

5. Solar Plexus

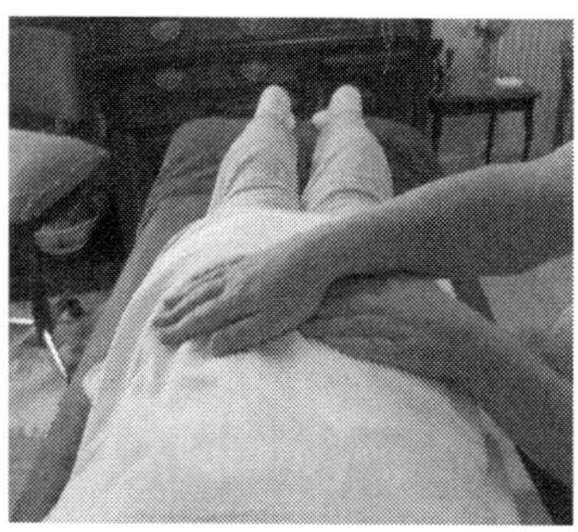

6. Sacral Chakra
(along ridge of pelvis)

HEALING OTHERS — BACK: 2

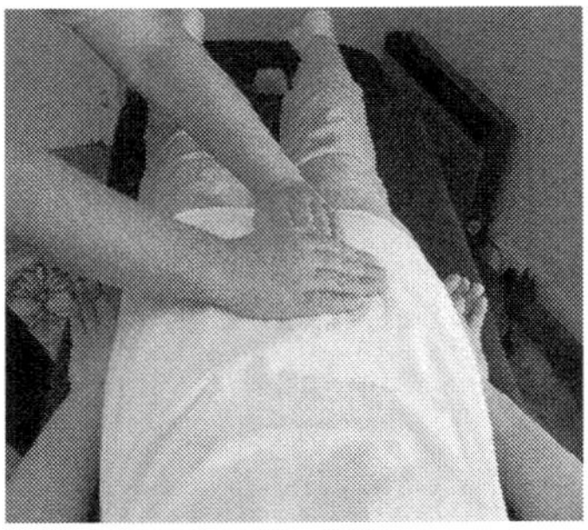

7. Base Chakra

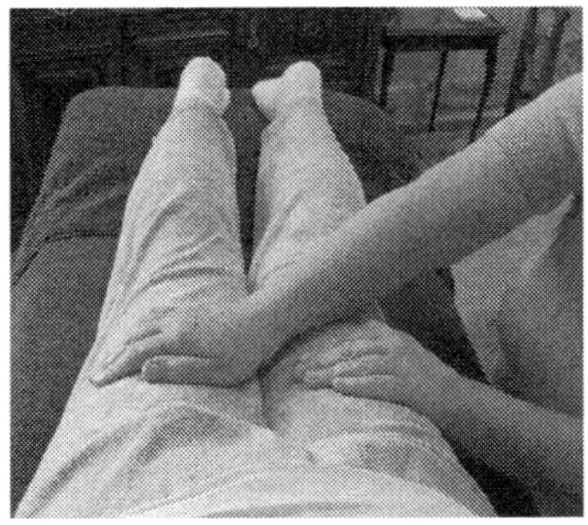

8. Thighs

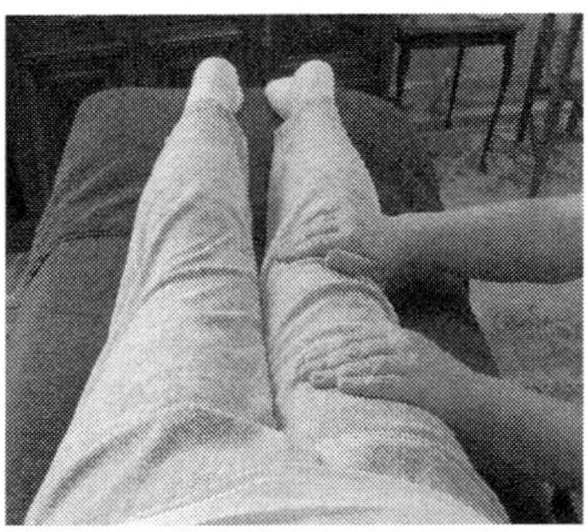

9. Thigh and Knee

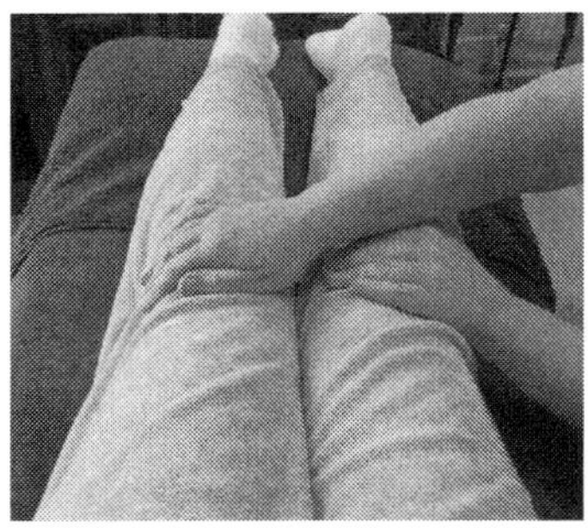

10. Backs of Knees
(repeat on other side)

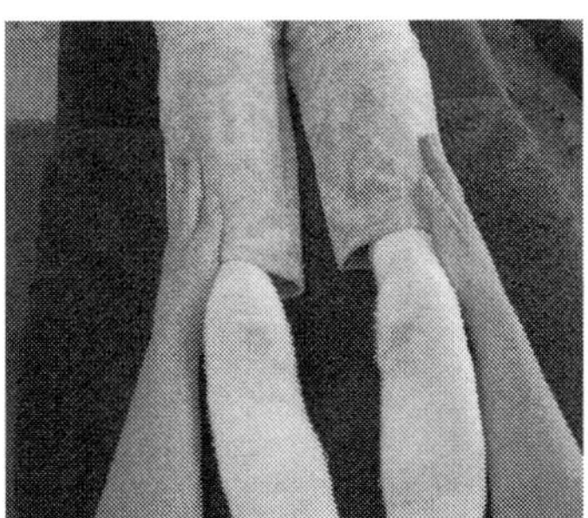

11. Ankles

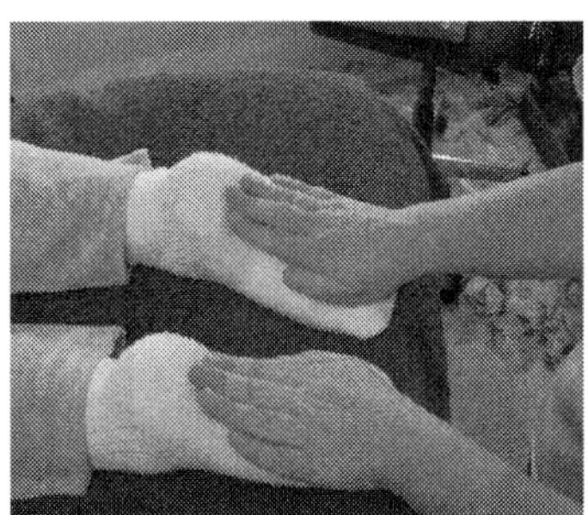

12. Soles of Feet

Acknowledgements

THIS BOOK WOULD not have been written had it not been for the many wonderful people to whom I have taught Reiki over the last twenty years or more. It has been an honour and privilege to share with them some of my joy and delight in Reiki. Each time someone opens to the healing energy of Reiki, the light of love that fills this wonderful planet of ours shines a little more brightly. So to all of them I offer my sincere thanks.

A number of them have encouraged me to write about Reiki, and I hope that, now I have found time to put fingers to keyboard, they will be pleased with the result. Thank you, from the bottom of my heart, for your perseverance, encouragement and help.

I also owe a deep debt of gratitude to my dear friend and sometime Reiki co-teacher, Reiki Master Teacher, Vivien Ford, with whom I have shared much of my Reiki journey. Together we have had fun, laughed and cried, and together we have grown into our spirituality. She has taught me much about kindness, gentleness and orderliness. Without her, I would never even have evolved a lesson plan.

Grateful thanks to her, Jenny Coote and Judith Thwaites for reading and re-reading the text of this book, patiently correcting my errors. Any that remain are mine alone, of course.

Finally, my deepest thanks to my husband, Richard Eaton, who constantly encourages and supports me in all that I do. Others have suggested that I write this book, but it was he who made me feel that I had something to offer to those who are interested in Reiki. As always, he has kept me supplied with numerous pint glasses of water, many cups of coffee and the occasional (!) glass of wine.

And finally, thank *you* for reading this book. I hope that it helps you along your Reiki journey. May you be richly blessed.

Thank you.

THE MYSTERIOUS MARSH SERIES

#1 WHEN THE CLOCKS STOPPED

When lawyer Hazel Dawkins decides to write a few wills while waiting for the imminent birth of her first child, little does she anticipate the dramatic events that her decision will set in train. But all too soon the dark and violent past collides with the sun-warmed present and Hazel finds herself pitted against an implacable ancient evil that has stalked the mysterious Romney Marsh for centuries.

As she fights with every fibre of her to right a great wrong, she knows that her very life is at stake, and with it, the life of her unborn baby. Yet to succeed, she must also change the destiny of a young woman who lived 200 years previously, for Annie's fate is interwoven with her own. And time is running out ….

For ebooks: www.books2read.com/WTCS

For paperback: www.amazon.co.uk/dp/1495931196

ISBN for bookshops: 978-0-9929752-0-3

#2 WHEN THE TIDE TURNED

August 1976. Soon after the birth of her daughter, young lawyer Hazel Dawkins finds herself covering holiday leave at the firm where she used to work. Almost immediately she discovers that a dark force threatens both her family and her country; and before long, the past and present intertwine in a rising tide of horrifying events.

What draws her to the painting depicting a sudden storm at sea on a night in 1803 as Napoleon prepares to invade England? What is the secret of the man pegged down to die on the incoming tide?

As Hazel seeks the answers to these questions, she faces evil and intrigue, her life and that of her baby daughter, threatened at every turn.

For ebooks: www.books2read.com/WTTT

For paperback: www.amazon.co.uk/dp/153466243X

ISBN for bookshops: 978-0-9929752-2-7

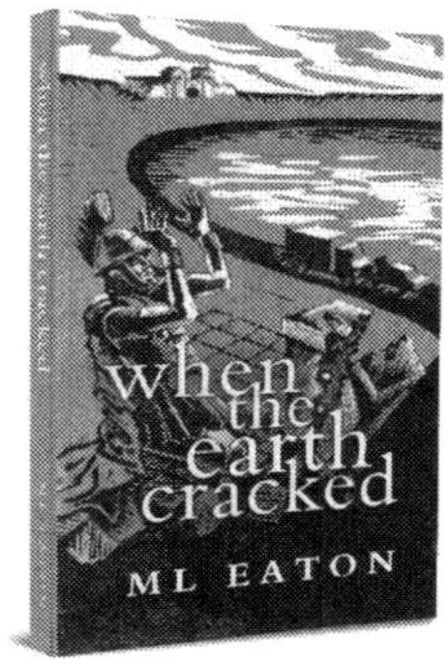

#3 WHEN THE EARTH CRACKED

As the winter of 1977 turns into spring, there is the promise of a beautiful summer on Romney Marsh in the south of England. But feisty young property lawyer, Hazel Dawkins, is unexpectedly caught in a web of frightening criminal intrigue that threatens the lives of herself and her family.

To her surprise, she finds herself ensnared in tragic events that occurred 1700 years earlier in a Britain ruled by the Roman Gallic Empire. There she confronts the power of the cult of Mithras as it wars with the Old Religion.

In the midst of an earthquake that shatters the fabric of both time and place, entangling worlds separated by nearly two millennia, Hazel strives to reconcile the ancient past with the present and to discover the meaning of forces that are seemingly beyond her understanding.

For ebooks: www.books2read.com/WTEC

For paperback: www.amazon.co.uk/dp/1533177481

ISBN for bookshops: 978-0-9929752-7-2

Faraway Lands Series

THE ELEPHANTS' CHILD – INDIA 1954

Always enthralling and exhilarating, at times sad and poignant, this is a story that captures the wonders of India as seen through the eyes and imagination of a young English girl.

Melanie is six years old when her parents take her to live in Bombay, (now Mumbai) where her father has been posted to undertake a Civil Engineering project but, anxious and unsettled, she finds it difficult to make friends.

Entranced by the emotive beauty of her surroundings, she unexpectedly discovers the love and friendship that banish her loneliness.

For ebooks: www.books2read.com/TEC

For paperback: www.amazon.co.uk/dp/B00K1ZWM50

THE LION MOUNTAINS – SIERRA LEONE 1956

Pounding with the vibrancy of African colour and music, occasionally sad but always engaging, this is a story that captures the heart.

Eight year old Melanie is spending several months with her parents while her father completes a civil engineering project. Swiftly enthralled by the primeval power of this beautiful African country, she soon discovers that, beneath its happy and apparently carefree exterior, there lurks danger and fear.

With the innocent eyes and intuition of a young English girl, Melanie learns of the bond of friendship that exist between people of different races.

For ebooks: books2read.com/TLM

For paperback: www.amazon.co.uk/dp/1507623291

THE SNAKING RIVER

BURMA 1934 - 1941

Teeming with the joy and abundance of life, the great Irrawaddy river is the life-blood of Myanmar, the country once known as Burma. From its myriad of sources high up in the jungle clad slopes of the mountainous hills bordering China, the 'River of Blessings' winds a thousand miles south to its fertile delta that opens into the Bay of Bengal.

To a little boy conceived in the Kachin Hills and living by the great river for his first five years, the country's fascinating wildness, creatures, culture and essence burns deep into his character, shaping the whole of his life.

For ebooks: www. books2read.com/TSR

For paperback: www.amazon.co.uk/dp/ 1516827139

A taste of THE ELEPHANTS' CHILD

'A gush of air bore the animal's spirit from her body. The earth quaked with the shock: after-tremors rocked the trees, rustling their leaves. Silence: bending trees slowly straightening.

In the aftermath of death there was a great stillness. Even the calf was still now, frozen in shock, bound in ropes, silent in its cage. The silence stretched: and stretched further. Until slowly, slowly, men crept out from behind trees and undergrowth. Others descended from the treetops. The white man, who had fallen full length upon the ground, slowly rose and gathered up his gun.

Silent in her prison, the elephant calf grieved for her mother, her freedom, her kind. Never again, she intuited, would she be free to roam the green and sacred land. Never again would she watch a lazy bird-of-prey circle between the green jungle hills; never again would she play with her kind in the crystal waters of the creeks – squirting water, bathing, drinking, playing. Ever after, she would be at the mercy of man, this puny creature who would beat and poke the spirit from her, until she did his bidding always.

When Melanie woke in the morning the dream was still upon her. A great weight crushed against her heart and she felt the agony of mother and child in every pore of her being, but she did not weep for the grief was too deep, too real for tears. And today was the day her mother was going away. It was her grief too.'

For e-books: www.books2read.com/TEC
For paperback: www.amazon.co.uk/dp/1507750781

GET YOUR FREE BOOK

Soliciting from Home

For a limited time you can get a FREE digital copy of ***Soliciting from Home***, the true but fictionalised story on which the Mysterious Marsh Series is based, direct from my website: www.marioneaton.com

Just enter, click or tap the link below to get started: http://eepurl.com/b9aPVf

Packed with authentic and endearing characters, unexpected romance and good old-fashioned country town drama, *Soliciting from Home* is an amusing, occasionally sad, but always warm-hearted account of a young woman setting up a legal practice in a small community in 1970s Kent.

Or to purchase an ebook, please follow this link: www.books2read.com/SFH
For a paperback: www.amazon.co.uk/dp/1499646127

Printed in Great
Britain
by Amazon

31401204R00181